If woman had been designed then what exactly was the brief? *Woman as Design* is a completely original reappraisal of that most familiar, yet mysterious, of things, the female body. What do curves mean? The breast – is there any more potent symbol? What are the correlations in architecture and design and what is meant by 'feminine line and detail'? In Part One: Before, Behind, Between, Above, Below, Stephen Bayley takes us from Aphrodite to the Delta of Venus and then to the industrialization of the breast (in bra form) and sexual identity. In Part Two he examines pin-ups, stereotypes, cosmetics, hemlines and heels and looks in detail at how design has appropriated the feminine form. Both provocative and beguiling, *Woman as Design* is an eclectic mix of design, cultural history, erotica, fashion, fetishism and sharp observation. Wonderfully designed and superbly illustrated this a compulsively attractive book and a modern study of the continuous conflict between the real and the ideal… in its most familiar form.

D1128680

DEC 2009

Page 2: Mannequin Factory, *Roger Mavity, 2008. The photographer has placed a real woman (in a rubber bald cap) among the lifeless, standardized mannequins to comment on the uncertain boundary between the real and the ideal. The picture was taken in the London factory of Adel Rootstein whose business – ironically – began sculpting artificial mannequins from life (including a young Twiggy) as a protest against the conformity of the fashionable female form.*

Page 4: The Venus of Urbino, *Tiziano Vecellio. This is one of the most sexually explicit paintings of the Renaissance. Commissioned by Guidobaldo della Rovere, Duke of Urbino, at some time before 1538, it was intended as erotic instruction for his young bride. Although known as 'Venus', the model has earthly rather than divine attributes. In his 1880 book* A Tramp Abroad, *Mark Twain described it as too foul, vile and obscene for a bordello and only suitable for a public gallery.*

Page 8: Nude Bent Forward, *Lee Miller, 1931. Miller took this photograph in Paris where she was in touch with the Surrealists. In Surrealist theory, a woman's body might be turned into sculpture to disrupt our sense of what is 'nature' and what is 'art'.*

Page 10: Roman women athletes wearing the mastodeton, a prototype bikini. Villa Herculia, Casale, Piazza Armerina, Sicily, 3rd–4th centuries.

First published in 2009 by Conran Octopus Ltd,
a part of Octopus Publishing Group,
2–4 Heron Quays, London E14 4JP
www.octopusbooks.co.uk

An Hachette Livre UK Company
www.hachettelivre.co.uk

Distributed in the United States and Canada by Octopus Books USA,
c/o Hachette Book Group USA, 237 Park Avenue, New York, NY 10017 USA

Concept and text copyright © Stephen Bayley 2009
Design and layout copyright © Conran Octopus Ltd 2009

All rights reserved. No part of this book may be reproduced, stored in a retrieval system, or transmitted, in any form or by any means, electronic, electrostatic, magnetic tape, mechanical, photocopying, recording or otherwise, without the prior permission in writing of the Publisher.

The right of Stephen Bayley to be identified as the Author of this Work has been asserted by him in accordance with the Copyright, Designs and Patents Act 1988.

British Library Cataloguing-in-Publication Data.
A catalogue record for this book is available from the British Library.

Publisher: Lorraine Dickey
Managing Editor: Sybella Marlow
Copy Editor: Sian Parkhouse
Proofreader: Colette Campbell

Art Direction and Design: Jonathan Christie
Picture Researcher: Anne-Marie Hoines

Production Manager: Katherine Hockley

ISBN: 978 1 84091 532 7
Printed in China

BEFORE
BEHIND
BETWEEN
ABOVE
BELOW

Woman as Design

STEPHEN
BAYLEY

 conran
OCTOPUS

MARGATE CITY LIBRARY

1889729   80.00

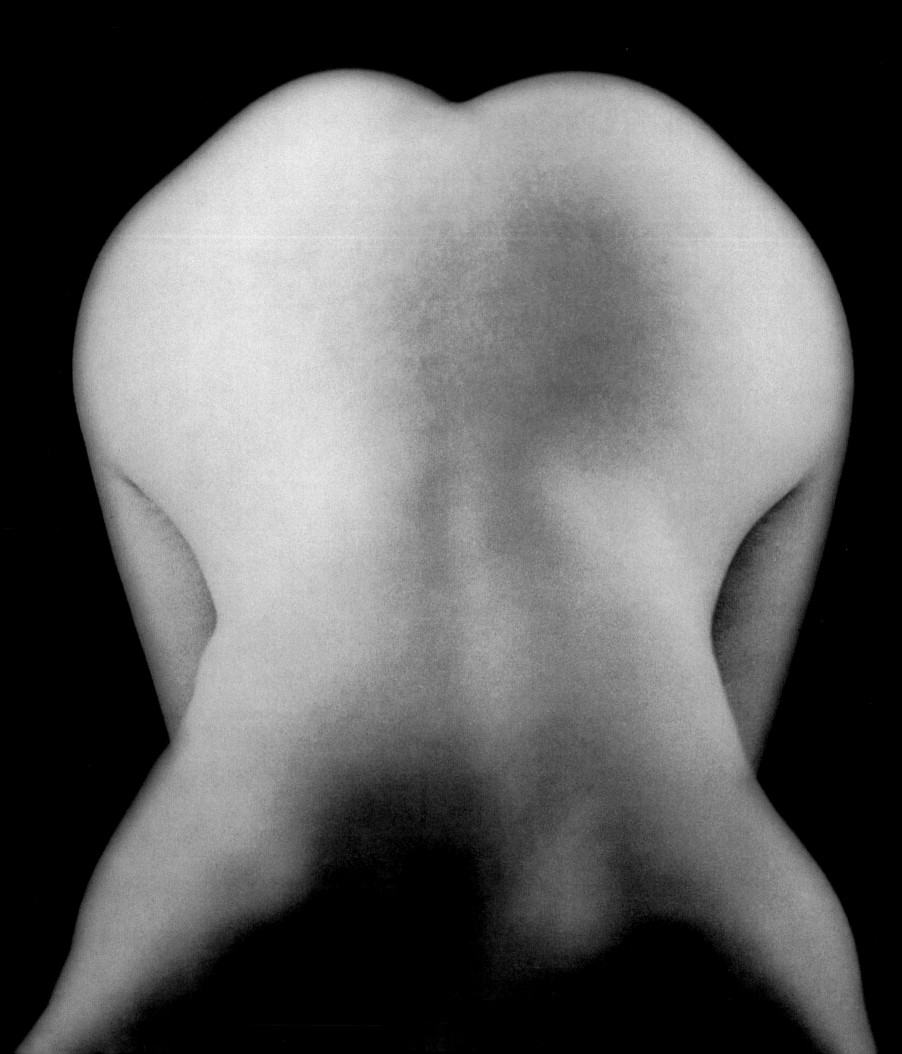

Introduction

12

'Licence my roaving hands, and let them go,
Before, behind, between, above, below.'
— JOHN DONNE, ELEGY XIX 'TO HIS MISTRESS GOING TO BED'

Opposite: John Donne (1572–1631) by Isaac Oliver, circa 1615. The English metaphysical poet wrote one of the first modern appreciations of a woman's body: erotic, elegant, explicit. The word 'clitoris' entered the language in Donne's lifetime.

Above: The striations of the kola nut, as well as the Callipygian curves of classical goddesses, influenced the shape of the Coca-Cola bottle.

This poem, unpublished in the author's lifetime and circulating only as a manuscript, was the first in the English language boldly to contain a line comprised entirely of prepositions. It was also the first in the English language unambiguously inviting someone to strip: 'unpin that spangled breastplate' the future Dean of St Paul's says to his mistress. 'What needst thou have more covering than a man?' he argues, successfully as it turns out.

And, as she willingly unpins and unbuckles her elaborate late Elizabethan costume, discards her innocent white linen and her busk, the poet considers the spectacle with anticipatory – then clear and present – delight. In a daring metaphor, he compares feeling her body with an adventure as ambitious and interesting as the discovery of America.

Later feminists might disdain the comparison of the womanly landscape to a mere continent as a coarse trivialization of female mystique typical of the crude, masculine need to commodify and objectify, to conquer, possess, cultivate and govern. But in the 1590s America itself was a daring proposition, a real *terra incognita*. To compare a woman to America was not to compare a woman

to a McDonalds or to a banal chattel such as a flowerpot: it was to compare a woman to somewhere exotic, strange, unknown, fascinating and distant. As Donne goes on to explain, what we are discussing here is a 'new-found-land'.

Besides, geography provides a whole atlas of useful morphological metaphors for discussing women's bodies. But working his way round that happy new-found-land Donne had to rely on established geographical fact to describe his discoveries. The gap between the breasts, for example, was compared by Donne in an earlier poem to the Hellespont, that epic waterway separating Europe from Asia. In terms of drama and excitement the allusion might have worked, but as an image it has some deficiencies.

Still, we all seem to find geography a source of useful metaphor in mapping the female body. The pleasantly bulging pubic area is known as the *mons veneris*, or, less elegantly in English, the venereal mountain. The clitoris itself (a word that only entered the language in John Donne's lifetime: 1615, according to *The Oxford English Dictionary*) may be derived from the Greek expression for 'little hill'. That English had no need for a word before the early seventeenth century may

suggest that this primal female sexual attribute was itself, like continental America, a discovery of the Elizabethan renaissance. More certain is the significance that in modern French the clitoris is known as *praline*, or almond. This is hilariously suggestive of the French preoccupation with food: in France, gastronomy even dominates the taxonomy of sex.

The female body is the most familiar, yet mysterious, of things. Our vision of it is as much influenced by modern artifice as by 'nature'. Those curves: what exactly do they mean? Why did we encourage them? The breast. Is there any more potent or ambiguous a symbol? Naked breasts suggest either a nurturing mother or a woman who is sexually available. The Chinese characters for 'mother' and 'whore' are very similar and each includes a pair of stylized square 'breasts'. The intensely flavoured neuroses arising out of this tormenting ambivalence have inspired and demented painters, writers, lovers, rapists, poets and sculptors, while providing super-abundant case-study material for clinical psychotherapists.

These same curves, proportions, fissures and orifices have also inspired architects and designers. But this is not a book not about women designers, rather it is about woman as design. It is about how we willed this most agreeable construct into existence. Of course, nature played its part, but so too did artifice and desire. The female body is a masterpiece of design: an eternal natural classic as well as an inexhaustible sourcebook of inspirational form and detail.

A conversation over dinner with my wife started me on this subject (although I can't deny it has fascinated me for as long as I can remember). She said, apropos of I can't quite remember what, did I think a modern product designer could have handled the complex mechanical, hydraulic and aesthetic problems of the area between a woman's legs?

Product designers often tell us how very adroit they are at melding form and function, of making junctions work, of handling contrasting textures and different materials.

They often do this quite well on food mixers or bagless vacuum cleaners, but nature's solution to the meeting of the legs and exhaust valves for waste, intakes and delivery channels is immeasurably more subtle. The Delta of Venus is a design solution that allows modesty to be retained until that moment when modesty is no longer an issue and becomes irrelevant in rapture. And with modesty abandoned, that neat detail when revealed becomes something both obsessively fascinating and existentially frightening. That the most offensive word in the language has the profoundest associations with birth and love is as weird as the ambiguous meaning of naked breasts.

Have any mortal designers ever achieved such an elegant and famous junction as that between the upper thigh and the gluteal mass? Car designers struggle to achieve a fraction of that elegance when adjoining a windscreen to a front wing. To understand the beauty and good sense of what has been achieved in woman as design, just consider that the female snail's vagina is in her head.

This conversation made me want to understand just a bit more about the woman's body than any son, husband or father might already know. I started musing about how the female body evolved. How can something so familiar equally also be so strange? How can the very same components respond to the vast, inexorable mechanics of reproduction, but also speak to the cultured subtleties and infinite varieties of erotic love? How on earth could you design such a thing, so flawlessly functional while infinitely beguiling too? But if woman is a design, then what exactly was the brief?

Left: Olympia, *Leni Riefenstahl, 1936. This film of the 1936 Berlin Olympics fused classical scholarship with racially coloured eroticism.*

Above: The Chinese pictogram for 'mother' (essentially similar to the one for whore) is based on a pair of stylized breasts.

Above: the breasts

With 1kg (2.2lbs) of sebaceous tissue, pectoral muscle, glands, blood and lymph vessels and nerves create dual, portable, self-sealing nutritional reservoirs allowing flexible responses to unpredictable demand cycles. These reservoirs to be placed on the ventral area of the female human and to have the subsidiary purposes of (a) symbols of aesthetic contemplation and (b) tactile objects exciting powerful, if confused, urges in males.

Behind: the bottom

A muscular system is required both to move and stabilize the hip joints. This system is to be covered by twin fleshy parts whose function is partly to act as a cushion and a cover for the gluteal muscles and the pelvic bone, but mostly to serve profound symbolic purposes. This part of the body is identified with locomotion, but also with reproduction and excretion. But this symbolism must not be explicit. Instead, it must be adapted to different cultural and social circumstances.

Between: the ano-genital delta

This is a complex, multi-faceted, highly innervated system of storage, transport and entertainment. Three functions must be combined into a compact area; the working apparatus to be enclosed beneath a cutaneous region covered with hair (optional). A layer of sub-cutaneous fat may be assumed to be available to give the area a pleasingly sculptural, domed aspect. Changes of surface texture must be carefully handled: external skin must blend imperceptibly with internal mucous membrane. Excretory orifices must be subtle and faired-in. Lubrication to be supplied in an on-demand basis. The major orifice must be flexibly commodious. Ample provision must be allowed for excretory ducts. The whole to be meticulously surfaced and carefully detailed.

The alarming feminist Andrea Dworkin explains and excoriates the male obsession with body parts, demonstrated so guilelessly in the passages preceeding. She writes:

'The love of or desire for or obsession with a sexual object is, in male culture, seen as a response to the qualities of the object itself.'
— PORNOGRAPHY, 1981

But that is merely to describe an aesthetic view of the body. I share Dworkin's views, but not her censorious attitude. The shape, meaning and influence of the superficialities of a woman's body is a story of limitless fascination and import. To enjoy the woman's body is not to exploit it; really, it is about understanding and appreciating its design.

There is a marvellous 1907 essay by Sigmund Freud where he analyses Wilhelm Jensen's short story *Gradiva* (1903). There is no better or culturally rich account of such a view that treats bodies and their motions as meaningful. Freud may have been wrong about a lot of scientific things, but he fully understood the poetry of how appearances might reveal underlying truths.

The essay is called 'Der Wahn und die Traume' in W. Jensens Gradiva' (Delusion and Dream in Jensen's Gradiva), and is a unique example of Freud psychoanalysing a fictional character, in this case the archaeologist Norbert Hanhold who is obsessed by the Gradiva, the 'walking woman' he knows from a low relief in the Naples Archaeological Museum. (The walk was specially significant in the ancient world: Greek prostitutes announced themselves with their distinctive footfall, their hard sandals making a loud noise on carpet-less floors.) In the story Hanhold dreams that he returns to Pompei to find her.

Freud explains that the sculpture:

'…represented a fully-grown girl stepping along, with her flowing dress a little pulled-up to reveal her sandalled feet. One foot rested squarely on the ground; the other lifted from the ground in the act of following after, touched it only with the tips of the toes, while the sole and the heel rose almost perpendicularly. It was probably the unusual and peculiarly charming gait thus presented that attracted the sculptor's notice and that still, after so many centuries riveted the eyes of its archaeological admirer.'

As Gradiva rivets our eyes now. She is an exquisite woman made into a sculptural pattern. A copy of the Gradiva (taken from the Vatican Museum) is in the Freud Museum in Hampstead, London. The same figure also inspired the

Below: 'Gradiva' or walking woman, a plaster cast belonging to Sigmund Freud from an antique original in the Naples Archaeological Museum. Freud was fascinated by the way a woman's locomotion expresses meaning.

Right: Salvador Dali Gradiva Rediscovers the Anthropomorphic Ruins –

Retrospective Fantasy, *1931. Freud's journeys into the unconscious fascinated the Surrealists, especially his analysis of a story about an archaeologist who falls in love with the Gradiva relief. Dali's* Gradiva *shows a humanoid form that is disturbingly lacking the face and genitals which would determine gender.*

surrealist André Masson, while 'Gradiva' was also Salvador Dali's pet-name for his demanding Russian wife, Elena Dirianoff, later known as Gala.

Freud is only the most famous of the dead white men whose thoughts on women, walking erect, or stationary and supine, framed in the nineteenth century, are still influential on us today. The others are Charles Darwin and Paolo Mantegazza, the Italian neurologist. The latter, one of Darwin's correspondents, is an outstanding candidate, in a very competitive field, for one of the most curious scientific figures of the nineteenth century. Another is Darwin's half cousin, the eccentric psychometrist Francis Galton, who was an enthusiast for eugenics (which term he coined) and a maniac for measuring. Galton once designed a Beauty Map of the British Isles, with the female population tabulated,

contrasted and compared according to his own system. Drawing on experience acquired when he measured 10,000 individuals for the databank in his Institute of Anthropometrics, Galton went about:

'classifying the girls I passed in the streets or elsewhere as attractive, indifferent, or repellent. 'Of course,' he conceded 'this was a purely individual estimate, but it was consistent, judging by the conformity of different attempts in the same population. I found London to rank highest for beauty; Aberdeen lowest.'
— MEMORIES OF MY LIFE, 1908

Absurd as Galton's commodification might seem, it was but a short step from his Beauty Map to twentieth-century beauty pageants. The first of these, Miss World, was established in

Above & right: The 1951 'Miss World' in London introduced a gasping public to the bikini; the 1953 competition helped fetishize women's legs.

Opposite above: Paolo Mantegazza (1831–1910) associate of Charles Darwin and pioneer Italian sexologist.

Britain in 1951. Miss America was founded in the same year but, after a dispute between the winner and the sponsor, Catalina Swimwear of Long Beach, California, the competition was re-configured as Miss Universe in 1952. Since 1996 it has been owned by Donald Trump.

Mantegazza, who was Professor of Anthropology at the Istituto di Studi Superiori in Florence and exchanged letters with Darwin for nearly half a century, did something rather similar to Galton's Beauty Map with his 'Aesthetic Tree of the Human Race'. He was a social and literary progressive, but an inspiration for political reactionaries, even while he was an anti-clerical liberal. A period in South America had given him, like Freud, an enthusiasm for cocaine (he wrote 'I would rather have a life span of ten years with coca than one of 10,000, 000,000,000,000,000,000 centuries without coca').

Besides much science, he was author of a liberal novel about a marriage of a couple with disease, but his Darwinianism made him argue for the primacy of the European (followed, in order of merit, by Polynesians, Semites, Japanese and 'Negritos'). In his *Fisiologia della Donna* (1893) Mantegazza cites a South American tribal chieftain who expressed a preference for European women, which in the twentieth century was confirmed by the global reach of Hollywood. His *Fisiologia dell' Amore* (1896) was a pioneering book on sexual medicine, the prototype of a still important publishing genre.

Just because no one reads Mantegazza – or, indeed, Darwin, Galton and Freud – any more does not mean they are to be dismissed. From Darwin's evolutionary theories we have acquired the assumption which lies very heavily on our culture that women crave stable relationships while men are

25

hard-wired to spread their DNA hither and yon. Or, as Gore Vidal, succinctly, if unpleasantly, put it: women want to lay eggs while men want to squirt. Egg-laying is best done stationary; squirting lends itself to mobility.

Also from Darwin was acquired the troglodyte ideal of the perfect woman: she must be youthful and flawless with expressive breasts and lips, the better to breed from. Chaucer had this as 'with buttokes brode and brestes rounde and hye'. In *The Descent of Man* Darwin argues that ideas of beauty are constant. He cites the traveller and Arabist Sir Richard Burton: 'a woman whom we [and by "we" he means educated, white, middle-class, English Victorian intellectual males] consider beautiful is admired throughout the world'.

We are not yet quite done with that idea. Indeed, it is tempting to suggest that since Darwin's ideas are so very robust, they may be of more than merely temporary significance. Steven Pinker of the Massachusetts Institute of Technology was reported in *The New York Times* on 21 February 1999 to have delivered himself of this uncompromising view of sexual relations:

'Most human drives have ancient Darwinian rationales. … A prehistoric man who slept with fifty women could have sired fifty children, and would have been more likely to have descendants who inherited his tastes. A woman who slept with fifty men would have no more descendants than a woman who slept with one … men should seek quantity in sexual partners; women quality'.

Pinker was discussing President Clinton.

Freud, it is now widely recognized, used pseudo-scientific diagnoses of his patients as a sort of wish-fulfilment. He often presents the fanciful as if it were real. In his magnificently contrarian book, *Why Freud Was Wrong*,

Richard Webster explains that Freud was fundamentally a physiologist and needed to have his sometimes very odd sexual theories rooted in biological fact. This has its contemporary equivalent in Marcel Proust's wonderful expression, in the Scott-Moncrieff and Kilmartin translation, about the body's 'terrible capacity for registering things'. Freud employed circular arguments. He put sex at the centre of the world, then referred everything back to it. His predecessor, the Frenchman Jean-Martin Charcot, put no such exaggerated emphasis on sex, but to Freud all nervous disorders were attributable to the '*secrets d'alcove*', or bedroom rituals.

Darwinism and Freudianism have given us a fixed concept of the ideal woman which advertising, movies, photography and fashion have tended to protect, project and advance. What is natural has in reality been designed. And what is designed is not natural. From pre-historic fertility votives to nurturing Renaissance Madonnas to Darwin via Freud and from Caresse Crosby and the modern bra to Charles Stine, the Du Pont executive who hired the chemist Wallace Hume Carothers who invented the nylon which led to tights, *Woman as Design* is a story of a notion of woman that has been willed into existence by appetite and desire.

Mother or lover? Two semi-circles and a dark triangle comprise a graphic that short-circuits the ego and plumbs the very depths of the id. The woman's body is familiar, but mysterious. Look at a Bronze Age statuette: chunky, schematized, ill-proportioned, gross. Has the physiology of woman changed in 5,500 years? Or have we nurtured another ideal? Have we designed woman?

This book is about the epic conflict between real and ideal as it takes place in underwear and cosmetics. The design of woman, in one way or another, or perhaps even in every way imaginable, defines our imaginative lives.

Left and above: An erotic postcard circa 1915 and a Calvin Klein advertisement, 2007. The fleshy bulk of the models has changed, but the pose is identical. But the first was covert erotica, the second imagery for mass-market consumption.

Right: Contemporary with Orientalist fashion, the Louvre's Aphrodite of Melos, known as The Venus di Milo, *became one of Paris' most popular sculptures. Our perception of her beauty is not compromised by her disabling lack of arms.*

29

Left: Jean-Léon Gérôme (1824–1904) was one of the first professors in Paris' hugely influential Ecole des Beaux Arts. His fashionable interest in Orientialism allowed a frank treatment of women as tradeable produce that would have been pornographic if his subject were contemporary Parisians. Slave Market in Rome *was painted in 1884 at just the moment French prostitution was becoming officially organized.*

Page 30: Allen Jones Table, *1969. The British Pop Artist uses full-size women models as structural elements in his furniture designs. Their distorting, exaggerating sado-masochistic outfits suggest compliance in this form of abuse.*

1

Before

34

Page 33: Rene Magritte Le Viol, *1934. This is one of the signal images of sexual identity: a woman's personality, as betrayed by the features of her face, is completely replaced by her sexual parts.*

The Venus of Brassempouy (above right) and The Venus of Willendorf *(opposite). Each is from the Upper Palaeolithic period of 22–30,000BC. Neither of these pre-historic votive figures is necessarily a goddess, still less a classical 'Venus', but nineteenth-century archaeologists wanted to fit these powerful figurines into a safe version of culture.*

The oldest works of art show women. The 'Venus' of Brassempouy in the Musée de l'Archeologie Nationale at Saint-Germain-en-Laye and the 'Venus of Willendorf' in the Naturhistorische Museum in Vienna are both discoveries of the busy men who ran nineteenth-century archaeology. They are both from the period 25–24,000BC and their interpretation is eloquent not so much of Stone Age woman herself as of nineteenth-century views of matriarchy and the ineffable Earth Mother.

This idea of the cave woman Earth Mother is a back-rationalization by nineteenth-century theorists from the already well-founded knowledge of the Greek gods. The scholars who wrote pre-history were educated in the classics and applied structural models derived from their formal schooling about Greek and Roman deities to rude hunter-gatherers of whom little was known. Thus, early anthropologists, including the Swiss J.J. Bachofen, established the Earth Mother idea. Doubtless, the intellectual invention of such a powerful matriarchal figure spoke to many of the queasy psychological realities of the nineteenth century as much as it reflected any historical

reality. Certainly, in the absence of any written evidence from the caves of Verzere, or the limestone *causses* of the Massif Central, the Earth Mother can at best be construed as a wistful interpretation of a social order of whose philosophy we are entirely ignorant.

What might an Earth Mother have looked like? The Venus of Willendorf may provide a suggestion. She is a 11.1cm (4⅓in) tall limestone statuette. She has a vast, pendulous stomach and enormous sagging breasts. While the breasts have no nipples, the labia are well-detailed. This indicates, perhaps, that other than as a generalized symbol of nutrition and well-being, the breasts of 25,000BC had not acquired any more specific meaning.

That this Venus is covered in red ochre is perhaps a reference to menstrual blood, although this is only speculation. Two things are obvious. One, that this is not a realistic image, not a portrait: it is more likely a generic totem or amulet concerned with maternity and may even have been carved by a woman. Two, that she does not represent either the Greek Aphrodite or the Roman 'Venus'. The use of the word 'Venus' in this context is a post hoc rationalization, a product

of modern archaeology. 'Venus' was first used in this way in 1864 when the Marquis Paul de Vibraye describes (one imagines ironically) another dumpy little statuette (with limbs missing) that, now in Paris' Musée de l'Homme, he found in the Dordogne.

Just as this Venus is a generalization, so the cave paintings of Paleolithic people are a form of sympathetic magic, or wish-fulfilment. Pictures of a successful hunt were designed to will such an event into existence; images of the Earth Mother were designed as tokens of fertility and its benefits.

Certainly, the first images of pre-historic woman verified by archaeology had little in common with Don Chaffey's modern concept of a cave woman presented in the 1966 movie *One Million Years BC*. Here Raquel Welch, in a torn wolfskin leotard, sculpted post-Willendorf breasts, elaborate pout and meticulously layered up-do (which gave rise to a flourishing Raquel Welch Wigs business), did not represent an abstract deity. She represented a construct as fanciful as the idea of naming a pre-historic votive sculpture – crafted, perhaps, by troglodyte cannibals – after the gorgeous and sophisticated Roman goddess of love.

We know almost nothing of the manners and morals of pre-history, but classical civilization has left us literary records which reveal an emerging idea of 'woman'. To what extent did woman have an ambivalent status in the ancient world? Hesiod, author of the *Theogony*, said it was, given the choice, best to buy a woman rather than marry one, since this means she could be sent out to plough the fields, if economic circumstances made this necessary. This has a curious similarity to a more recent remark by another Greek, the shipping tycoon, Stavros Niarchos. Much dismayed by the costs of running yachts, private aircraft and serial divorces, Niarchos' advice was 'if it, floats, flies or fucks… rent it'. Clearly, he was drawing on a cultural memory of the temple prostitutes of classical Greece.

Semonides of Amorgus has left behind a seventh-century BC text on Women which by way of illustrative comparisons, mentions bristly sows, wicked vixen, busybody bitch,

Left: Raquel Welch in Don Chaffey's 1966 movie One Million Years BC. *Hollywood's concept of primitive woman has proportions and features different from the Upper Palaeolithic soapstone 'Venus' (right, 6cm (2¹/2in) tall) found in the caves of Balzi Rossi, Italy.*

37

stubborn, decrepit donkey, short-necked ape. In this misogynistic view, everything about woman is messy. Additionally, she has become fat and malodorous through her custom of sitting on dunghills. Traditions of gallantry and courtly love were still 2,000 years in the future.

But a divine woman was one of the most powerful figures in the classical landscape. '*Aphros*' means foam and Aphrodite, the Greek goddess of love, beauty and procreation, sprang from the sea, thus making pre-historic claims to a profound connection between the experience of ego-loss in sex and the Oceanic sensibility. Stepping out of the foam was the moment Botticelli dramatized in the picture he made for Lorenzo di Pierfrancesco de Medici's Villa di Castello in 1482. Aphrodite became a divine celebrity; she was the first woman to be worshipped.

The Aphrodite cult flourished chiefly on the mainland in Corinth and on the island of Cythaera. While Aphrodite herself may have been an intangible divinity, her cult had an unambiguously sexual character. You have to imagine inside the temple that there were slaves (more than 1,000 in Corinth alone) and you have to be told that these slaves were, when they had finished burning frankincense and other priestly functions, sexually available for worshippers. This in the name of Aphrodite. Yet to call them mere prostitutes is to short-change the contemporary subtleties.

Outside the temple, choruses of maidens would sway and sing in myrtle groves, as a sort of advertisement: according to the first-century AD account of Rufus of Ephesus, worshippers would have made an explicit association between the myrtle and the labia. What did these harlots do in their temples? The historian Catherine Johns has drawn figures from a Samian vase which shows a naked woman sitting on a waist-high altar, her legs wrapped around a male worshipper. This, Johns says, is a temple prostitute at work. Meanwhile, in the distance, a hairy capryl-scented shepherd god Pan would be scouting the scene. Pan had a way with women and music, was much given to the seduction of nymphs and shepherdesses, but men found him disturbing. The anxiety we sometimes feel in lonely country places is called 'panic' on account of this.

The Aphrodite cult could be tailored to local cultural preferences or geographical necessities. There were, for example, Aphrodite Ourania (Heavenly); Aphrodite Aidos (Modesty); Aphrodite Pandemos (Democratic) and Aphrodite Morpho (Buxom).

38

Below: Woman as sex object and votive statuary combined. Worshippers from a Gaulish Samian-ware pot, second-century. This drawing is by Catherine Johns, a British Museum archaeologist.

Right: The Erotic Trinity: Aphrodite, Pan and Eros. A first-century BC sculpture excavated on Delos, 1904.

Opposite: A detail from Le Bain Turque, *1863 by Jean-Auguste-Dominique Ingres (1780–1867). French painters and poets were fascinated by the libertine regimes of the Ottoman Empire's bathhouses, where women would be hennaed and depilated so as to conform to a Pasha's ideal. Besides the obvious nudity, there is a further implied sexual element: the* Koran *requires bathing after intercourse.*

Left: The Aphrodite of Knidos (sometimes Cnidus) by Praxiteles, circa 350BC. Considered illusionistically realistic, the Goddess of Love actually looks like a man.

The second-century topographer Pausanias gives a splendid description of a temple devoted to the goddess of love, this one in Sikyon :

'In the temple of Aphrodite, into which enter only a female verger, who after her appointment may not have intercourse with a man, and a virgin, called the Loutophoros [bath-bearer] holding her scared office for a year. All others are wont to behold the goddess from the entrance and to pray from that place. The image [of Aphrodite] is made of gold and ivory, having on its head a polos [headdress] and carrying in one hand a poppy and in the other an apple. They offer the thighs of the victims, excepting pigs; the other parts they burn for the goddess with juniper wood, but as the thighs are burning they add to the offering a leaf of the paideros. This is a plant in the open parts of the enclosure, and it grows nowhere else either in Sikyonia or any other land. Its leaves are smaller than those of the esculent oak, but larger than those the holm; the shape is similar to the oak leaf. One side is a dark colour, the other is white.'
— DESCRIPTION OF GREECE

Prostitution is the oldest profession. Thus, not only was a woman the very first subject of art, but a woman was the very first professional. Greek prostitutes were in three categories, reflecting the divisions and hierarchies in Greek society. There were the Dikteriades who were slaves, the Auletriades who were flute-players and the more sophisticated Hetaires who enjoyed full civil rights. One such Hetaira was Phryne, said by some sources to be the model for Praxiteles' sculpture now better known as the Aphrodite of Knidos. This Aphrodite was the first life-like nude in art. She bends, she looks, she feels. There is psychology in the marble; you sense a real person, not a stereotype. So life-like, in fact, was the Knidian Aphrodite

42

Left: The Artemis of Ephesus was the ultimate symbol of womanly fertility. This bronze and alabaster polymastic figure from the second century has perhaps 15 pendulous breasts. Confusingly, some archaeologists claim the breasts are, in fact, bulls' testicles: evidence of a different sort of female power.

Right: Jewellery on this African tribal figure emphasizes the neck, not the breasts.

that, according to Polybius, the goddess herself recognized some revealingly accurate minor flaws in her representation and demanded 'Where did Praxiteles see me naked?' From the time of its making in the mid-fifth century BC, Praxiteles' Aphrodite was the most famous classical sculpture.

The original is long since lost, assumed to have been exported from Knidos to Byzantinium and destroyed there. It is known only from copies and variations, the best-known being the one in Rome known now as the Capitoline Venus. She is in the form of Venus pudica, which is to say, a naked woman making a small gesture of modesty as a hand delicately covers her groin. But in all essentials we might assume this is the Ideal Woman of the fifth century BC. She has a large almost masculine frame, ample flesh, small, firm breasts and big legs. The depredations of time have left us only with bare stone copies of the Parian marble Aphrodite, but Praxiteles' original would have been brightly coloured and jewelled, just like a harlot or a temple prostitute.

The Greek Aphrodite became the Roman Venus, as well as the Phoenician Astarte who then became the Jewish Esther. There were temples to Astarte in Tyre, Sidon and Heliopolis. Figurines of Astarte were often represented as a tree with breasts. Aphrodite as a concept was a sophisticated evolution of the fertility cults which dominated early religious life, although the preoccupation was based, perhaps, more on survivalist practicalities than any real mystical interest in procreation.

Other goddesses, besides Aphrodite, helped frame a concept of 'woman'. To the Greeks, Artemis, the Roman Diana, was associated with childbirth, but the Artemis of Ephesus who is mentioned in Acts XIX, 23–41 in the Bible is not the same deity, although the famous polymastic (multi-breasted) statue of her in Naples' National Museum makes clear that

she too is a fertility symbol: she has perhaps 15 breasts, mixed with stylized bees and grapes. Sometimes she is known as Artemisia Hypermammia on account of this bountiful super-abundance. It may be noted that some commentators have claimed that what appear to be Artemisian breasts may, in fact, represent skinned bulls' testicles which are also powerful symbols of fertility.

While the Aphrodite cult represented a veneration of woman, the Amazons represented the opposite: gynophobia, the fear of women. The name may derive from the Greek words for lacking a breast: the story is that the Amazons voluntarily had a breast removed by cauterization, the better to draw the strings of their military bows when in battle. There are no sources to suggest this is anything other than a revealing myth whose survival illuminates an enduring prejudice: when a woman assumes an 'un-natural' role – such as soldier-archer – she loses an element of her sexual identity.

This assumption by woman of a hitherto masculine role as a soldier features often in classical art: the popularity of the Woman as Warrior image shows that a single concept of femininity had not been fixed by the third century BC when, perhaps, the last Amazon image occurred in Greek art. The name was revived in 1956 by the Volvo Car Company of Gothenburg: the first modern Volvo, designed by Jan Wilsgard, was called 'Amazon'. At the time, the woman's social role was being rapidly redefined in Western countries. Volvo called the car 'Amazon' in order to project an image of competitiveness and aggression in a tranquil social democracy: the Swedish Amazon was not inspired by the house beautiful theories of Ellen Kay, but by the American 1953 Kaiser Dragon Hardtop Sedan.

A Roman sarcophagus from the third century BC showing the traditional battle between Greeks and Amazons. The Greek warriors have familiar masculine attributes; the Amazons' womanhood has been compromised by elective breast removal. As a symbol, Amazons perhaps reveal the unease Greeks felt when women stepped outside conventional roles.

The figure of the Motherland *on Mamayev Hill is a memorial to Stalingrad (now Volgograd). In female warriors, naked breasts indicate the struggle for 'liberty'.*

Three hundred years after the last war-like Amazon appeared in Greek art, the image of woman had again stabilized. The figure of the Terra Mater (a Romanized Earth Mother) on the glorious Ara Pacis Augustae (consecrated 9BC as a memorial, explicitly, to Augustan Peace and, covertly, as a shrine to fertility) established a prototype of the beautiful, nurturing divine woman that fed directly into the most potent image of woman before the pin-up: the Virgin of Christian art.

The Catholic Virgin seen by painters is by far the most familiar version of woman in art and the second most familiar image of all, excepting only Jesus. She was the very first thought in the mind of God. But the familiarity of the woman-and-child image cannot disguise some of the layered contradictions, mysteries and paradoxes in what this divine woman actually represents. So far from dignifying women, the ubiquitous images (beautiful, serene) and the baffling theology (we will come to this shortly) have made some modern women recognize it as constraining and limiting. In her magnificent critique of 'Mariolatry' *Alone of All Her Sex* (1976), the Roman Catholic cultural historian Marina Warner finds herself 'subtly denigrated' by the oppressive Cult of the Virgin. The Virgin is not so much an inspirational role model as a too firmly applied template.

The image of the Christian Virgin as the ultimate nurturing mother has pagan origins. The Egyptian goddess Isis, that culture's chief deity, suckled a child. She evolved into an all-purpose nature goddess, a sort of SUV among deities, and then was absorbed into the Greek goddess Aphrodite.

Opposite: Barbara Hepworth
Mother and Child, *1934.*
The biomorphic form is readily
interpreted as 'feminine'.

Left: A late period Egyptian
bronze of Isis with an infant
Horus. Pagan votive statuettes of
this kind were direct influences
on the iconography of the
Christian Virgin and Child.

Opposite: A detail of Madonna and Child *by Hans Memling from the Diptych of Maarten van Nieuwenhove, 1487. Above: Robert Campin (The Master of Flémalle)* Madonna and Child, *first half of the fifteenth century. Flemish Virgins – the Queens of Heaven – at least the sort found in paintings, were perhaps the most beautiful women a villager might ever see.*

Milton has Aphrodite among the Fallen Angels, although as suckling goddesses derived from Isis are familiar figures in many non-European cultures she is also the distant source of the Virgin's iconography. But while Isis has many mysterious attributes ('to lift the veil of Isis' means to penetrate something obscure) the Catholic Virgin is a nursing mother. The only other thing she does besides breast-feeding is crying. The Queen of Heaven is therefore rather limited.

The theology of the Virgin insists on the idea of immaculate conception: that she is sexually intact means she is saved from Original Sin, but also provides the source of the essential mystery of Christianity: the simultaneous humanity and divinity of her Son. If her hymen is in place, how can Jesus have been born? That we never know the answer means science is replaced by faith, but it also means that this version of woman became 'the staple antidote to love on earth', according to Marina Warner. How extraordinary that we worship a woman who represents a frank denial of sex! Warner writes:

'Whether we regard the Virgin Mary as the most sublime and beautiful image in man's struggle towards the good and the pure, or the most pitiable production of ignorance and superstition, she represents a central theme in the history of western attitudes to women.'
— ALONE OF ALL HER SEX, 1976

The very first image of the Christian Virgin and Child may be a wall painting from the catacombs of Santa Priscilla on the via Salaria in Rome. It dates from the second century of the Christian era and is a protoype of the *Maria Lactans*, the divine nursing mother whose image was eventually treated by

53

Left: Adam and Eve in The Fall *from Master Bertram of Minden's Grabow Altarpiece, 1379–81. Here is a depiction of Original Sin. Master Bertram's theology is weak; both Adam and Eve have navels, suggesting human, not divine, birth.*

Right: The Ara Pacis Augustae, *or the Altar of Augustan Peace, was commissioned 13BC. Its sculptures describe a Golden Age of Roman administration and includes the Terra Mater (Earth Mother), a symbolic figure of fertility which fed directly into Christian iconography of the Virgin.*

St Mary of Egypt

Another sensational Mary – with a clear relationship to the
Magdalene story – was the Egyptian girl who lived in
profitable and pleasurable sin in Alexandria. She joined a
seaborne pilgrimage to keep the Festival of the Exaltation
of the Holy Cross in Jerusalem, but did so not for religious
purposes, only to continue her 'evil practices' on board.
When she landed in Jerusalem, a mysterious power was
repulsed from a church she intended to visit. Suddenly, her
past life appeared before her in all its vileness. On application
to the Virgin herself she was allowed in and was given
instructions to cross the river Jordan. Here she received the
Sacrament and then decided to live in the desert for half a
century, entertained only by a diet of roots and herbs. A lion
dug her grave with his paws. Like the Magdalene, she is
shown in art with flowing long hair, a token of wantonness
turned into penitence. She was so popular that her body
parts were spread as relics throughout Italy. The covent of
St Maria Egizia in Naples has her head, the larger part of her
body is in Urbino and the rest in Cremona. Pietro da Cortona's
painting of her (*St Mary of Egypt*, circa 1650, right) lying dead
while the lion digs her grave is in Florence's Pitti Palace.

every major European Renaissance artist in both the north and the south. The influence of the type is unfathomably deep. A Flemish Virgin and Child, for example, represented an ideal of womanly beauty that would have utterly transcended the everyday squalor of life in rural Brabant. A serene Virgin by Dirc Bouts or Hans Memling or Robert Campin would simply have been the most beautiful image a Flemish villager would *ever* see, as well as the most colourful. And while no true records of facial types exist from the fifteenth century, it is a reasonable speculation that a Flemish Virgin was an artistic ideal that did not faithfully represent a farmer's wife in a hovel near Gaasbeek.

As the Renaissance matured, there were fewer images of the Maria Lactans. (And, indeed, apart from Caribbean kitsch, there are none today.) Paintings of the Virgin in Western art became progressively more worldly, more secular, as the emerging reality of the modern woman evolved. Although it is significant that as the act of nursing became a less popular image, so – necessarily – the breast itself retreated under cover. This is because the breast was becoming sexualized: less the property of the infant than the lover. During the later Middle Ages the Virgin's milk was one of the most popular of relics (widely distributed samples are claimed to exist in Aix-en-Provence, Walsingham, Paris, Naples and elsewhere), but by 1500 the breast did not indicate a means of nourishing the Christ-child, but had become instead an element of the erotic vocabulary.

The Nineteenth Ecumenical Council of the Roman Catholic Church, usually known as The Council of Trent, was held between 1545 and 1563. Among its many deliberations was a ruling that nudity – which essentially meant bare breasts – should be banned, at least in art. Accordingly, Michelangelo's assistant Daniele da Volterra was commissioned post-mortem to cover-up the nude parts of the Sistine Chapel ceiling. This he did in a way most critics think of as ham-fisted, although his energy and application must be applauded. In a secularizing world, the image of a

nursing Christian mother became ever less significant and the cult of the Virgin, or at least its treatment in art, declined.

But while the graphic presence of the Virgin declined, the philosophical idea endured. Mary the Virgin, who imposes chastity while she also espouses motherhood, has her exact opposite in the equally contradictory Mary Magdalene, the first witness of the Resurrection, but a figure of richly ambiguous status with a confused multi-cultural identity. (Made more confused still by Dan Brown's sensational *The Da Vinci Code*.) The Magdalene is the matron saint of weak and penitent women. She was absolved from all her very many sins by her love of Jesus. Indeed, in some versions of her story this love, as Dan Brown surmised, had found physical expression.

The histories tell of her colourful life. Put in a rudderless, oarless boat with her brother and sister, Martha and Lazarus, Mary Magdalene landed in Marseille. Promptly after landfall she converted the local population and then went out to a convenient desert where she lived for 30 years without sustenance, nourished instead by celestial food and songs sung to her by angels in Heaven. Her remains were found in the thirteenth century and the cathedral church of St Maximin-la-Ste-Baume (51km [32m] from Marseille) is her architectural memorial.

Mary Magdalene is usually shown with an alabaster box of ointment (purpose unspecified) and always with profuse long hair, on her account now held to be a symbol of carnality and lasciviousness in women. As a saved woman and penitent, she is sometimes shown contemplating a skull. The 'baume' in St-Maximin-la-Ste-Baume in Provence refers to the 'balm' or soothing ointments for which the Magdalene became famous.

She is the prototype of the prostitute who turned out to have a heart-of-gold while the Virgin is the sempiternal blameless mother, either suckling in her adoration or weeping in her misery. Because of the Virgin Mary and Mary Magdalene, for millennia the virgin/whore choice was the only career option open to single women. And as Marina Warner dolefully noted, it was a definition of women in terms only of their relationship to men (who designed them).

Opposite: The Council of Trent
in an eighteenth-century copy
of an original from 1545.
The Ecumenical Council of
the Roman Catholic Church
banned nudity in art.

Warhaffte Abbildung des Heil: Concily oder Kirchen-Versamlung zu Trient, so Angefangen.
A° 1545. Und geendet 1563. Wie solche Herz oberster Melchior Lussy Ritter Und Landaman
Alls gewester Abgesandter von den 7. Loblt Chatt Cantonen in seinem Wohnhaus hate
Abmahlen Lassen: Disere Taffel hat Herz Haubtman Felix Leonti Keyser Alt Land-
aman zu Ehren und gedächtnus Hochermelten Herren Lussis als seines gewesten Uran=
Herren Copieren, und in das Capuciner=Convent Ubersetzen Lassen A° 1769.

59

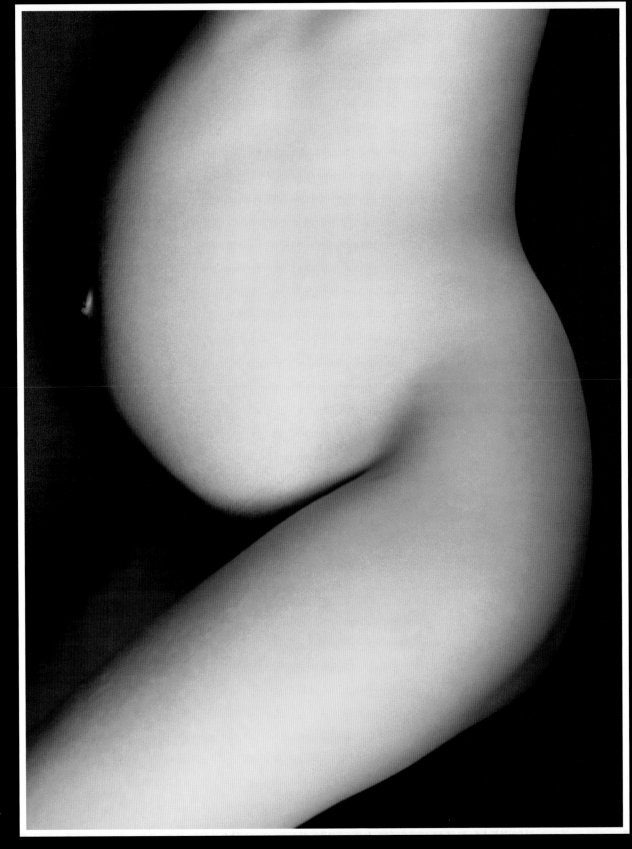

Left: Piero della Francesca
The Madonna del Parto *from*
Monterchi, circa 1460.
Pregnant Madonnas had been
painted by earlier Italian
masters, but Piero's fresco is
unusually straightforward.
The Queen of Heaven,
beneficiary of the divine
Immaculate Conception, is
presented as a real woman. This
is prototype modern pregnancy.

Right: Pregnancy may destroy WHR
(Waist-to-Hips Ratio), but
enhances glorious curves while
exciting confused responses about
motherhood and lust.

THE
EROTICIZED
BOTTOM

Behind

Above: Aesthetic possibilities of the bottom extend from numerology to sculpture. A figure '3' flipped ninety degrees suddenly evokes one of nature's most familiar shapes.

Opposite: By disconnecting this model's bottom from the rest of her body and framing it in an apartment window, Jeanloup Sieff wittily isolates formal perfection: not scatlogy, but sculpture. A la fenêtre, *1973.*

The Board of Commissioners of St John's County, Florida, were much exercised in the early 1990s by the question of public nudity becoming a nuisance to chaste retirement communities. As fashion and taste progressively revealed more flesh, guidelines were required to establish what was and was not acceptable in terms of exposure.

In reaching their decision to ban the airing of 'private' parts in public, they established an epic definition of the bottom. With the pseudo-scientific zeal of a nineteenth-century biometrist mingled with the raw nerve-endings of a tub-thumping seventeenth century puritan bent on discovering affronts to propriety, it was determined that a bottom was:

'The area at the rear of the human body (sometimes referred to as the gluteus maximus) which lies between two imaginary straight lines running parallel to the ground when a person is standing, the first or top such line being a half inch below the top of the vertical cleavage of the nates (i.e. the prominence formed by the muscles running from the back of the hip to the back of the leg) and the second or bottom such line being a half-inch above the lowest point of the curvature of the fleshy protuberance (sometimes referred to as the gluteal fold) and between two imaginary straight lines, one on each side of the body (the "outside lines") which outside lines are perpendicular to the ground and to the horizontal lines described above, and which perpendicular outside lines pass through the outermost point(s) at which each nate meets the outer side of each leg. Notwithstanding the above, buttocks shall not include the leg, the hamstring muscle below the gluteal fold, the tensor fasciae latae muscles, or any of the above described portion of the human body that is between either (i) the left inside perpendicular line and the left outside perpendicular line or (ii) the right inside perpendicular line and the right outside perpendicular line. For the purpose of the previous sentence, the left inside perpendicular line shall be an imaginary straight line on the left side of the anus (i) that is perpendicular to the ground and to the horizontal lines described above and (ii) that is one third of the distance from the anus to the left outside line. (The above description can generally be described as covering one third of the buttocks centred on the cleavage for the length of the cleavage).'
— HARPER'S MAGAZINE, JUNE 1992

The perfect shape for female buttocks is a question that goes very deep into myth and psycho-history. A synonym is 'behind' because it is secret. Both people and houses have facades as well as secret gardens. Evolutionary biology also has a lot to say, not all of it terribly scientific, about the bottom. The conventional view is that because of a readily made association in the male mind between wide hips and child-bearing potential, generous buttocks gave positive signs to predatory hunter-gatherers in search of a fertile mate. And from the merely functional-survivalist search for a breeding partner, culture soon laid many different meanings on that perfect rear.

The classical statue of Aphrodite Callipygos is the starting point for any cultural history of the eroticized bottom. Known in several versions, it may be an illustration of an ancient story about two sisters from Syracuse who were engaged in a conversation over who it was had the prettiest bottom. We do not know that this was a popular topic of everyday conversation in the world, but the fact that the story has been transmitted to us does suggest that bottoms had acquired an amount of semantic significance by, say, the fourth century BC. Anyway, the sisters decided to ask a passing youth to make the judgement and end their dispute. And 'his choice' was to be 'his reward' as Francis Haskell and Nicholas Penny nicely put it in *Taste and the Antique*.

The youth chose his preferred bottom and, presumably, claimed his reward. The second sister, miffed that her bottom had been rejected on aesthetic grounds, asked another passer-by to make the same judgement. He chose the second sister, perhaps because the first was otherwise engaged at the time. Both couples got married and built a temple to Aphrodite of the Beautiful Bottom.

The proportions of the buttocks of Aphrodite Callipygos were examined in the seventeenth century by pioneering bio-statisitician Gerard Audran, who found them to be exceptionally distended in the vertical axis. We may make our own judgements from Lord Leighton's *Psyche* (1890), which is based on a reliable (although not original) antique version of the Aphrodite. By the standards of the early twenty-first century, at least as expressed in fashion magazines and advertisements for tights, Aphrodite's bottom is large and dependent, slung rather lower than the tastes of twenty-first century art directors dictate.

An important element fundamental to the understanding of the bottom is its multiple meanings. Here is a body part that has a trinity of associations: with walking, excretion and reproduction. Plus sitting. It has a practical function as a fleshy cushion, but also a critically important symbolic role.

Frederic, Lord Leighton was a celebrity artist of Victoria's Imperium. His Psyche, 1890, *(right) is just one example of his pre-occupation with generous flesh. His source for this gorgeous image of Cupid's lover was the ineffable* Aphrodite Callipygos *(opposite) which he saw in Naples. She is the starting point for any discussion of the beautiful bottom.*

62

64

Left: An erotic postcard of circa 1900. The ample callipygian bottom passed into European popular culture, but not into African. The astonishing profiles of steatopygic Hottentots (opposite) clearly show that ideals of womanly shape are not universal.

Some ethologists, including Desmond Morris who became a celebrity amongst British children in the Fifties as custodian of an apparently unchallenging, but culturally determinist, black-and-white television programme called *Zoo Time*, have argued that the bottom is the most significant erogenous zone of all.

Human females, Morris argued, on what scientific basis was never made quite clear, only acquired breasts after they abandoned the knuckle-dragging quadruped crouch and began to walk on two legs. With a better view of the distance, human beings expanded their horizons. This new upright posture tended to make the sexually alluring buttocks relatively less apparent, so ventral mammae were promptly grown in compensation. While the buttocks had been an authentic target for the male, directing him to the primary sexual feature, the breasts became a surrogate. Salvador Dali made play with this idea when in 1938 he proposed some dress designs with false breasts in the back.

With its shifting role and meanings, unsurprisingly we feel a deep ambiguity about the bottom. That word is singular, but the English 'buttocks' and the Latin 'nates' are plural. Are there one or two of them? Those triple associations mean the bottom is more than it seems.

As the first generation of European explorers evolved into the first developmental biologists, the bottom ceased to be merely a focus of fetishistic erotic speculation, but became a marker of cultural difference. When it was noticed, for example, that Kalahari bushwomen enjoyed a greater vibratory movement of the buttocks, it was a pseudo-scientific way of saying that a fat arse rather suggests primitivism.

Darwin has a story about a Somali man lining up 20 potential wives and assessing their allure on the basis of quite how much their bottoms projected from that same imaginary line described the Board of Commissioners of St John's County. Projections come and go, but a well-proportioned and curvaceous rear has ever been a desirable feature in life and art. The question, of course, is at what point do the mathematical determinants of 'well-proportioned' skid off into the treacherous territory of gross and mis-shapen? And when, exactly, do pleasing curves sicken into the pain of a lardy butt? Neuro-aesthetics may have a clue.

Steatopygia

From the Greek for fat rump. First used circa 1818, it is a condition best described by the statistics of the anthropometrician. It exists if the projection of the buttocks beyond an imaginary vertical line exceeds 4 per cent of an individual's overall height. Nineteenth-century researchers, finding steatopygia a dominant trait of Kalahari Bushmen, the Khoikhoi and Andaman islanders, quickly identified it with 'primitivism'.

In Western art, the breast acquired a recognizable profile before the bottom. The image of Maria Lactans, the nurturing mother, allowed painters to experiment with mammarial form. But when painters decided to treat the Garden of Eden, the opportunity to depict Adam and Eve naked (and naked it was, since nudity, the absence of clothes, was theoretically impossible before clothes existed) they had an iconographically valid reason to paint bottoms as well as breasts. Thus, paintings by van Eyck and Cranach, to name only the absolute masters of the subject, were early experiments with the design of the European bottom.

And if, for example, the *Ghent Altarpiece* (1434, Sint Baafskathedraal, Ghent) and Cranach's *The Close of the Silver Age* (1527–35, National Gallery, London) are exemplary, then the European bottom was modest, symmetrical and firm.

If van Eyck's Eve has a bottom which hangs a little lower than Cranach's mythological types then this may be a question of fashion. Eve also has (like the same painter's Giovanna Cenami in *The Arnolfini Wedding*, National Gallery, 1434) a putative pregnant bump. This was in Flemish vogue at the time.

Since about 1500, bottoms have become ever more familiar. Visitors to London's National Gallery will know (mature, as opposed to infant) bottoms by, and this is a random, although alphabetical, list: François Boucher, Angelo di Cosimo (Bronzino), Paul Cezanne, Cornelis van Haarlem, Antonio Allegri (Correggio), Lucas Cranach, Hilaire-Germain-Edgar Degas, Jean-Auguste-Dominique Ingres, Damiano Mazza, Michelangelo, Iacopo Palma, Nicolas Poussin, Guido Reni, Pierre-Auguste Renoir, Peter Paul Rubens, Andrea Schiavone, Jacopo Tintoretto, Tiziano Vecellio (Titian) and Diego Velázquez.

Left: Jan van Eyck The Arnolfini Wedding, *1434. Scholars dispute whether Giovanna Cenami is pregnant, or simply nurturing a fashionable bump under her clothes.*

Lucas Cranach's The Close of the Silver Age, *1527–34 (above) and Jan van Eyck's Eve from* The Ghent Altarpiece, *1432 (right). Each shows that the ideal early European bottom was lean and tight.*

Left: Antonio Canova
The Three Graces, *1814–17.*
Canova frequently sculpted from
live nude models. Beauty, Charm
and Joy are his sitters. Each has
a perfectly proportioned neo-
classical bottom… in chaste,
snowy marble rather than
coarse, pink flesh.

Right: Man Ray's Monument
to D.A.F. de Sade, *1933.*
This monument to the French
aristocrat who gave his name to
sadism imposes an outline
crucifix onto the cleft of a
woman's bottom. Look again
and the crucifix assumes the
profile of an aggressive phallus.

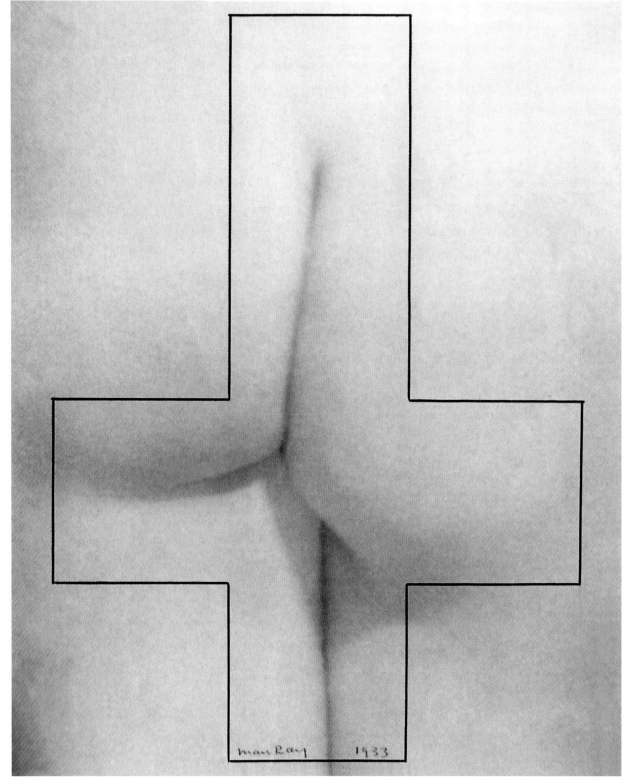

But while this is a list that provides the eager connoisseur of the aesthetic Euro-bottom with magnificent raw material for study and comparison, it is also a rather short one. Given the vast size and range of the National Gallery's (essentially pre-modern) collections, it is remarkable on any visit how very few bottoms are actually treated in art before the twentieth century. Indeed, the evidence is so weighted as to give reasonable support to a thesis that maintains the bottom became a preoccupation only during the twentieth century.

In such a thesis, Freud would inevitably be cited as an influence since he attributed so much significance to what he was pleased to call the anal stage of a child's development. Additionally, the Surrealists found a rich source of ideas, association and validations in Freud's apparently 'scientific' insistence on the creative vitality of the unconscious. At the same time, the Surrealists' fascination with the female body as an artistic mystery provided a firm basis for the elevation of the bottom to art.

Brassai photographed bottoms and gave them a formal perfection that loses nothing in comparison with the sculptor Constantin Brâncusi's biomorphic sculptures. Alas, Sigmund Freud never wrote about Salvador Dali's *Young Girl Auto-Sodomising Herself*; it would, one imagines, have confirmed many of the great man's prejudices about modern desire and modern motivation. Hans Belmer's trussed and truncated dolls reveal a darker side of this interest. But it was the great Surrealist photographer Man Ray who made bottoms his own.

His *Monument á D.A.F de Sade* appeared in *Le surrealisme au service de la revolution*. It is a close-up photograph of a woman's bottom; the vertical cleft and the horizontal folds making a lop-sided cross. This itself is framed in a geometrically perfect cross, an up-ended Christian symbol containing a design of the perfect buttocks. As Jane Livingston wrote, this astonishing image 'arouses simultaneous feelings of tension and resolution' (*Amour Fou,* 1985).

And it was simultaneously blasphemous and provocative, as it was intended to be. In about 1935 Man Ray used exactly the same design for the binding of his own copy of de Sade's *One Hundred and Twenty Days of Sodom*. And Man Ray's great disciple was the American photographer, Lee Miller. A nude of about 1931 by Miller is in the Julien Levy Collection at the Art Institute of Chicago. It is a highly stylized formal composition of a crouching woman seen from above. The orientation is upside-down and the head is invisible below the x-axis. Her bottom is at the top of the picture, as perfect as a peach.

The aesthetic is abstract-industrial, clearly based on a 1930 Man Ray nude known as *La Priére*, now in the Lee Miller Archives in Sussex. That a woman's bottom might be so dehumanized, indeed, objectified into a stylized design was entirely consonant with the spirit of the age. In 1927 Brâncusi had to persuade US customs authorities that his erotic biomorphic sculptures (many resembling bottoms) were 'art' with no duty payable, as opposed to industrial components which carried the obligation of paying import tax.

Left: Hans Belmer (1902–75) Les jeux de la poupée, 1935–8, currently exhibited in the Centre Pompidou, Paris. Belmer's transgressive images of sadistically distorted puppets took the Surrealist interest with womanly form to dark destinations.

Right: Salvador Dali The Young Virgin Auto-Sodomised by Her Own Chastity, 1954. Dali (whose name actually means 'desire' in Catalan) thought 'eroticism must always be ugly'. In the Fifties Dali was preoccupied with rhinoceros horns which both comprise the Young Virgin's body while threatening to violate her. The painting was once in the collection of the Playboy Mansion, where its bizarre eroticism may have had a curious influence over the design of girly centrefolds.

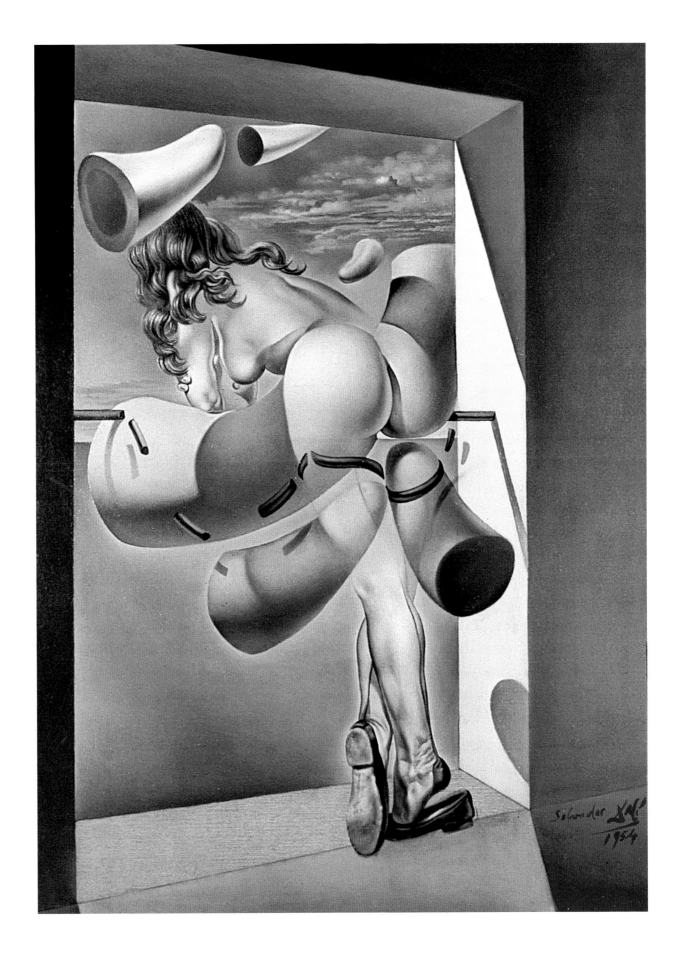

71

BEHIND: THE EROTICIZED BOTTOM

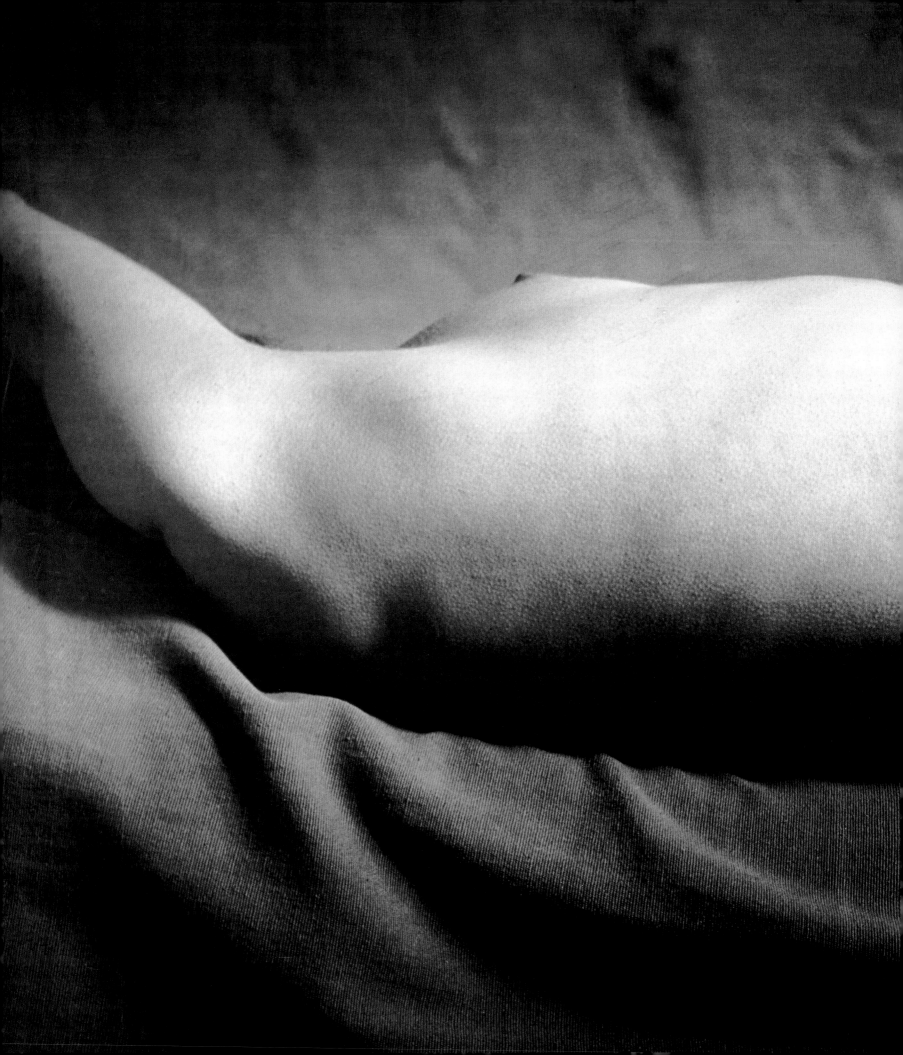

Page 72–73: Nu. 116, *as seen in the Centre Pompidou, Paris. The photographer Halász Gyula (1899–1984) was better-known as Brassaï. His nude photographs, often of Paris prostitutes, became surreal compositions.*

Left: This 1976 poster-girl by Martin Elliott has some claim to be the most reproduced photograph of modern times. Ms Fiona Butler's naked bottom on a Birmingham University tennis court was inspired by a wardrobe malfunction at a second round Wimbledon match between Emmanuelle Galgliardi and Kristina Brandi. Elliott had previously worked as a motor industry photographer.

Opposite: The sculptural treatment of the woman's body came full circle, culturally speaking, with the cult of industrial design. Herbert Read's Art and Industry *(1934) celebrated the raw beauty of industrial components, including ship's propellers (this one belongs to RMS Queen Mary). And in 1947 Read collaborated with Roland Penrose, Lee Miller's husband, to found London's Institute of Contemporary Arts. In this way Surrealism influenced the popular conception of design.*

And this treatment of a woman's body was contemporary with another form of aestheticized objectification: the new cult of 'industrial design'. The mid-Thirties saw a rash of new books inviting readers to see in industrial components – perhaps a roller bearing or a ship's propellor – the very same artistic qualities they might find in the new abstract art. Among the most influential of these books, at least in England, was Herbert Read's *Art and Industry*, 1934. In 1947 Herbert Read founded the Institute of Contemporary Art with Roland Penrose, the collector, critic and wealthy champion of Surrealism. Penrose was Lee Miller's second husband. So it is not too ambitious to claim that the Surrealist vision of how a woman's body might be seen as design fed straight into the British establishment's interpretation of contemporary art.

Among painters, Stanley Spencer and Lucien Freud have given us epic interpretations of the bottom although each treats flesh with a sort of loathing rather than the sort of beautiful deference employed by, say, Man Ray. Spencer's flesh looks like cold, clammy, lardy bacon. Freud's often looks as though it is rotting, or at least corpulent, gross and decadent. In contrast, photographers have been better able to capture the strange formal beauty sensed by the Surrealists. China Hamilton, an English photographer says 'nothing quite feeds the primal desire for curving lines'.

Jeanloup Sieff was one of the most influential reporter-photographers of the later twentieth century, with a spell at the Magnum agency and a portfolio including work for *Vogue, Elle* and *Jardin des Modes*. He has made the eroticized bottom a special subject, publishing a monograph called *Derrieres* in 1993. The 'soft curves of buttocks' define for Sieff a woman's beauty. He writes:

'Some posteriors belong to the mythology of the body, and one of the finest definitions that can be applied to them is the one that Proust gave of beauty, which is… "the complementary quality which our imagination overwhelmed by longing bestows on a fragmentary and fleeting woman passing by." '

Sieff was first stirred when, aged 12 or 13, he discovered a statue on the rue Delessert, near the Trocadero in Paris. In 1974, as his interest in the subject hardened, he wrote an essay called 'Derrieres after 1968' in which he paid

Opposite: The annals of nineteenth century psychology – in search of behavioural theories - recurrently attribute to adipose hips a strong sexual character. In the twentieth century, photographers treated the same feature as voluptuous abstraction.

tribute to a part of the body he felt had been neglected. He explained:

'Doing a portrait consists, more often than not, in depicting a face or a bust in familiar or neutral surroundings. The face is the most exposed part of the body, the most visible and the most used in social life. It has become a hypocritical mask which can be made to express whatever we like, which can laugh when we are sad, appear interested when we're dying of boredom, or take on a stony air when we're bored with passion. This is one of the reasons I became interested in derrieres.'

Because the bottom is the most protected and secret part of the body, Sieff found in it special value for interpretation. The woman's bottom 'retains its childhood innocence which

the look or the hands have long since lost. It is also, in a plastic sense, the most stirring... made up of curves and promises; it is memory.'

In his book Sieff chose 93 bottoms because he liked the way the figure '3' rather suggested a visual pun on his subject. He believes that bottoms are as diverse as the individuals to whom they belong. Sometimes they are merely functional cushions. Instead, he was looking for elegance and aristocracy, bottoms that are 'the Romanesque vaults of body architecture which enable us to find original faith in a woman in God's image'.

Proust believed that having a body is a threat to the mind. Jeanloup Sieff chose his *derrieres* for their 'plastic, intellectual and moral' qualities. What is beautiful, he argued, does not have to be stupid.

Above: Model Elle MacPherson became known as 'The Body' on account of her comely figure. In a heroic act of self-exploitation, she extended her personal brand to a range of lingerie supposed to offer customers access to her attributes via knickers and bras. Photograph by Rankin, 2003.

Page 78: An Edwardian bottom from 1906.

Page 80: An 'odalisque' is an Ottoman pleasure-girl whose purpose was to supplement Islam's allowance of four wives. François Boucher (1703–70) painted many different versions of them for private clients in search of titillation. The decorative flourishes of his Rococo style obscure the blunt sexual invitation of the pose. Of this particular 1745 painting Diderot said Boucher was prostituting his own wife.

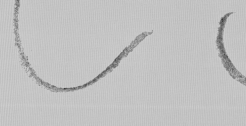

THE
DELTA
OF
VENUS

Between

Above: 'Woman' is immediately brought to mind by the very simplest visual language.

Opposite: Nero di Bicci The Ascension of the Virgin, *1465. The Virgin is surrounded by a mandorla, the almond-shaped device that suggests the vagina and the birth canal.*

'Woman' can be immediately signified in a rapidly sketched ideogram showing two semi-circles above a dark triangle. The circles are the breasts. The triangle is even more complicated, fascinating and psychologically resonant. Conflicting functional demands are beautifully reconciled in neat detail.

One of the most curious episodes in consumer psychology occurred in Detroit in the late Fifties. Imaginative officers of the Ford Motor Company decided to launch a premium product to enhance the prestige and profitability of the business.

With surprising civic responsibility, Ford tried to introduce seatbelts in the mid-Fifties, but its customers saw no enhanced prestige. So Ford took the cupidity route. The Edsel (named after Henry Ford's son) was aimed somewhere between youth's taste for hot-rods and the middle-aged taste for luxury. Never had any product ever been so thoroughly consumer-researched. All this research cost $250m (at a time when the car itself cost about $4,000). Introduced in 1958, it was ignominiously withdrawn from production two years later.

The marketers said it was the wrong car at the wrong time, but the motivational researchers were keen to find underlying reasons. Aesthetics was one. Someone said the tail-lights looked like ingrown toenails. But it was the car's face that caused the problem. The vertical grille resembled a horse's collar. Someone else said it looked like an Oldsmobile sucking a lemon. But what this chromed mandorla really looked like was a vagina. Although the vagina is a continuous source of fascination to men, it is also culturally associated with fear and threat. The early Christian writer Tertullian said women are the 'ianna diaboli' or the Gates of Hell. The idea of the *vagina dentata*, which is to say one fitted with teeth, appears in several cultures. In *The Great Mother* Erich Neumann explains that a hero is the man who overcomes the Terrible Mother by breaking the teeth out of her vagina. These myths may be sourced in memories of the trauma of birth or may even represent a metaphor of man's anxiety about sex. But what is certain is that when the grille of your 1958 Edsel Ranger Villager Station Wagon excites primitive and repressed fears of a vagina that bites (as hypnosis of selected consumers revealed), then you have a commercial disaster on your hands.

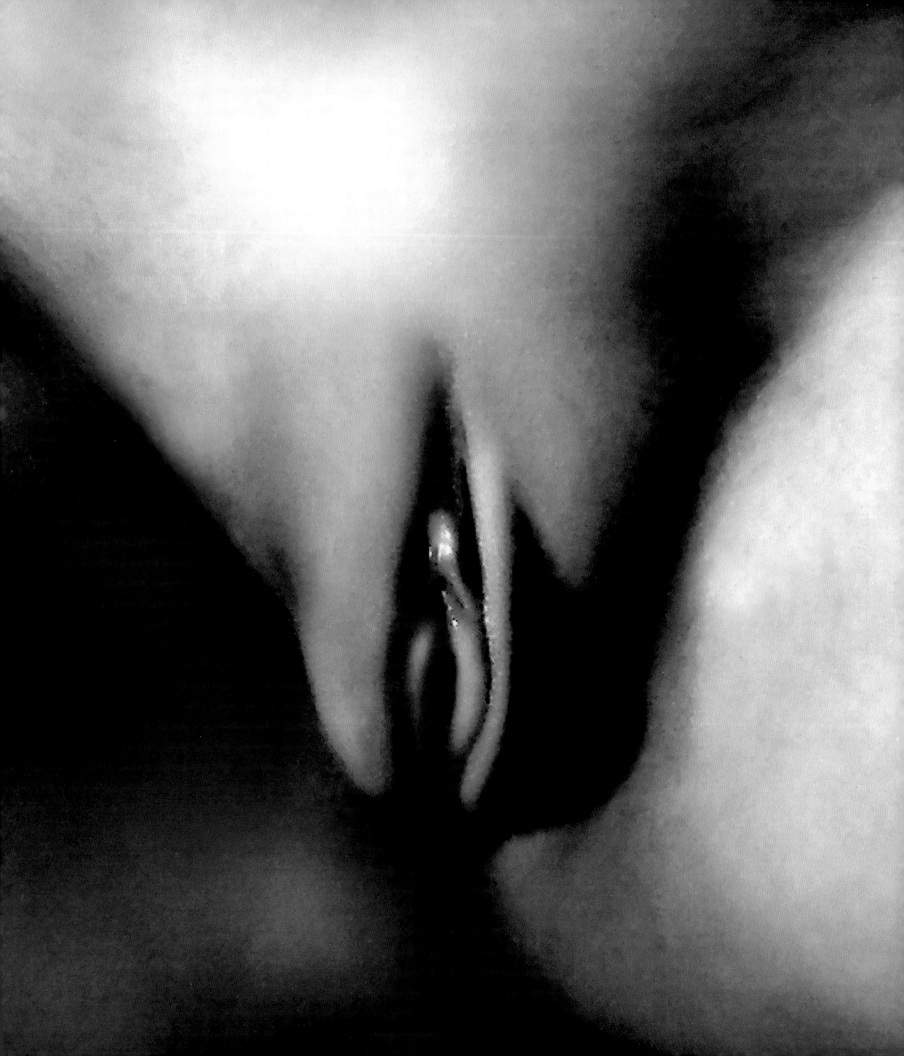

Eventually, Edsel became a metaphor of failure. In 1966 Walker Percy in his novel *The Last Gentleman* described the commercial calamity as 'the last victory of the American people over marketing research and opinion polls'. In 1971 the poet Karl Shapiro wrote a novel about an American academic who considered his life a personality calamity. He titled it *Edsel*. In the same year, when the Du Pont experiment with Corfam, a sort of artificial leather, tanked, it was described by *The New York Times* as 'Du Pont's $100m Edsel'.

The difficulty of naming this part – or is at an area? – is richly fascinating. Artists avoided a precise treatment of the pubic area until the nineteenth century, perhaps rushed into a fury of competitive activity by the new generation of erotic photographers whose new medium had no traditional constraints. The grim sexologists Masters and

Johnson called the Delta of Venus a dense bulbar vascoconcentration. Aristophanes searches the whole range of animal and vegetable (and even mineral) metaphors. So we have box, piggie, pomegranate, rose, garden, delphinium, meadow, thicket, celery, mint, fuzz, gate, circle, pit, gulf, vent, sea urchin, hearty, brazier, hot coals, boiled sausage, barleycake, pancake, thrush, mousehold, bird's nest and gravy boat. Many classical authors mixed up words for pig and pudenda. Imagists with Oriental tastes sometimes refer to the Jade Pavilion.

To revert to geographical metaphors, which have so often been useful in circumlocuting anatomical fact, contemporary colloquial Australian has the pubic bush as a 'Mapatasi', being a conflation of the expression A Map of Tasmania, a name given on account of its morphic similarity

Page 85: The radiator of the grille of the commercially catastrophic 1958 Ford Edsel was an unconscious reminder of the vagina dentata, *the vagina with teeth which appears in several different cultures. The modern photograph makes clear the unconscious source of the Edsel designer's iconography, eventually revealed to researchers after experiments with hypnosis and recovered memory.*

Right: Australian demotic for the female pubic triangle is 'mapatasi', a contraction of 'Map of Tasmania'.

Opposite: Examples of the bizarre variety of imagery used by Aristophanes to describe a woman's sexual parts.

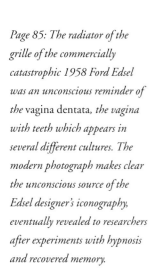

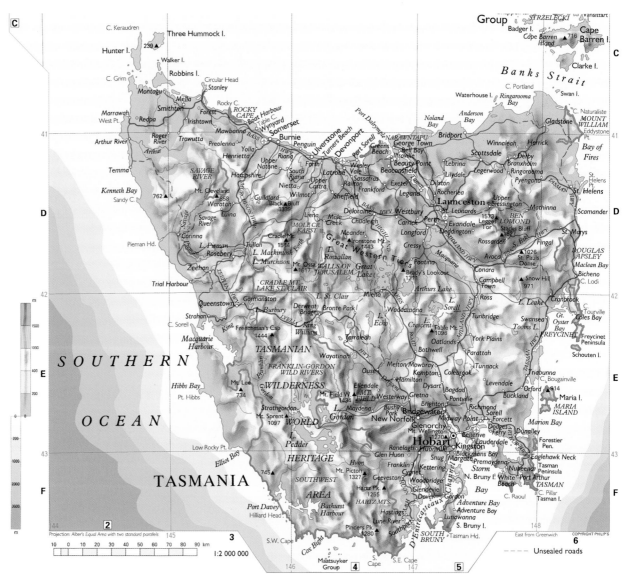

with the South Australian island. Or it can be the pudendal cleft, but this is an expression with neither the advantages of technical accuracy or poetic charm. No one surely, not even in the helpless transports of amatory bliss, has ever actually muttered 'pudendal cleft'. This may be on account of residual etymological memory: pudenda in Latin means that of which you are ashamed. To compound this ambiguity there is the curiously mixed etymology of words related to venereal: '*venenum*' is Latin for poison… but is also Latin for an aphrodisiac.

Our complex reactions are based on the curiosities of female human anatomy. The multi-functional character of the intercrural area was gloomily commented upon by a depressed Burgundian monk called Odon of Cluny: '*inter faeces et urinam nascimur*'. That we are indeed born between outlets of bodily waste perhaps accounts for many phobias and acute anxieties, yours, mine and Freud's included.

Curiously, the defining female anatomy arises out of shared componentry in the womb. At the very earliest stages of life, male and female are indistinguishable. In foetal development, the gender-indeterminate labioscrotal swellings which evolve in the first six to eight weeks of pregnancy eventually separate into the female labia maiora and the male scrotum. So the Bible is entirely wrong to say that Eve sprang from Adam's rib. Every human egg is female.

When the male seed enters the egg at the moment of conception, the resulting zygote can be either gender. At about seven weeks, testosterone masculinizes the brains of future males and specific sexual characteristics begin to evolve in the embryo. So, against all religious and cultural prejudices, the biological truth is that, in the beginning, Adam was Eve. In compensation for this sex change, the vernacular French '*con*' is masculine. While a common vulgar expression in British and American English refers to a small feline creature, the French can also call it a cat. Again, a masculine word in the French language.

In early nineteenth-century Paris, speculation about primitive sexuality became a popular collective fantasy. Manners may have deterred popular open discussion about sex, hence the scandal of *Madame Bovary* and the furtive popularity of the *maisons clos*. But the observation of tribal behaviour offered a convenient camouflage for open speculation about sex and, more particularly, the woman's sexual parts.

The unfortunate focus of this pornographic speculation was a tribal nomad girl from south-west Africa captured by a Dutch ship's surgeon in 1810. He gave her the Netherlandish name Saartje Baartman. Her case became known as the Hottentot Venus. Fascination with her steatopygic rump was matched only by horrified fascination with her dramatically enlarged labia: the case of Saartje Baartman illustrates our simultaneous fascination with and revulsion from the uro-genital area.

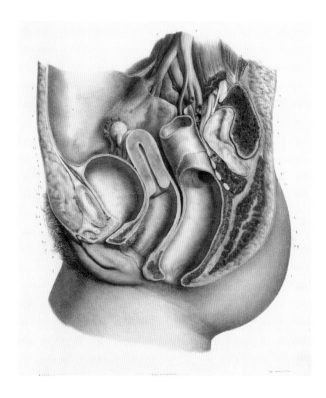

Left: Stripped of allure, mystique, decorum and eroticism, gynaecological illustrations present the complexities of woman as design in terms of infrastructure, rather as if the subject were a petro-chemical plant.

Right: The mysterious coming together of functional exhausts with pleasure centres has long been noticed: the Burgundian monk Odon of Cluny sighed, 'inter faeces et urinam nascimur'. Or, bluntly, we are born between excrement.

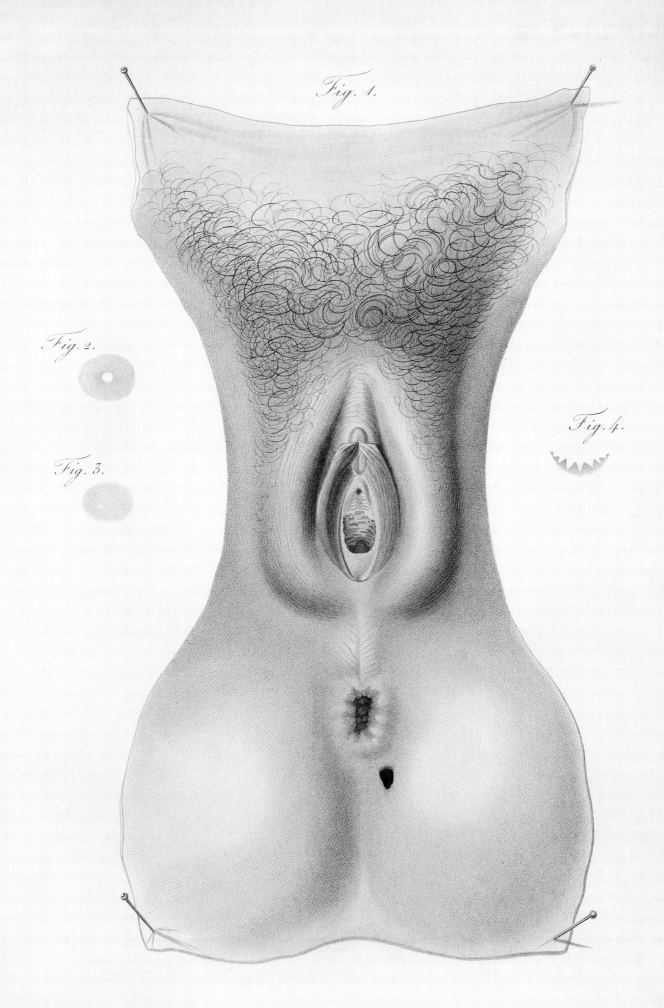

Pl. 10.

Fig. 1.

Fig. 2.

Fig. 3.

Fig. 4.

The Baartman freak show circus moved to England. In the home of parliamentary democracy she was placed on a 60cm (2ft) tall plinth so curious visitors could prod her bottom (she was very short). In Paris she was similarly put on show in the rue Neuve des Petits Champs. Scientific investigation, of a sort, now began. There was speculation that Saartje (who had become Sarah as she was tri-lingual) might represent the 'missing link' since, in the days before anthropology had become a proper academic discipline, this was a focus of much sloppy research.

The great anatomist Georges Cuvier was the leader of a scientific group who were eager to trace Sarah as being a descendant from the orang-utan, while also keen to investigate her astonishing genitals. Her 'Hottentot Apron' comprised labia that were distended by about 10cm (4in). Cuvier devoted 16 pages to her in the *Memoires du Museum d'Histoire Naturelle* (c.1816). Only one paragraph was devoted to her brain, but a whole nine pages were taken up describing her genitalia, breasts and buttocks. After Sarah died (it was said of syphilis, described as an 'inflammatory and disruptive illness') the two 'wrinkled fleshy petals' of her labia were preserved in a bell jar in the Musée de l'Homme. Here they remained until surprisingly recently.

Progress in ethnic stereotyping as well as advances in conceptions of woman became features in popular French art. So far from being a missing link, an African woman as romantic revolutionary heroine soon became acceptable. A sculpture called *Pourquoi naitre esclave?* is a splendid example of this improvement. The artist was Jean-Baptiste Carpeaux, a nineteenth-century hack from Valenciennes whose work was mostly given to sculptures of winsome Neapolitan fisherboys. His highly romanticized *Slave* is in the Chapelle de Chartreux, Douai: she is posed dynamically, looks to the future and has a triumphalist air. She is also highly sexualized. Despite the precedent of the biometricians' relentless investigations into Ms Baartman's vulva, Carpeaux did not speculate on the uro-genital area of this new model of African womanhood, but he does give her a dashingly exposed breast, now a symbol of liberty and independence. Carpeaux's design is still popular: the fashionable candle store Cire Trudon in Paris' rue de Tournon will sell you a wax copy.

Contemporary with the *Slave* and 50 years after the Hottentot Venus, it was possible for a leading French artist – although, admittedly, one of a contrarian disposition – to paint a groin shot of a woman. The most explicit painting in the world of museum art is Gustave Courbet's *L'Origine du Monde*. It was painted in 1866 for the bathroom of Khalil Bey, a Turkish man-about-town, and is now exhibited in the Musée d'Orsay, Paris. Without the *cordon sanitaire* of a

90

Right: Georges Cuvier, the French biologist who was determined to show that African women descended from the orang-utan.

Far right: While some French academics were coldly measuring the horrible distortions of 'The Hottentot Venus', some French artists were busy liberating African women from restrictive stereotypes. Jean-Baptiste Carpeaux's Pourquoi Naitre Esclave? *(Why am I a Slave?), 1868, shows a frankly romanticized and none too subtly eroticized version of a negress.*

L'Origine du Monde

Painted by Gustave Courbet in 1866, born Ornans (Doubs), France, 1819, died in La Tour-de-Peilz (Vaud), Switzerland, 1877. Oil on canvas, 46cm x 55cm (18in x 22in) Originally, it was in the collection of Khalil Bey (also owner of Ingres' *Le Bain Turc*), Paris. By 1955 it was in the collection of influential psychoanalyst-philosopher Jacques Lacan, where it was part of the furniture. It has been in the collection of the Musée d'Orsay since 1995. Christine Orban's 2000 novel *J'etais l'Origine du Monde* says the model was the mistress of J.M. Whistler. A Canadian television documentary made in 2000 suggested – on account of the colouration and a bit of engorgement here and there – that the model had been masturbating.

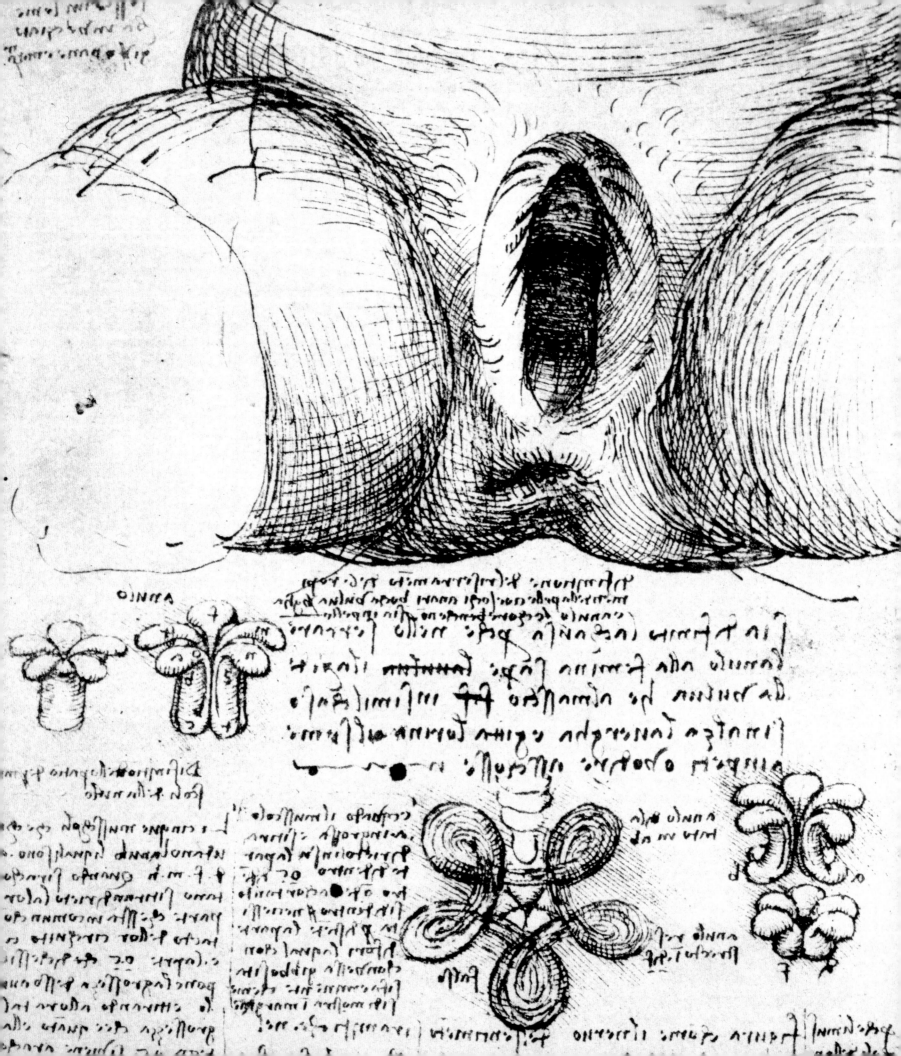

global reputation, without the prestige of one of Paris' great museums, Courbet's astonishing image of the pudendal cleft would be pornographic.

It shows the naked torso of an amply proportioned woman in the days before bikini waxing was either technologically available or fashionable. The radical Courbet's intention was to shock and to be ironic. But, despite his art-historical label as a realist, the details of *L'Origine du Monde*, while fearlessly frank, are not quite anatomically correct. Courbet presents the pudendal cleft as a continuum with the gluteal cleft, as if two fleshy hemispheres. His model lacks the perineal no-man's-land which separates the vaginal opening from the anus. This is a strange lack of observation from Courbet, who was well-used to nude models and a trenchant heterosexual. Leonardo da Vinci, who was not a trenchant heterosexual, made no such mistake. His female anatomical drawings in the *Quaderni d'Anatomie* of 1511–26, while not flattering, are accurate. Courbet could easily have had access to contemporary French anatomical studies: the final volume of Constantin Bonamy's *Atlas d'Anatomie Descriptive du Corps Humain* was published in exactly the same year *L'Origine du Monde* was finished. Instead, he chose to idealize. Despite or, perhaps, because of this, Courbet's painting is the best-selling postcard in the Musée d'Orsay.

But the history of the vagina's (sometimes disguised) role in art is much more ancient. Early Christian gynaecology suggested that the vagina was, anatomically speaking, a penis turned inside-out, a conceit approximately related to our modern understanding of foetal development. In Renaissance paintings the Virgin is often surrounded by an almond-shaped aureole, known as a 'mandorla' on account of its essential similarity to the nut. James Frazer explains that in pre-Christian art the virgin nymph Nana was impregnated with an almond placed in her bosom by Attis. In Byzantine art the mandorla device often surrounds both the Virgin and her Son. With curious gynaecological equivalence, in some Byzantine art the mandorla are painted in concentric patterns getting darker and darker towards the centre. This corresponds both to the anatomical reality of the vaginal canal, but also to the theological doctrine that, as holiness increases, the only way to depict it is by darkness. Meanwhile, in the Musée de Cluny in Paris, there is a fine thirteenth-century ivory plaque from a German coffer showing Christ in Majesty in a mandorla, surrounded by symbols of the Evangelist.

To Hildegard of Bingen, the first woman celebrity musician, the mandorla represented the Cosmos. Sometimes this is composed of seven doves to illustrate the seven gifts of the holy host, but more often it is a graphic of

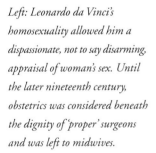

Left: Leonardo da Vinci's homosexuality allowed him a dispassionate, not to say disarming, appraisal of woman's sex. Until the later nineteenth century, obstetrics was considered beneath the dignity of 'proper' surgeons and was left to midwives.

Right: A pregnant woman from a fifteenth-century Anathomia, *by 'pseudo' Galen (Galen of Pegamum, the Roman physician and anatomist).*

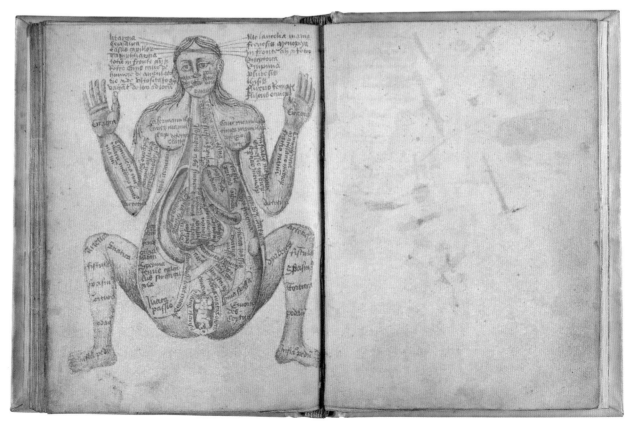

the vagina. Nero di Bicci's *Ascension of the Virgin* (1465), for example, may lack correct anatomical detail, but is no less explicit for that. The Virgin crowned in the birth canal is a profound symbol of the Christian themes of life, death and resurrection. A sacred moment that transcends time and space? Sex and the loss of ego at the *moment critique* may, it seems, have a cultural and bio-medical link to the Resurrection and the Transfiguration.

Discussion and depiction of the Delta of Venus retains a strong element of taboo. Publishing the demotic word led to the most famous obscenity trial in British legal history. In *Lady Chatterley's Lover* the heroine is confused by the rough language of Mellors, who, a fumbling oik, has become her lover. Aristocratically, she demurely asks him 'What is cunt?' He replies 'It's thee down theer.' To Henry Miller, it was rather ungallantly 'a crack with hair on it'. In *The Prisoner of Sex* (1971) Norman Mailer wrote a ferocious attack on Miller's crude fascination and unsympathetic objectification:

'…faceless, characterless, pullulating broads, in all those cunts which undulate with the movements of eels, in all those clearly described broths of soup and grease and marrow and wine which are all he will give us of them – their cunts are always closer to us than their faces – in all the indignities of position. The humiliation of situation, and the endless presentation of women as pure artefacts of farce, their asses all up in the air, still he screams his barbaric yawp of utter adoration for the power and the glory and the grandeur of the female in the Universe.'
— CITED DWORKIN PORNOGRAPHY, 1981

The power to shock remains. We take a mondain and sophisticated interest in Gustave Courbet's groin shot, yet much of the shock and force of Charlotte Roche's cult bestseller *Wetlands* (2007), about a teenage girl and her relationship with her own body, was based on introductory pages which carry a frank and disturbing description of an accident suffered by its grotesquely unhygienic heroine while shaving her pubic hair.

Roche, who is also a television personality based in Germany, may be reacting against the hyper-aesthetics of the fashion industries. She said she wrote the book to be sexually arousing, but then deliberately deflated that sensation by adding long and sensational passages that were deliberately anaphrodisiac in their vividly disturbing descriptions of dirt and smell. Roche explained:

'It's not feminist in a political sense, but instead feminism of the body, that has to do with anxiety and repression and the fear that you stink, and this for me is clearly feminist, that one builds confidence with your own body.'
— INTERNATIONAL HERALD TRIBUNE, 6 JUNE 2008

Roche presented her female audience with a 'language for lust'. That's as may be, but ideas of purity and sacredness also attach to this anatomical area: the concept of the Christian Virgin is the profoundest concept of them all. And it is based on a design that both employs multiple functions and carries every imaginable nuance of meaning.

Left: Henry Miller (1891–1980) was the Francophile American novelist who helped liberate popular discussion of sex. What Gustave Courbet called L'Origine du Monde, *Miller called a 'crack with hair on it'.*

Right: Figures known as 'Shelagh na Gig' are familiar in Romanesque churches throughout Ireland, but also appear in, for example, Church Stretton, Shropshire. The origin and meaning of these strange quasi-erotic figures is not agreed, but what is certain is that they depict grotesque women audaciously displaying their vulva to churchgoers.

BRAS
ARE
FOR
MEN
OR
THE
INDUSTRIALIZATION
OF
THE
BREAST

Above

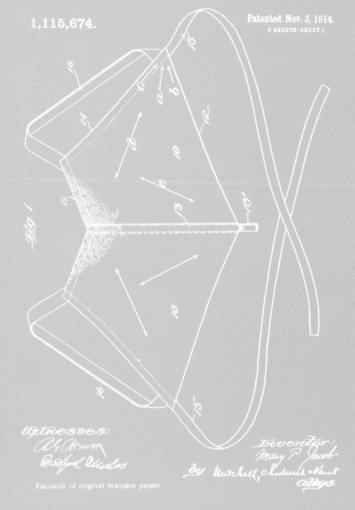

Facsimile of original brassière patent.

Above: The bra is an elaborate device employing cantilevers, load-paths and shock-absorbers. Its purpose is not so much to contain the breast as to advertise it. This is Mary Phelps Jacobs' patent of 3rd November, 1914.

Opposite: The Bestform bra. No finer fit at any price was the promise of this temporary prosthesis from the Thirties.

Bras are for men. This most womanly garment isolates, emphasizes, moulds, packages and presents breasts in a fashion that men find desirable. The functional requirements of stabilizing two dynamic sacs could be met by other solutions, but the fabulous bra creates a preferred sculptural ideal. It is part of the process that Hoag Levins called the industrialization of the breast. In a bra, the breasts are designed: on delectable display, like a sandwich in an automat. To confirm this perception, the French even have an expression for how to undo a bra with one deft flip: *l'art du decrochetage*. A bra presents woman in a package ready for consumption, with its hook and eye like the ring-pull on a tinnie of beer.

'Pneumatic bliss' was what T. S. Eliot found in the uncorseted bust he wrote about in *Whispers of Immortality* (1920). Three centuries before, Robert Herrick noted with great approval 'that brave vibration each way free' as his friend Julia (in the days before the restraining influence of the bra) ran towards him. In Zoonomia (1794–6) Erasmus Darwin (Charles' grandfather and an important source for his

evolutionary theory) wrote of 'the softness and smoothness of this milky fountain'.

Whether inflated or vibrating, soft or smooth, the breast is a matter of compulsion: a near-universal source of pleasure. In 1752 the Swedish botanist Linnaeus coined the term 'mammae'; six years earlier he had declared that the human female breast was the defining characteristic of advanced quadrupeds. Sigmund Freud's very last words were hand-written notes about the breast.

Appended to the ventral area between the bottom of the rib cage and the neck are a pair of fleshy sacs which weigh on average about 0.5kg (1lbs) each. They are, according to Gershon Legman in his *Rationale of the Dirty Joke* (1969) 'the principal fetish of male attraction'.

The word 'bosom' is significant. There is a sort of onomatopoeia in its rounded, voluptuous, generous sound. Additionally, the twin 'o's give the word a full-frontal symmetry that is graphically suggestive of its subject. The French, appropriately so for a nation which has made taxonomy and hierarchy into national sports, have a large variety of words

PRODUXIT ENIM TERRA GER-
-MEN, HERBAM PRODUCENTEM
SEMEN JUXTA SPECIEM SUAM,
ET ARBOREM FACIENTEM FRUC-
-TUM, CUI INERAT SEMEN SUUM
JUXTA SPECIEM SUAM VIDITQUE
DEUS QUOD ESSET BONUM.

Gen: C.I.v. 12.

Left: In 1752 the Swedish botanist and taxonomist Linnaeus coined the term 'mammae' for breasts. They define the type which is why mammals are called mammals.

Above: The alarming chrome protuberances on Fifties American cars became known as 'Dagmars' after the popular comedienne-hostess of an early US television show.
Above right: Dagmar had dramatically conical breasts and presented herself as the 'dumb blonde', thus forging a connection between voluptuousness and stupidity.

Page 100–101: An udder. An object of aesthetic delight perhaps only to bulls.

for breasts. *Poitrine* is a sexless chest. But *ropolopots*, *nichons*, *miches*, *tetons* and *doudounes* are all more suggestive of delight. In vulgar English,'tit' can be traced to an eighteenth-century expression for 'pleasant' fellow, later appropriated, according to lexicographer Eric Partridge, into colloquial Australian.

These same Australians use the word 'nork', derived from the image of a cow with an ample udder which featured on packets of Norco, a brand of butter. Americans are perplexed by the breast. An internal memo circulating in Fox Television in 1993 told producers and editors that while the words 'tits and knockers are not allowable, no exception would be taken to the use of boobs, bazongas, jugs, hooters and snack-trays'. On such exquisite niceties, such finely drawn preferences, such elite nuances, such perfect sensitivities is civilization built. 'Bazongas' are, incidentally, defined by the online *Urban Dictionary* as hairy, pendulous testicles. This may point to serious confusion in the mind of Fox TV's in-house *arbiter elegantiarum*. In the Fifties, the dramatic chromed conical protuberances on many Detroit cars were known as 'Dagmars', after the busty hostess of Broadway Open House, a popular Fifties television show. Originally, the General Motors design boss, Harley J. Earl, had asked his designers to mimic artillery shells to provide customers with an interesting symbolic feature. Iconographic

thefts from the military were routine in Earl's design department, but by about 1958 when Buick sold the Fashion-Aire Dynastar the artillery shells had become chromed norks and explicitly recognized as such by consumers and commentators. The muddle between weaponry and erotica is as profound as the oedipal confusion between lactation and desire.

For most of an adult woman's life, her breasts are redundant fatty tissue of no practical use. Indeed, the human female is the only animal to have permanent external mammae. More accurately, they are an encumbrance which has created a huge international support industry. Their permanent place in culture can be understood not merely as erotic props for male enjoyment, something which is, in fact, a relatively late development, but also in religious and social terms.

There is a universal understanding in what used to be called 'primitive' cultures that large breasts were a reliable guarantee of fertility. Thus, the breast was a part of art's iconography from about 25,000BC. And before 25,000BC there really was no art.

In the glory days of early sexology, the late nineteenth-century, German scientists tried to prove the connection between the breast and sex which had been the basis of Sigmund Freud's and scientifically thin speculations. In order to demonstrate hard-wired neural links between the breasts and the sexual organs, electrodes were clamped to nipples.

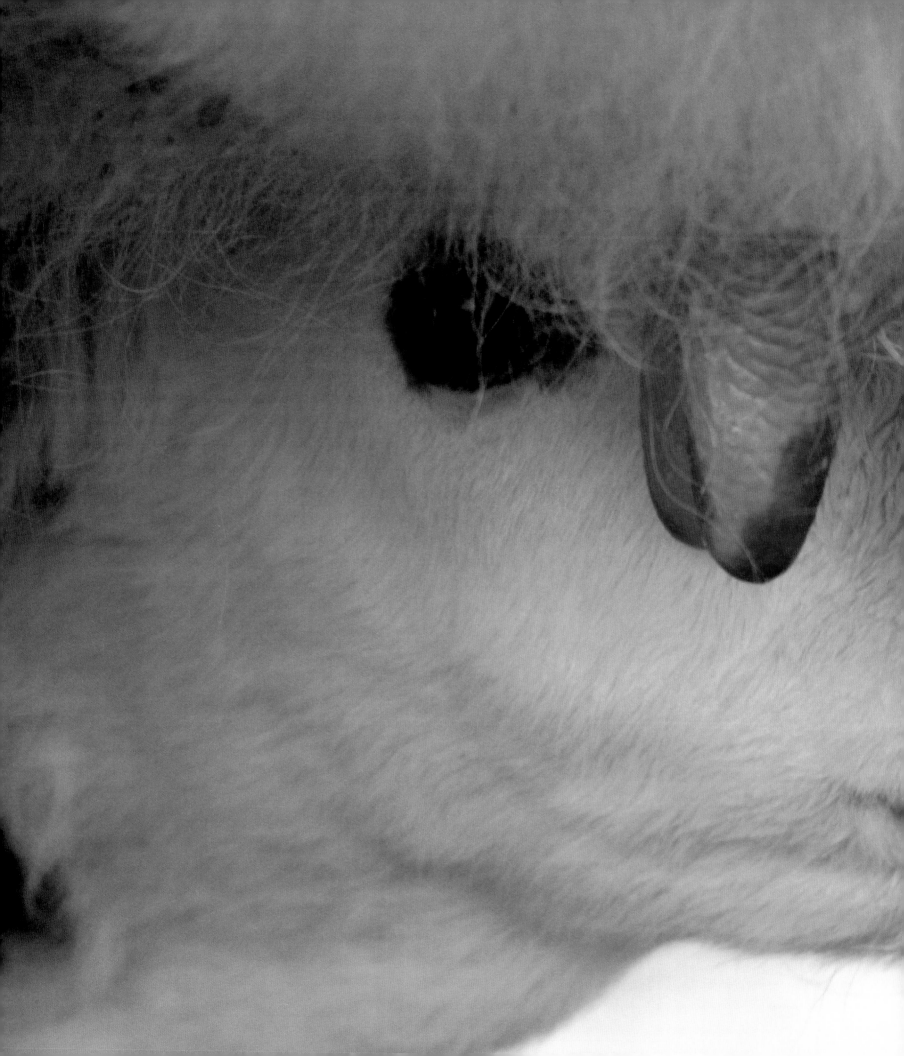

At the throw of a switch, a current passed through the volunteer's central nervous system causing, in many cases, a spontaneous contraction of the uterus. The sceptical might see this as merely as a painful spasm, but our sexologists felt it proved that the act of suckling an infant produces a voluptuous sexual response. What Freud had theorized with reference to Leonardo da Vinci – the penis/nipple confusion – was proved by men in lab coats with several volts of direct current at their disposal.

There is a crude interest in breast size. In a study of London prostitutes published in 1865, Johann Friedrich Blumenbach claimed that their professional activities (which he sniffily dismissed as 'precocious venery') caused enlargement, thus confusing cause and effect. In his 1972 novella *The Breast*, Philip Roth picks on a Kafkaesque theme of transmutation. His hero is turned into a giant, autonomous six foot breast. This at the time when feminists were burning bras and arguing that anatomy-is-destiny.

In cultural history, there are good and bad breasts. Ezekiel, the original prophet of doom, said you could tell that the women of Samaria were wanton because of their breasts. But the breasts of Aphrodite and, later, of the Virgin Mary, are symbols of beauty, fertility, nutrition, motherhood and, in general, all good things. Although his own attitudes to parental nurture may be construed from the fact that he abandoned his own children to an orphanage, Jean-Jacques Rousseau made a fuss about breastfeeding as a necessary part of the simple life which he so influentially popularized as a theory.

The breast properly emerges in the nineteenth century. Eugène Delacroix's *Liberty leading the People*, his

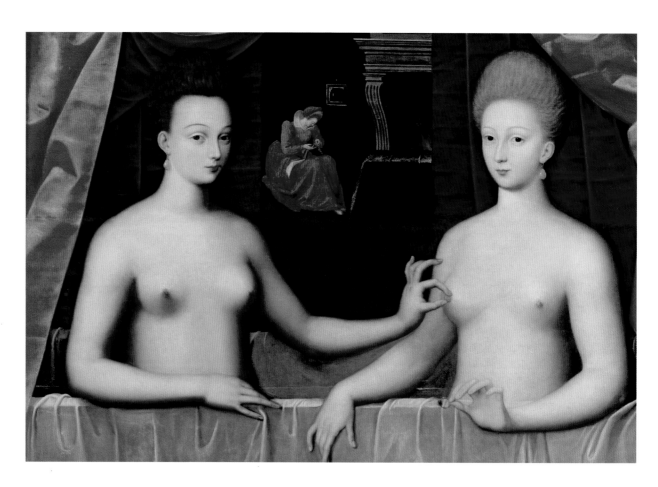

Above: Gabrielle d'Estrées, shown on the right with her sister in this 1594 double portrait by an anonymous artist, was a favourite among France's Henry IV's 56 mistresses. The tweaking of the nipple is a motif unique in art (perhaps accounting for the picture's popularity in the Louvre), but the formula of the bagno was already familiar in Italy. It gave the sanction of art to nudes.

Right: Annie Sprinkle is a 'post-porn' performance artist famous for her Bosom Ballet. 'I stretch, pinch, squeeze, twist, rock, roll and jiggle my breasts to music, usually The Blue Danube Waltz, under a pink spotlight.' Sprinkle is not only post-porn, she is post-feminist too, unabashedly turning her breasts into delightful theatrical props. Commodified, but in a good way.

ABOVE: BRAS ARE FOR MEN OR THE INDUSTRIALIZATION OF THE BREAST

monumental canvas in the Louvre, shows Marianne, the spirit of France, trampling over the barricades in the July Revolution of 1830. Her naked breasts are a direct suggestion that 'Liberty' – almost literally – feeds the people. An inheritance from Rousseau and his enthusiasm for 'primitive' breastfeeding was an association of the naked breast as a symbol of defiance.

Delacroix's topless revolutionary was perhaps inspiration for Frédéric-Auguste Bartholdi's 1886 Statue of Liberty, or 'La Liberté eclairant le monde' as Bartholdi had it. In America, Liberty was not topless, but is presented, in the words of

Emma Lazarus' 'New Colossus' (a terrible poem attached to the statue on a plaque in 1903) as 'A mighty woman with a torch, whose flame/Is the imprisoned lightning'.

Although her chaste covering (not to mention atrocious associated poetry) may have retarded taste in the United States by almost four generations, Liberty was, after the Virgin and before the movies, the world's most important female image. She came to prominence at the same moment that the murky soup of gynophobia and patronizing lust had reconciled bad breasts and good breasts into an attractive image of the modern woman. In the telling of this

Opposite: Ferdinand Victor Eugène Delacroix Liberty Leading the People, *1830. Delacroix's most famous painting shows the pivotal event of the July Revolution. It is 28 July 1830, and the emblematic figure of 'Liberty' chases down the demoralized troops of Charles X. Her status as a popular revolutionary figure is proven by the thrillingly exposed breasts.*

This page: Frederic Bartholdi's Statue of Liberty, *1886 (US Patent D11,023) takes Delacroix's imagery a step further, although her breasts are covered. The poet Emma Lazarus, who described 'the wretched refuse of your teeming shore' in the poem inscribed on the base, wanted Liberty to be called Mother of Exiles. This pioneering gesture of radical feminism was rejected.*

AGNÉSSOREL

stage in the design of woman, the history of the bra has pre-eminent importance. It was, in Marion Yalom's memorable words, the moment when 'the full force of capitalism… seized upon the breast as a profit-related object.' (*The History of the Breast* 1997) Of course, breasts had been, as it were, manipulated before the invention of the bra. Although the addition of money to the already potent mix of motherhood and eroticism is of special interest.

Cycladic idols had stylized breasts. Minoan snake goddesses wear pre-corset devices that give an impressive up-thrust to the mammae which has nothing to do with hygiene or nutrition, but a firm connection to a version of eroticized aesthetics still recognizable today. Sicilian mosaics in the Villa Romana del Casale show women athletes in bikini-like garments with a band helpfully retaining their breasts during dynamic exertions, but the history of the bra really begins only in the fourteenth century when a bifurcation occurred in European dress that had the shapeless tunics hitherto worn by both men and women abandoned in favour of garments that identified the sexes.

The male cod-piece of folklore had its origins at this moment and so too did garments that more-or-less exposed – or, at least, evidenced – the female breast. This outraged conservatives, including Dante who has a short passage in *Purgatorio* denouncing strumpets for what we would call flashing their tits. In his more elegant Tuscan, this was rendered as '*mostrando con le poppe il petto*'. At about the same time, the authorities in Venice – more exotic, more sensuous than Dante's austere Florence – issued an order that prostitutes should stand topless on the Ponte delle Tette (in the Carampane district of San Polo, by the Sotoportego e Corte de Ca' Bollani) in order to discourage the then fashionable sodomy, or what was called in judicial Latin '*abominabile vitium sodomiae*'.

No records exist to account for how many Venetian homosexuals were deterred from their practices by bare breasts, nor how effective a deterrent against homosexuality the strategy might have been, but here is clear evidence that the breast was no longer a child's teat, but an eroticized attribute. In France, Charles VII's mistress, Agnes Sorel, had the title of '*dame de beaute*'. Sorel is the model for Jean Fouquet's *Virgin of Melun* of 1450; she is on the right-hand panel of a diptych now separated between Berlin and Antwerp. Sorel's Virgin has her magnificent left breast ceremoniously exposed; all the iconographic elements of the virgin-and-child are present, but this is unambiguously erotic.

Left: Agnes Sorel, (circa 1422–50), lover of France's Charles VII, was known as a 'dame de beaute'. She was often painted by fifteenth-century French artists, frequently with one breast exposed. It is an ambiguous motif: is she displaying vulnerability or authority?

Right: Roman women athletes from the Villa Herculia, Casale, Piazza Armerina, Sicily, third–fourth centuries.

Left: Jean Fouquet's Virgin and Child, *1450, from the Melun Diptych. Again, the sitter is assumed to be Agnes Sorel. Despite the Christian iconography, this is not a nurturing breast, but an audaciously erotic one.*

Above: Janet Jackson's 'wardrobe malfunction' at the 2004 Superbowl XXXVIII, Reliant Stadium, Houston, USA also led to a popular exposed breast. The voyeurism of a French King and the voyeurism of the

MTV audience united in a single gesture. The breast retains its ability to shock.

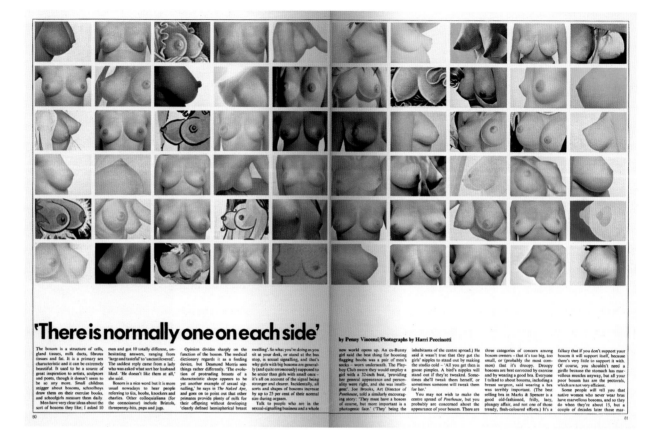

Above: David Hillman and Harri Peccinotti 'There is normally one on each side' Nova *magazine, November 1971. From 1969–75 David Hillman was art director of* Nova, *a short-lived, but very influential magazine which took Sixties sexuality and made it high style. Photographer Harri Peccinotti offered 'real' girls £5 to lift their shirts; the resulting pictures were mixed with famous art historical breasts. Journalist Penny Vincenzi explained that the new liberality now meant that 'bosom' might also be referred to as tits, boobs, knockers or charlies.*

This is not a feeding breast, but an advertisement of sexuality, painted perhaps to enhance the King's status and provide him with aesthetic gratification in addition to the regular carnal pleasures.

The breast's adventures continued into the next century. Pierre de Ronsard's *Amours* contain ample mentions of ample breasts. In 1535–6 the poet Clément Marot wrote 'Le Beau Tetin'; his verse was a development of the *blazon* poetry of the troubadours which celebrated, besides breasts, other evocative body parts including knees, hands and thighs.

Even as they admired the physicality of the female body, with its delicious features comparable in poetry to ripe fruit, the troubadours were at the same time trapped in a melancholy belief that all earthly love is a temporary, therefore tragic, delusion. If a woman is fruit, then she too is also liable to physiochemical spoilage by nasty bacilli, to bruising caused by careless handling and, ultimately, to turn into rotting flesh. As the alchemist Paracelsus knew, putrefaction is the 'change and death of all things'.

Despite, or perhaps because, of the harrowing evidence that fruit is fragile, fruity metaphors continued to tempt poets in pursuit of the woman's powerful, but elusive, qualities.

Clément Marot writes: 'A little ball of ivory/In the middle of which sits/A strawberry or cherry'. Here the strawberry and cherry metaphor applied to sexual parts introduces another dominant idea: the notion, alarming and attractive, of 'forbidden fruit'. John Donne's line of prepositions wherein he invites himself to explore his mistress' body with the determination of a contemporary navigator on the high seas, has its artistic precedents in this first generation of frankly erotic verse.

Just too late to assist Robert Herrick's Julia, whose brave vibrations so impressed him, versions of supportive underwear arrived in Britain from Spain. It was on the Iberian peninsula that an artificially imposed slimness was first acquired from unyielding whalebone with paste-stiffened linen corsets which pinched tightly at the waist and emphasized the breasts. By the early nineteenth century these corsets had been industrialized: some claim to be the pioneer of the mass-produced corset may be made by Jean Werly, whose factory at Bar-le-Duc was making corsetry available to the working classes by the late 1830s. Underwear might constrain the workers as tightly as their production regime.

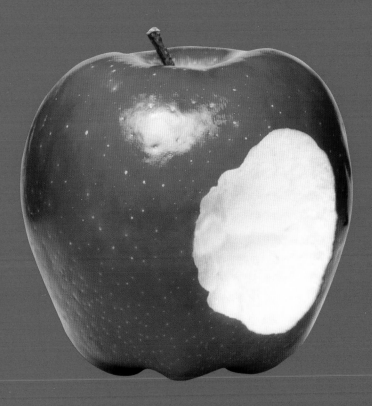

Fruit and Sex

– Since acquiring the role of Forbidden Fruit in *Genesis*, the apple has had a sexual character.

– Juno gave apples from the Garden of Hesperides to Jupiter as a wedding present.

– A golden apple was Paris' reward for judging the Three Graces.

– A neglected sixth-century BC poet known now as Paul the Silentiary, but perhaps known then as an old bore, had a narrator deploring the fact that he was holding apples given to him as gifts when he could, instead, have been holding his lover's apple-like breasts.

– Henri II's mistress, Diane of Poitiers, maintained her sexual appetite with a diet of fruit and vegetables, disdaining the new fashionable rich food of her lover's court.

– Freud noted that apples and pears frequently occur in sexually nuanced dreams.

– In his magisterial book *The Nude* (1956) Kenneth Clark frequently compares the female curves with pumpkins, strawberries and pears.

ABOVE: BRAS ARE FOR MEN OR THE INDUSTRIALIZATION OF THE BREAST

Top: Carese Crosby (1892–1970) was the Boston socialite who has, perhaps, the most legitimate claim to be the inventor of the modern bra. Here she is in 1964 being carried around her Roman estate at Roccasinibalda, enjoying the proceeds of industrializing the breast.

Right and opposite: Early advertisements for corsets and brassieres emphasized new, you and sex: the trinity that advertising experts know commands immediate attention from consumers.

From the corset, the bra was an inevitable development. Its precise history is a matter of dispute, but what is indisputable is that by the late nineteenth century the breast had achieved such cultural, artistic, erotic, social, fashionable significance that there was international consumer demand for undergarments that lifted, separated, emphasized, and sculpted the breasts. Certainly, Thorstein Veblen (the polymath critic of 'conspicuous consumption') regarded the figure-flattering bra as a form of mutilation.

Indeed, surgical associations of another sort at first attached to the bra. In France it was known as a 'soutien-gorge', or throat support, which sounds like a prosthetic rather than a cosmetic device. Veblen's influential *Theory of the Leisure Class*, a thundering critique of consumerism and its various postures, was published in 1899. At the beginning of that decade, the Sears Roebuck mail-order business was already selling 'falsies' to its flat-chested customers.

Although the French may claim the invention of the bra (many were on display at the great Paris Exposition of 1900), and *Vogue* was using the word by 1907, the bra as we know it was successfully commercialized by the American Mary Phelps Jacobs. A patent for her soft, rather than punitive, supportive garment (the prototype was made out of handkerchiefs) was given in 1914. But Jacobs, a Boston Brahmin, lost interest and sold the rights to Warner Brothers Corset Company for $1,500. Jacobs went onto become another part of twentieth-century American folklore when she married Harry Crosby, a cousin of Henry James and prototypical American in Paris whose Black Sun Press published, among other authors, Ernest Hemingway. She re-branded herself as Caresse Crosby.

The history of the bra continued. In 1935 Warner established 'cup' sizes. Du Pont's public introduction of nylon was at the 1939 New York's World Fair. The publicity said it was fine as a spider's web, but as strong as steel. Its first application was to replace animal bristle in toothbrushes, but soon its suitability for the supportive bra was realized. The modern bra is a hybrid instrument of torture and seduction.

It was Russell Birdwell, the veteran Hollywood publicist, who span the story of Howard Hughes having, on aircraft construction principles, to design a special bra to cope with the special support needs of Jane Russell, the full-figured actress who starred in Hughes' 1943 western, *The Outlaw*.

A 'shabby, contrived, cornball' movie (according to *TV Guide Online* 2000), loosely based on the story of Billy the Kid, *The Outlaw* was nonetheless a marvellous curiosity. One story has it that Hughes had discovered the 19-year-old Jane Russell from publicity stills showing her bending over to pick-up a

Bandeau Type

Outsize Type

Outsize Type

Dress Shield Type

Surplice Back Type

Bust Girdle Type

Close Fitting Type

Bandeau Type

Bust Supporter Type

Underbodice Type

Bandette Type

Bandeau Type

Outsize Type

De Bevoise
Brassieres that Beautify

DO justice to your figure and gowns—wear a De Bevoise. It adds a charm and beauty to your appearance that nothing else can supply. For smartness of line, perfection of fit, excellence of materials and beauty of workmanship—for durability, comfort, health and all-around satisfaction—the De Bevoise insures you the utmost possible brassiere-value for your money.

There are De Bevoise types scientifically designed to beautify *your* figure. Each type comes in a wide variety of styles and prices, to suit every purse and preference. Write for our free illustrated booklet. It will help you select *your* brassiere type. The De Bevoise is made, labeled and guaranteed by *Chas. R. DeBevoise Co., Newark, N.J.,* world's oldest and largest brassiere specialists.

Original   *Best*

50¢ up
Ask your merchant for the debb-e-voice

De Bevoise
Brassiere

INSIST always on this Label of Highest Quality

ABOVE: BRAS ARE FOR MEN OR THE INDUSTRIALIZATION OF THE BREAST

pair of milk pails, revealing an impressive pair of pendulous mammae. The contrarian Hughes wanted to use the busty Russell to test censorship. As soon as it was released in San Francisco, local puritans had the film closed down (to Howard Hughes' delight).

What is certain is that Hughes hired Russell Birdwell – once described as an old-fashioned hallelujah and hellfire shouter – to promote his brazen film. Birdwell had cemented his reputation with his PR for *Gone with the Wind*. Hughes wanted to replicate its success. When he saw the rushes of the movie, Birdwell was impressed by the sight of Russell lolling in the hay. He sold the photograph to *Life* magazine. He had poster-sized blow-ups sent all over the world. Censors had ordered 102 cuts which, they felt, focussed too warmly on Russell's majestic bosom, but Birdwell hired a Columbia University mathematician to compare and contrast the exposure of other starlets and negotiated the cuts down to two. It was eventually released only in 1946 and the ads asked a slathering public: 'What are the two reasons for Jane Russell's rise to stardom?'

'I love women. I love their curves,' said Frederick N. Mellinger, founder of Frederick's of Hollywood, the Los Angeles lingerie business that began as mail order in 1947, acquiring retail premises on Hollywood Boulevard by 1952. (Coincidentally 1947 was the year of Dior's New Look.) Among his first bras were items with helical stitching, producing a cup that was nearly conical. Whether this was a more or less unconscious memory of military artillery shells, no one can say, but Frederick's catalogue was certainly a reliable indicator of contemporary taste and preoccupations. Some years ago they would sell you Riot Squad Bikini Panties, Conquistador white leather thigh boots, Dagger Dance five-inch spike heels, Sheik's Choice slave-girl harem pyjamas and Cuddle Puff slippers. The white thigh leather boots were advertised – quite without irony – with the tag-line 'You'll need a whip to beat the men off'.

It was Frederick's intention to perfect what nature had left flawed, although (absurdly) the Frederick's commercial material maintained that the Lurex, Spandex, taffeta and sequinned under garments actually created a 'natural look'. What was the source of this version of 'nature'? Clearly, Frederick Mellinger had some sort of symbiotic relationship with the movies. His customers – sagging and surging, skinny and flat-chested, puckered and wrinkly – were assured

Above: Frederick Mellinger, founder of lingerie specialist Frederick's of Hollywood, in 1976. He is inspecting a regular mail-order item, perhaps intended for a housewife in Fort Wayne, that will help Middle American Woman look like an exotic belly dancer. The Frederick's of Hollywood mail-order catalogue (right) promised curvaceous delight via Spandex.

This page: Jane Russell in
Howard Hughes The Outlaw.
Release was delayed until 1946
because censors felt Hughes and
his publicist focussed too closely
on Russell's impressive bosom,
described as the two reasons for
her rise to stardom.

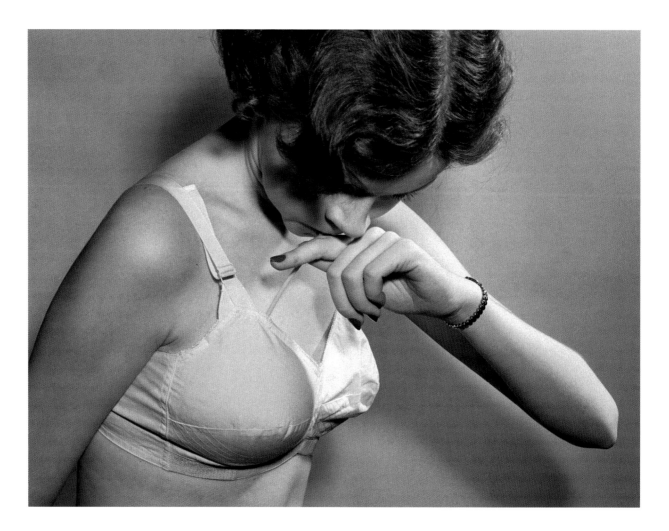

Above: In 1951 an inflatable bra was launched in the United States. The pneumatic system allowed for variable shape-making, depending on sartorial need: beach, sport or cocktails.

Opposite: The National Women's Liberation Party picket the Miss America Pageant in Atlantic City, 7 September 1968.

that with his underwear they might achieve the Hollywood-look that, it was assumed, all men craved. The breast fixation had found its Michelangelo.

Mellinger's appetites were formed in the privation of military service during the Second World War. He dreamt of girls in satin and lace slips, camisoles and night-gowns. He theorized about why breasts drooped. Wish fulfilment was always part of the retail offer: even as a location-free mail-order business, Frederick had insisted on the important 'Hollywood' toponym.

But more significant still than this bizarre repertoire of yearning nomenclature, is the insistence on 'body sculpting'. Frederick's can also sell you an Air-Lite inflatable bra. This was one of a number of cosmetic-prosthetics which allowed customers to change their dimensions and profiles from day to day. The object, whatever its dimensions, was always clear: breasts should be clearly separated and symmetrical, must point upwards, must have prominent nipples, be symmetrical and generously proportioned. 'We change fashions,' Mellinger said, 'to glorify and re-glorify a woman's

figure.' Even pneumatically (although one imagines Frederick Mellinger was, perhaps, not a reader of T. S. Eliot).

The psychology of liberation can be written in terms of the bra. While in 1970 feminists started burning them as symbols of masculine oppression, in 1949 one American manufacturer was running ads saying 'I dreamed I went shopping in my Maidenform bra.' Currently, Frederick's of Hollywood is offering via its website 'Hollywood Naughty Knickers', 'gartered mesh crotchless panties' and 'Tulle Ruffle Skirt Crotchless Panties' – all at $18.

The Barbie doll was introduced at the 1959 New York Toy Fair as a 'shapely teenage fashion model'. Hitherto, dolls had been modelled on babies and had few or no distinguishing sexual characteristics, but Barbie wore eyeliner and nail varnish, had a pert bottom, debuted in a striped, close-fitting *maillot* flattering her pert bottom, wore spike heels and, magnificently, had enormous breasts.

She was the creation of Ruth Handler, daughter of an immigrant Polish blacksmith who lived in Denver, and may have been inspired by a German sex toy called Lilli.

The Bra

– The mastodeton worn by Greek women athletes, fifth century BC.

– Roman women use a mamillare to disguise large breasts; Roman girls wear a band of cloth (a fascia) to control growth.

– US Patent 24033 filed by Henry S. Lesher of Brooklyn for a device to create symmetrical rotundity of the breast.

– Herminie Cadolle bisects the corset to create two piece underwear, shown at the Great Exhibition of 1889.

– 'Brassiere' first appears in *The Oxford English Dictionary*, 1911.

– Mary Phelps Jacobs combines silk handkerchiefs with pink ribbon to create a form-hugging 'Backless Brassiere', patented 1914. ('Brassiere' is derived from the French for military breastplate.)

– Ida and William Rosenthal collaborate with Enid Bissett of New York to create the Maidenform company, manufacturers of the first modern bras, 1920. The monobosom disappears in favour of separated and individualized breasts.

– Cup sizes established, 1935.

– Nylon launched at New York World's Fair, 1939.

– Betty Friedan publishes *The Feminine Mystique*, 1963. Bras now seen as oppressive, not supportive.

– Russ Meyer, soft-porn film producer, launches *Mondo Topless*, 1965. Friedan's arguments against the bra are taken in a surprising direction.

– Feminists demonstrate at Miss America, 1968.

– Germaine Greer says 'bras are a ludicrous invention', 1970.

– Sara Lee Intimates, a division of a company best-known for cake mixes, acquires Wonderbra licence for United States, 1994.

Left: The very first bikini was shown 7 July 1946, at Paris' Piscine Molitor in the 16th arrondissement, near Roland Garros. Designer Louis Reard used a 'dancer' from the Casino de Paris as his model.

Right: The exaggerations and distortions of the body industry were parodied in the 1958 horror movie, Attack of the 50ft Woman. *An abused wife becomes a giant after an alien encounter and goes on the rampage after her faithless hubby. This reads like a digest of the psychology of the lingerie industry. (At just the same time, Detroit exaggerated the proportions of its cars shown in advertisements to make them more 'sexy'.)*

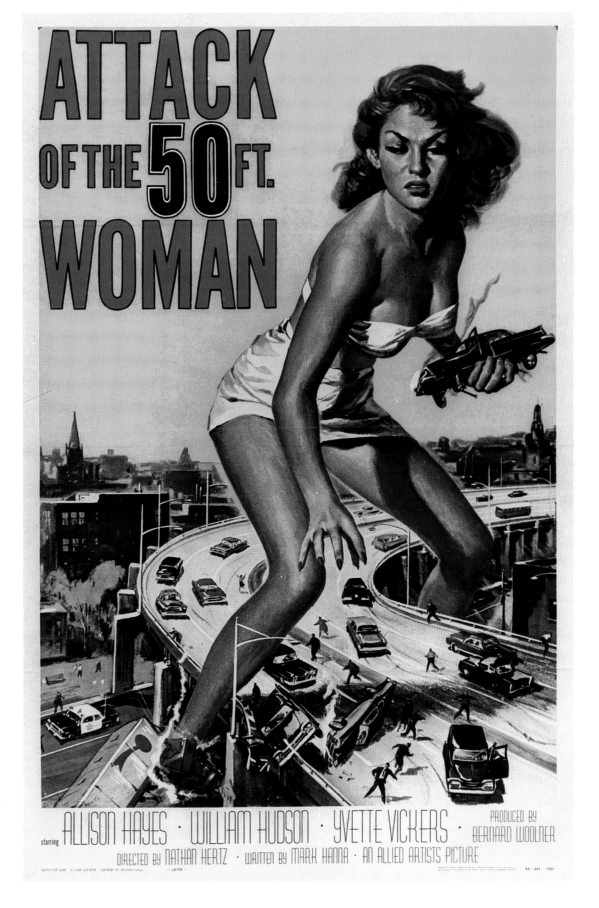

Handler told *The New York Times* in 1977:

'Every little girl needed a doll through which to project herself into her dream of the future. If she was going to do role-playing what she would be like when she was sixteen or seventeen, it was a little stupid to play with a doll that had a flat chest. So I gave it beautiful breasts.'

Experts have calculated that, scaled-up to human size, Barbie's beautiful breasts would be equivalent to a stonking 99cm (39in) bust (with a 53cm (21in) waist and 84cm (33in) hips). Feminists criticised Barbie for sexualizing childhood and exciting unrealistic expectations among innocent children, but this matter of scale and distortion affected all of America in this period. Advertising agency illustrators routinely distorted the proportions of their (already woefully exaggerated) Chevrolets and Pontiacs to make them appear ever wider and lower.

In her autobiography *Dream Doll: The Ruth Handler Story* (1994) Ruth Handler wrote:

'My philosophy of Barbie was that through the doll, the little girl could be anything she wanted to be. Barbie always represented the fact that a woman had choices.'

One choice Barbie only acquired in the Sixties was a mate. This was Ken, named after Handler's son (who died of a brain tumour in 1994). Ken did not have genitals. Commenting on her decision to start manufacturing prosthetic breasts for women who had experienced mastectomies, Handler said 'I've lived my life from breast to breast.' The prosthetic product was poignantly called 'Nearly Me'.

120

Above: Ruth Handler (1906–2002) was the creator of Barbie. Her plan was to give young girls a means of imagining their future which, in Handler's interpretation, involved imagining large breasts.

Right: Ruth Handler and her husband, Elliott. With his partner Matt Matson, Elliott Handler created the Mattel toy company which manufactured Barbie.

This page: If Barbie was to be scaled-up to human size, she would have a 39in bust and a 21in waist.

Page 122–123: Barbie's Bust: magnificent in size and proportions, but deficient in detail.

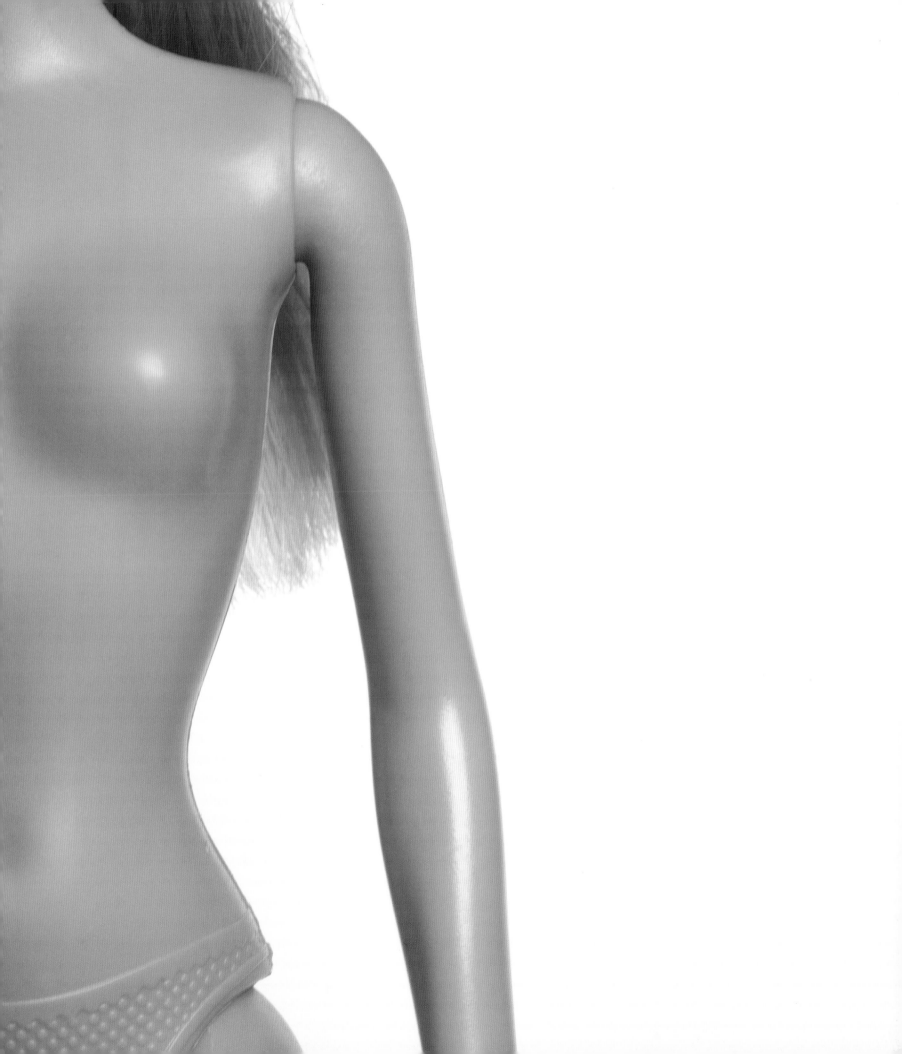

125

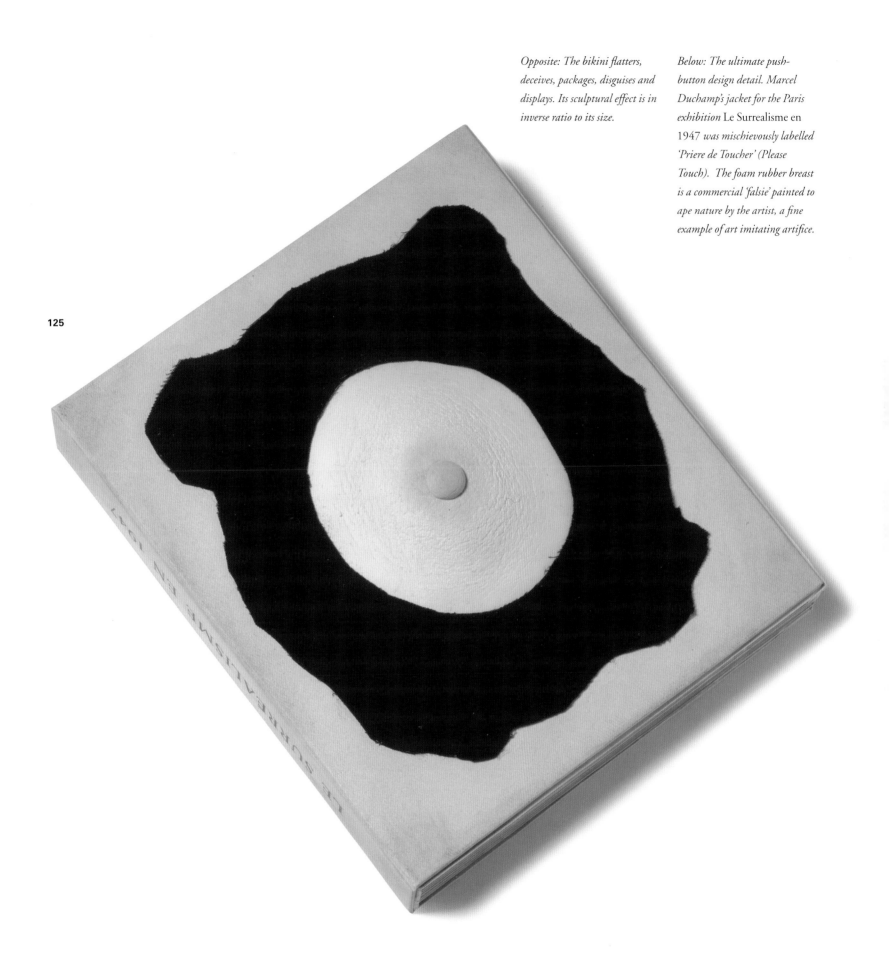

Opposite: The bikini flatters, deceives, packages, disguises and displays. Its sculptural effect is in inverse ratio to its size.

Below: The ultimate push-button design detail. Marcel Duchamp's jacket for the Paris exhibition Le Surrealisme en 1947 was mischievously labelled 'Priere de Toucher' (Please Touch). The foam rubber breast is a commercial 'falsie' painted to ape nature by the artist, a fine example of art imitating artifice.

While the modern bra created a covert sexuality, its external equivalent was the bikini. This curious garment externalized underwear. This happy invention we owe to a French mechanical engineer called Louis Réard and his collaborator, Jacques Heim. The name bikini derives from the notorious US Army nuclear weapon tests on the Pacific island of Bikini held 1 July 1946. Using only 76cm (30in) of fabric in a design that comprised only 4 triangles, Réard's bikini was patented 17 days after the nuclear tests. As a mechanical engineer, Réard's patent includes nicely ironic general arrangement drawings. Bikini was also known as '*atome*' because of its tiny size.

Although the bikini became identified with post-War liberalized pleasure (and in particular the cult of St Tropez), Réard's first model was a nude dancer from the Casino de Paris called Micheline Bernardini. Acceptance went in stages. Cole of California was manufacturing bikinis by 1959; the year after, Brian Hyland celebrated this in his hit single 'Itsy Bitsy Teenie Weenie Yellow Polka Dot Bikini'. In 1962, Ursula Andress playing the role of Honey Ryder in the Bond movie, *Dr No*, emerged from the foamy sea in a striking white bikini, a very self-conscious take on Aphrodite iconography. In 1964 Pope Paul VI banned bikinis in Catholic countries, but in a bold counter-move, fashion designer Rudi Gernreich introduced the monokini in the same year. In 1967, in a well publicized event, Brigitte Bardot put St Tropez on the map when she took off her bikini top around the pool of the Byblos Hotel.

This she described as shedding prejudice.

Opposite: 1 July 1946 saw the explosion of a nuclear weapon on Bikini Atoll. This put minuscule atoms in the news and, through a small gymnastic conceptual manoeuvre, a 'bikini' became a minuscule swimsuit.

This page: Ursula Andress as Honey Ryder, the first Bond girl, in the 1962 movie Dr No. *Andress, then aged 26, emerges in a bikini from the sea in a style that deliberately evokes the classical Aphrodite.*

This page Bulk reservoirs in the oil industry: this is how technology answers the questions of storage and retrieval demanded of a woman's breasts.

Below

Above: The Chevalier d'Eon, whose coloratura cross-dressing tested conventions of male and female identity.

Opposite: Pierre Bonnard's (1867–1947) photograph of his model and muse, in fact his wife, 'Marthe au tub', circa 1908, currently exhibited in Musée d'Orsay, Paris.

Page 132: The Chevalier d'Eon, an enthusiastic swordsman, in a duel. He is dressed as a woman.

Beneath the clothes is underwear. And beneath the underwear there is the eroticized bottom, the Delta of Venus and the industrialized breast. But what lies below the psychological surface?

Charles Genevieve Louis Auguste André Timothée d'Eon de Beaumont changed sex twice. His eighteenth-century contemporaries described him as a shrewd, but impetuous intriguer. And, naturally or otherwise, inclined to effeminacy. Given the presentational advantages conferred by his easily misconstrued gender, the Chevalier d'Eon, as (s)he became known, was invited on an espionage mission to Russia disguised as a woman. He later joined the French Embassy in London where he became as much a celebrity as he was in gay Paris. The French King saluted him for serving his country just as well in a woman's clothes as the ones custom would require him to wear.

The celebrity of the Chevalier d'Eon – whose cross-dressing adventures began just as women were very slowly assuming an identity – illuminates an interesting area of gender history. The fixed points are less secure.

Of course, at the centre of this discussion is the meaning of the body. By which I mean the skin and bones. Since Kenneth Clark and up to and including Anne Hollander, art historians have argued that there is a significant difference between naked and nude. Waggishly, the poet Robert Graves said that naked is sacred, but nude is rude. Our utter subjugation to the idea of fashion, or, perhaps more humbly, just to the idea of wearing clothes, means that when we see a body without clothes… we assume them to be missing. Another poet, this time a darker one than Graves, used to ask his mistress to strip to nothing except a necklace. That way, she appeared more thrillingly nude. This poet was Charles Baudelaire. A vision of Edenic purity is no longer available to us. A body without clothes is not neutral; it has very specific meanings.

Naked simply means to be without clothing, just as Adam and Eve were in Eden. Innocent, uncorrupted. At least for a while… Eventually, Eve was so identified with evil that the serpent in the Sistine Chapel in Rome has female features.

Nude has more meaning and intention. Nature left you naked, but you are nude as an act of will. Accordingly, attitudes to nudity are a reflection of prevailing values. And since these attitudes change, the interpretation of the ideal woman's body is not constant: a short history of nudity is a version of woman as design. Natural innocence versus conventions, fabrications and abstractions. Of course, it is the latter that are the most interesting.

Which body parts were most meaningful? Fashions for naked breasts have come and gone. In the fourteenth century Queen Isabella of Bavaria was applying rouge to hers, a practice which suggests an inclination towards exposure. The Renaissance acknowledged four different types of nudity:

Nuditas naturalis	*The innocent nudity of the baby*
Nuditas temporalis	*A nudity that foreswears possessions*
Nuditas virtualis	*Nudity as a symbol of innocence*
Nuditas criminalis	*The nudity of lust and vanity*

While in the early seventeenth century a largely exposed breast might be construed as a pious suggestion of virginity, by the end of that century naked breasts were seen as pernicious and unseemly. Naked breasts were modish novelties at least as wicked as powdering the hair. In 1678 Edward Cooke published a book whose title is amply revealing of a constipated consciousness: *A just and seasonable reprehension of naked breasts and shoulders written by a grave and learned papist*. Perhaps grave and learned papists were very much on the lookout for offences, but the existence of so rarefied a title (print run unknown) clearly suggests that 'naked breasts' had somewhere become a familiar outrage against decency.

Perhaps inspired and legitimized by the 'pink fictions' of seventeenth- and eighteenth-century art – the chubby nymphs and mistresses of Rubens, Boucher, Fragonard – Josephine Beaumarchais (later Bonaparte) danced in the nude. In public. Madeline Hamelin, evidently a little more modest than the future Empress, walked down the Champs-Elysée stripped to the waist. The advanced tastes of the Directoire may have made nudity a matter of gesture politics, but in an England undisturbed by revolution it was possible for Regency gentlemen to enjoy nude women who were not their wives in clubbable privacy.

Spectacles of nudity were cloaked under the respectable mantles of art and the classics or horticulture. In his magisterial *Encyclopaedia of Gardening* (1822) J.C. Loudon gives some background to the idea of the Temple of Pleasure.

Below: Charles Baudelaire (1821–67) and some art photography nymphs (opposite), captured cavorting in aesthetic poses on 1 January 1905. Baudelaire was fascinated by the nuances and meanings of nudity and nakedness. He wrote a poem requesting his mistress to strip to nothing other than her necklace, the remaining jewellery serving to emphasis, not to diminish, her lack of clothing.

*Opposite: Corradino d'Ascanio's
design for the 1947 Vespa scooter
included a step-through frame so
that priests, women in dresses and,
crucially, nuns, could get on board
with no compromise to dignity.*

*Left: Mary Wortley Montagu
(1689–1762) in Turkish
costume. Montagu was an
adventurous traveller in
Ottoman lands and enjoyed
dressing in Turkish costume
whose asexuality, she said,
facilitated intimate encounters
in the souk and bazaar.*

Some Notable Cross-Dressers

– Celibate clerics wear vestments in a feminine style. When the Vespa scooter was launched in Italy in 1946, its distinctive step-through frame was designed to allow both women in dresses and priests in their smocks to mount the scooter maintaining modesty intact.

– The Abbé de Choisy, a member of the court of Louis XIV, was dressed as a girl by his mother. Genuine young girls copied his style.

– The Duc d'Orleans, son of Louis XIV, was a short, pot-bellied individual who wore high heels, women's clothes, perfume, rouge and an unusual amount of jewellery.

– Lavinia Edwards, actress.

– Jenny de Savalette de Lange, French nineteenth-century socialite.

– The Smiling Bandit Queen of Chicago.

– The Night Queen of Montmartre.

– Amelia, Countess of Derwentwater.

– Mary Wortley Montagu, who used to wear harem trousers and Turkish costume in the bazaar of Constantinople, the better to facilitate anonymous romantic assignments.

– The Chevalier d'Eon who swapped petticoats for a dragoon's uniform on a regular basis. He is buried in St Pancras Old Church.

– Madonna wearing gentleman's pin-stripes with a Jean-Paul Gaultier conical bra in the movie *Truth or Dare* (1991).

BELOW: THE CHEVALIER D'EON'S FROCK

William Hogarth, An Orgy
from The Rake's Progress, *1735.*

He directs us to Ezekiel xiii 20 where the Lord saith 'I am against… Your luxurious cushions, wherewith ye ensnare souls in flower-gardens.' An ideal garden is, of course, literally a 'paradise'. Here, in ideal circumstances, Venus would be worshipped by a company of nude women. And, paraphrasing Loudon's source, the beauties of nature would be converted into the instruments of sin. At one point in history, gardens were symbols of virginity. To the cultivated Regency mind, they also suggested sex.

Actual temples of pleasure existed in London. Miss Fawklands could offer Aurora, Flora and the Mysteries to her customers. There was, in addition, a vigorous trade in virgins in eighteenth-century London. A book called *The Battles of Venus* was published in 1760. It originated in The Hague and was even briefly (and optimistically) attributed to Voltaire. In it you can read a description which by today's standards is paedophiliac, but by its contemporary ones was an idealized account of nudity:

'Yet no ringlets deck the pouting mount, but all is like her lily hand, both bare and smooth, before the periodical lustration hath stained her virgin shift, while her bosom boasts only a general swell rather than distinct orb.'

'Posture girls' became an eighteenth century fashion. Hogarth shows one in *A Rake's Progress*: she is getting undressed and is ready to be transported and then consumed on a serving dish. A Dr James Graham ran a so-called Temple of Health. Among the healthy activities practised here was posing in the nude. A leading poseuse was Emma Hamilton, whose habit it was to imitate the attitudes struck by dancers, prostitutes and athletes on her husband Sir William Hamilton's collection of Attic red-figure vases.

WOMAN AS DESIGN

The old communist regime of Albania colluded with peasant tradition to create an ambivalent sexual identity: the sworn virgin. Since women were traditionally worth less than cattle, great advantage could be acquired for their families if they denied female identity and lived as men. The practice continues.

Hamilton also posed nude for Thomas Gainsborough and Joshua Reynolds and once danced nude on the dining table at Uppark, Sir Harry Featherstonehaugh's seat in Sussex. Hamilton was also exhibited nude at Ranelagh Gardens in Chelsea. (Despite these successes, her rackety finances forced her to live in Calais as a debtor. Here one of Britain's most famous nudes has her memorial in the grim Parc Richelieu.)

The idea of posture girls lasted into Victoria's era. The concept was disguised in art classes where nude women would strike '*poses plastiques*' which were said to be edifying. Emma Hamilton may have done little to encourage virginity, but the trade in virgins remained rife in nineteenth-century London, described by *The Pall Mall Gazette* in 1885 as 'The Maiden Tribute of Modern Babylon'. William Gladstone, four times Prime Minister of Modern Babylon between 1868 and 1894, became preoccupied with fallen women.

Meanwhile, the nude became established in painting. While the Chevalier d'Eon was putting frocks on for the love of his country, Ingres, and later Manet and Renoir, were refining the genre of nude painting. Before Ingres there are only rare examples of nudes in European art. In the northern

143

Far left: Miss Chudleigh (1720–88) posing as a nude Iphigenia at a masque of the Venetian Ambassador in 1749. Theatrical identities allowed adventurous society women to disport themselves nude.

Left: A 1910 nude by Eugène Atget, in an 'artistic' pose.

Right: The splendid and notorious Lady Hamilton striking one of her nude 'attitudes', as seen by Thomas Rowlandson circa 1790. Her very popular nude displays were inspired by her early experience of working in London brothels.

Renaissance both Jan van Eyck and Lucas Cranach painted beguiling naked Eves. Since no clothing was available in the Garden of Eden, this version of nudity was sanctioned by a faithful interpretation of biblical facts. In his *Last Judgement,* Giotto paints an unfortunate woman descending into Hell; her ludicrously cartoonish breasts are – so oddly for the artist who established observation as a principle of art – not based on anything he might ever have seen. Then there is Velázquez's *The Rokeby Venus,* and any number of lardy Flemings in classical roles. The Judgement of Paris allowed painters to play with nudity. Goya's Naked and Clothed Maja are famous for establishing in painterly terms the absolute meaning of nudity.

But as a proper genre in painting, nudity was only fully established in the nineteenth century. Thus it joined landscape and still-life as a major category of art. But it needs to be said that nudity means female nudity. And it was, without exception, painted by men for the pleasure of other men. The Anglo-Swiss artist Henry Fuseli included an account of the perfect female shape in the Aphorisms he collected between 1788 and 1818:

'The forms of virtue are erect, the forms of pleasure undulate. Minerva's drapery descends in long, uninterrupted lines; a thousand amorous curves embrace the limbs of Flora.'
— EUDO C. MASON, THE MIND OF HENRY FUSELI, 1951

Ingres made a profession of painting Odalisques. These were, in the Ottoman world, the pleasure girls with whom a gentleman might supplement his inadequate religious allowance of four wives.

Opposite: Giotto The Last Judgement, *1304–1305, from his Scrovegni Chapel, Padua. The absurd triangular breasts of the woman condemned to perdition suggest that Giotto had not actually seen a naked woman.*

Above: Diego Velázquez The Rokeby Venus, *1648–51. Nudes were very rare in seventeenth century Spanish art and Velázquez may have been inspired to his quintessentially erotic composition by a visit to Italy. The mirror is held by Venus' son Cupid, creating a narrative about vanity.*

145

This page: Francisco de Goya's
Maja Vestida *and* Maja Desnuda
*were painted between 1797 and
1800. Their source and subject
remains a mystery, but what is
clear in the Nude Maja is a fine
painterly rendering of pubic*
*hair. In 1815 the Inquisition
declared this 'obscene'. The US
Government still thought it so in
1930 when letters from Spain
carrying stamps employing this
famous bush were puritanically
returned to sender.*

BELOW: THE CHEVALIER D'EON'S FROCK

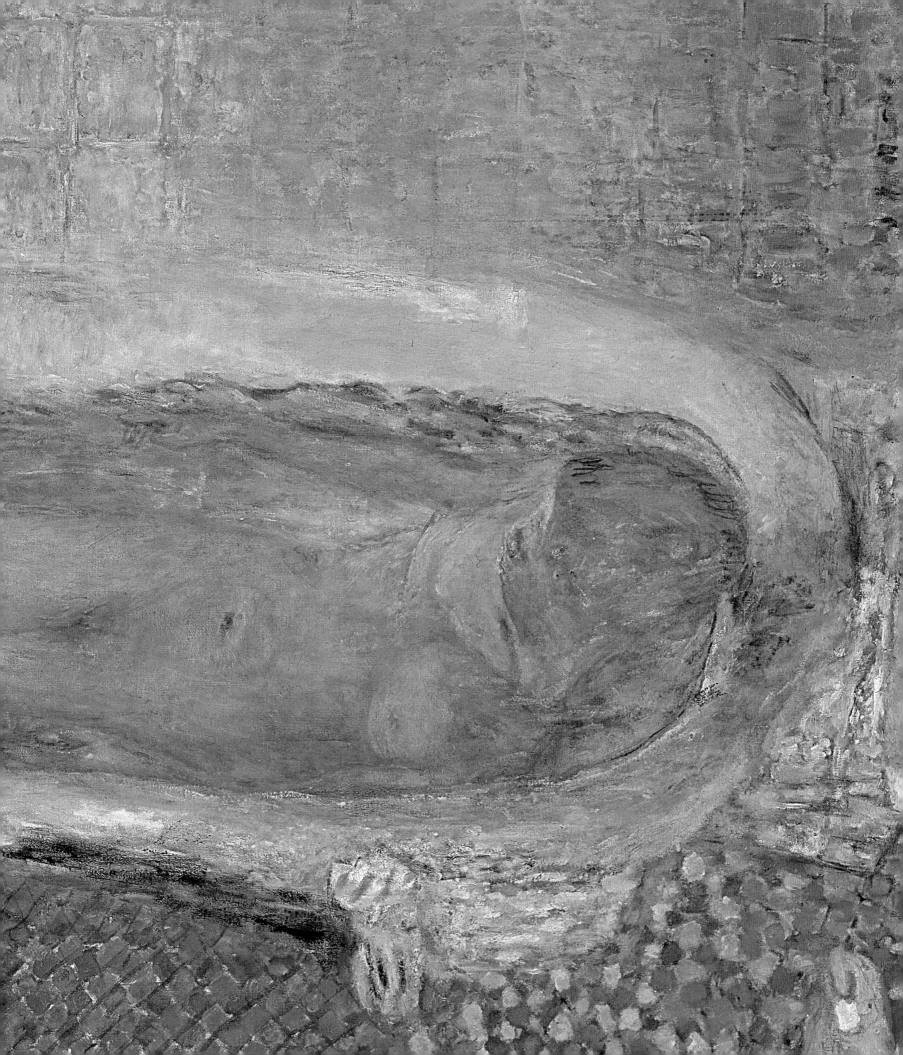

Since prostitution was illegal in Turkey until the late nineteenth century, the law was undermined by the odalisques being bought as slaves. In 1867 the French Orientalist Jean-Léon Gérôme painted a *Slave Market* (now in the Sterling and Francine Clark Art Institute, Williamstown, Massachusetts) which nicely captured the eye-witness accounts of the markets and their curious morality: potential odalisques were often displayed nude for purposes of inspection, but they were also allowed certain powers of veto and of negotiation over their pricing.

Ingre's most celebrated pleasure girl is now known as *La Grande Odalisque*, painted in 1814 and on show in the Salon five years later. She is a design of amorous curves. She hints at the sexual licence of the Orient so dutifully researched by contemporary travellers. But she is a graphic invention rather than a true description of a woman. Her flesh is like marble and her anatomy is deranged: critics visiting the Salon complained that she seemed to lack blood and muscle. Recent research suggests she may actually have three or four more vertebrae that Nature intended. Certainly, her head is an improbably long distance from her hips, hinting perhaps at a certain emotional disengagement.

For the true depiction of flesh, the nineteenth-century amateur had to wait for William Etty, Ingres' Scottish contemporary. Engorged by the chromatic experience of a trip to Venice, Etty returned to London and became a leading specialist in nudes. In particular, he made realistic nipples as much a specialization as Ingres had made improbable anatomy. After Etty, Ingres' marmoreal and geometrical mammae were forever replaced by fleshy examples with pink pinnacles.

And pubic hair? Cranach's *Nymph of the Spring*, painted in 1537 and now in The National Gallery in Washington, has modest pubic hair and engravings made in the seventeenth century by the great Bolognese painter Agostino Carracci show women with ample pubes. And in the Japanese tradition of *Shunga* a woman's pubic hair is often exploited as an emphatic decorative device. But when Ingres was painting, Japanese watercolours and prints were not so well-known. The Ingres Odalisque has neither public nor axillary hair. The conventions of the early nineteenth century, which tolerated men ogling women with no clothes on, would not allow a frank revelation of hirsute womanly reality. Men who wanted to look at nudes (at least in public) had to do so through the idealizing filter of art. Renoir's friend Théodore Duret said his nudes were 'the ideal mistress – always sweet, gay and smiling… the true ideal woman'. And generally hairless.

Page 148: The Grande Odalisque *by Ingres, 1814. Ottoman 'pleasure girls' were a recurrent motif for the painter. Odalisques were sex slaves, but with empowerment. Ottoman custom gave them the right to pick and choose their vendors. They enjoyed higher status than other domestics and could spend freely on luxurious clothes, although Ingres has pointedly painted a nude Odalisque.*

Page 150: Pierre Bonnard Femme Nu à la Baignoire, *1936. Bonnard paints his partner, Marthe, in her bath in the house they shared near Cannes. The curious angle and perspective turn the naked woman into a decorative motif. By the mid Thirties, painterly expressions of pubic hair were not controversial in Europe.*

Above: The Scottish Painter William Etty became an unlikely specialist in voluptuous breasts. He is specially admired for his gorgeous treatment of nipples.

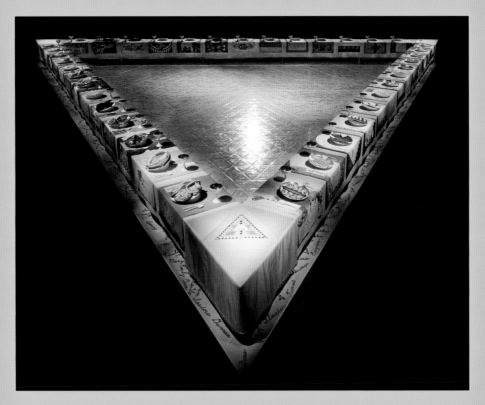

Left: Judy Chicago's Dinner Party, *1974–9, was the first major feminist art installation, now in the Brooklyn Museum. The triangular setting has a* placement *that includes celebrity women from myth and history, including Hrosvitha and Virginia Woolf. Plates are decorated with a fluttering butterfly motif, to represent the omnipresence of the vulva in feminist thought.*

Some Notable Women Artists

According to Pliny, Greek women painters included: Timarete, Eirene, Kalypso, Aristarete, Iaia and Olympias. Medieval manuscript illuminators include: Ende, Guda and Claricia. The Italian Renaissance allowed personalities to emerge: Marietta Robusti was Tintoretto's daughter; Sofonisba Anguissola acquired a reputation in her own right. In Protestant Holland, Judith Leyster was a contemporary of Rembrandt. In seventeenth-century Italy, Artemisia Gentileschi painted nearly as well as Caravaggio. In England, Angelica Kauffmann was one of the founders of the Royal Academy in 1768. The nineteenth century provided: Berthe Morisot, Kate Greenaway, Mary Cassatt, Suzanne Valodon among painters while Julia Margaret Cameron was a pioneer of photography. The twentieth century saw women clearly established as artists of originality and interest: Sonia Delaunay, Georgia O'Keefe, Frida Kahlo, Barbara Hepworth, Elisabeth Frink, Tamara de Lempicka, Bridget Riley. And with photography established as an art form, Lee Miller, Dorothea Lange and Diane Arbus. Judy Chicago's *The Dinner Party* of 1974–9 is often claimed to be the first feminist work of art.

BELOW: THE CHEVALIER D'EON'S FROCK

Left: Georgia O'Keeffe's Black Iris of 1926 uses a flower as sexual symbol, a conceit later very fully exploited by the photographer Robert Mapplethorpe.

Below: My Nurse and I, *1937, Frida Kahlo. This is one of the many autobiographical pictures of Kahlo, bi-sexual wife of Diego Rivera and lover of Leon Trotsky. It hints at a feral sexuality: 'I never painted dreams,' she said, 'I painted my own reality.' Her own reality was profoundly sexual.*

Page 156: A Shunga woodblock print of 1785 by Yoshido Shunsho. 'Shunga' literally means 'images of spring', but is the generic term for eighteenth-century Japanese erotica. Explicit sexual detail is turned into decorative graphics.

155

Pubic Hair

Public hair is a physiological mystery: there is no functional explanation for its existence,
something which confounds evolutionists. Some argue that it is a survival from a
phylogenetic stage of man's development. Leg hair and pubic hair have troubled poets.
Robert Herrick preferred his Julia's legs to be as white and hairless as an egg. *A Genuine
Letter from the Earl of Rochester to Nell Gwynn* is a 20-page poem about how hateful pubic
hair is. It is always assumed that John Ruskin's sudden impotence was caused by the sight,
on his wedding night, of Effie's pubes. Ruskin, whose knowledge of women's bodies was

Left: A shunga wood block print, circa 1855, by Utagawa Kuniyoshi. The Satisfied Woman illustrates the Japanese fascination with pubic and axillary hair.

Below: Paola Borboni, the actress who pioneered public nudity in Italy. Photograph by Wanda Wulz, circa 1935.

159

But public nudity still has the power to shock. The Italian actress Paola Borboni became known as 'Paola of the Scandals' when, in a 1925 performance of Carlo Veneziani's *Alga Marina* she surprised the audience by hoiking her breasts out in a scene that did not call for such liberating gestures. She said 'I was neither sensual nor vulgar. I was just young and my bare breasts didn't bother anyone, not even Il Duce.' Towards the end of her life Borboni said 'After 90, intelligent women reduce their sexual expectations.'

The tools which different cultures devise either to inhibit or, indeed, encourage successful fornication are richly illustrative of prevailing orthodoxies about sexual identity. You have to construe the shape and functions of the female body in a particular way in order to design tools to deter or enhance its potential for pleasure. And the versions of technology employed in this inhibition or encouragement are equally revealing of the limits of the contemporary imagination.

Thus, the chastity belt: evidence, perhaps, of oppressive masculine regimes. But evidence also that women were expected to enjoy sex with or without the company of their husbands. Thus the latter might take steps to inhibit this path to pleasure. Certainly, the chastity belt – which carries the suggestions of constraint and restriction – suggests a temperamental opposite to the cults of voluntary chastity that were popular in the early Christian period. This version of romantic chastity – which celebrated the freedoms to be found in solitary virginity – is often described in the bloodthirsty and often hilarious hagiography *Acta Sanctorum*.

But since so much of the speculation about the chastity belt can be sourced in romantic pseudo-histories of the nineteenth and twentieth centuries, the existence of the chastity belt in our imaginative lives is evidence, perhaps, of our back-projection of our own fantasies and desires onto

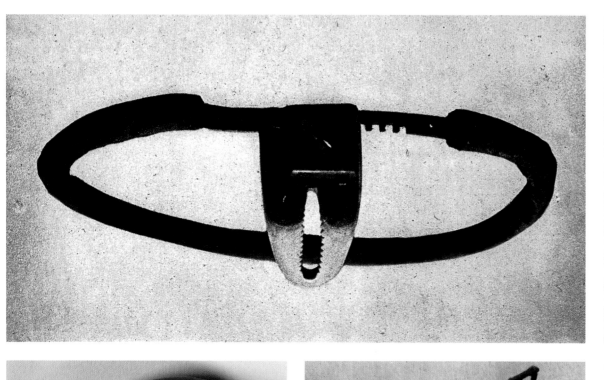

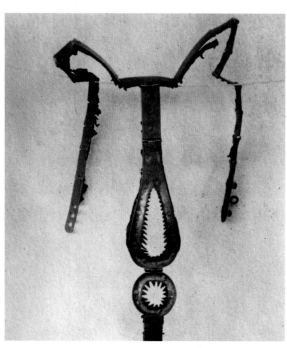

history. There is, according to S. Talalaj and J. Talalaj in their book *The Strangest Human Sex Ceremonies* (1994) some evidence that though the Amerindian Cheyenne used a device comparable to a chastity belt, it is overwhelmingly a product of the European imagination.

The myth is that European knights called-up for the Crusades felt required to strap their stay-at-home wives into a device that was part garment, part machine. It would lock and the wearer could only be released when the person carrying the key returned, perhaps after a Middle East tour lasting several years. However, as medieval blacksmiths possessed the equivalent of bolt-cutting technology and could easily remove a chastity belt from Guinevere or Gwendolyn as soon as the key-holder's barque had slipped over the Channel horizon, the idea of 'locking' and 'restraint' and years of sexual privation have a symbolic rather than a practical reality. Significantly, whether myth or reality, our concept of the chastity belt belongs to the same historical period that daring deeds in the field of chastity were becoming less popular. It was in the popular twelfth-century story *Aucassin and Nicolette* that, as Havelock Ellis puts it, we find that 'the chaste refinements of delicacy and devotion were possible within the strictly normal sphere of sexual love'.

Thus the chastity belt may be seen as the origin of a culture of sexual awareness that brought us to, among other places, Frederick's of Hollywood. As no true account of the design, manufacture or, indeed, wearing of a chastity belt is certain, it is not certain whether their primary function was to deter masturbation or prevent rape and infidelity. Indeed, very little is certain about chastity belts except that men seem to enjoy believing in them since the necessity of locking-up your wife's uro-genital area during a business trip abroad suggests the existence of a very strong sexual appetites needing mechanical restraint. However, the historical authority for their existence is so slight that examples once on display in the Germanisches Nationalmuseum in Nuremberg and the British Museum in London have long since been withdrawn. Authorities in the British Museum now believe their chastity belt is a nineteenth-century fake.

Another example was once on display in the Doge's Palace in Venice. A description of it will meet the purposes of deconstructive myth-making. A leather belt passed around the waist and hanging from it at the mid points front and rear are two dependent metal pieces, hinged (rather uncomfortably one imagines) at the perineum. The anterior metal piece has a generous orifice to match the vagina. The posterior one, to match the anus. Each allows the necessary evacuation of waste, but each is also fitted with rearward facing teeth or barbs. The function of these would be to rip to shreds any intromittent organ which had not already been deterred from its target by so clunking a security system. So here is a ghost of a memory of the *vagina dentata*.

Opposite: Historical evidence for the existence of chastity belts is sketchy. Some historians believe that they are a projection of unhealthy nineteenth-century fantasies about domination and supplication. True or false, surviving examples are a graphic representation of conceptions of womanhood.

Left: Increasing consciousness of the particularity of the woman's body and soul during the later nineteenth century saw the appearance of countless pseudo-technological appliances designed to moderate 'hysteria'.

Right: The form and style of sex accessories is revealing of cultural preoccupations. This woman is using a root vegetable as a dildo.

Opposite: In any age, the surrogate penis reveals the dominant conception of woman. By the twenty-first century, the dildo was a stylized, feminized, technologically advanced high concept device somewhere between jewellery and personal hi-fi.

Page 164: An officer returning from the wars is avid for gratification in this masterpiece of Edwardian kitsch. His woman has been left, while he is on campaigns, in shackles of chastity. To greet him she proffers the keys to release her, establishing a none too subtle narrative about master, mistress and controlled access to pleasure. Such were the dominant fantasies suggested by the chastity belt.

The same historical period that invented the idea of the chastity belt in order to accommodate its ever-enlarging concept of female sexuality was also the period when sex machines came onto the market. At the same moment in history when women were inching towards emancipation, and the liberating prospect of birth control was no longer a taboo subject, an entire industry arose whose purpose was to redesign the female body. Garments such as the 'electric corset' spoke of the Victorians' queasy relationship between primitive sexuality and modern technology. The mid-Victorian woman was engulfed by technology in the home.

Andrew St George writes:

'The home provided mid-Victorian England with a concept wide enough to outflank the realities which challenged it… the omnivorous domestic scene absorbed dissent, continually recreated itself as technologies (mass production of furniture, gas and then electric lighting, integrated plumbing) required the household ethics to change as the house evolved.'
— THE DESCENT OF MANNERS, 1993

The various evasions and camouflages and quackery used to disguise the real purpose of the startling variety of hydro-pneumatic-oleo-electro-therapeutic devices that were commercialized in the nineteenth century is both comical and pathetic. They were never called 'vibrators' (that is a much more recent vulgarism), but their purpose was nonetheless to provide a reliable means of sexual gratification for an individual Victorian woman. If this tells us as much about the insensitivity and failings of the individual Victorian man as it does of female self-identity and appetite,

then it is no less valuable a part of the story of the sexual woman as something willed into existence by conscious desire, not just by accident of nature.

In *Mechanization Takes Command* (1948), his majestic study of the role of the machine in modern architecture and design, the Swiss historian Siegfried Giedion illustrates a nineteenth-century pelvic douche. Here, a powerful jet of water is aimed at the patient's vulva. Some occult 'hygienic' purpose is presumed, but the effect and likely results may be guessed at from the presence of the word 'percussion' on the original drawing.

The solitary woman was, according to the conventional mores, one not allowed the pleasures of sexual release. It is code for virgin/celibate/frustration and the condition and its nervous side effects were known as 'hysteria'. In *The Anatomy of Melancholy* (1621) Robert Burton says this malaise tends to effect maids, nuns and widows. In other words, women without men. (Burton does not mention the problems of those women confined in chastity belts.) Industrialization was to bring relief, often electrically powered. Disguised as a domestic appliance, vibrators were actively marketed in the sort of journals maids, nuns and widows might read: *Women's Home Companion, Modern Women* and *Needlecraft*. They allowed occult mass produced masturbation through hydro-therapy below, while other patent electrical devices promised to harden and embolden the bust above. When it was declared that 'all physicians agree that every family should have an electric battery in their house' its real meaning was that every house should have a sex toy for the use of its women. 'Hysteria' was only removed from the American Psychiatric Association's list of diseases in 1952.

2

FROM
THE
VIRGIN
TO
PAMELA
ANDERSON
(AND
KATE
MOSS)

Pin-Ups

Page 166: Tom Wesselmann's series The Great American Nude *(this is Number 70, 1965) reduced women to a flat graphic logogram: lips, tongue and nipples are given prominence over the eyes. Thus, the windows of the soul were judged inferior to mucous membrane and erectile tissue. Wesselmann's stylized nipples and lips are the exact equivalent of Mary Quant's stylized underwear.*

Opposite: Bettie Page in 1955, the original professional 'pin-up'. She was affectionately known as 'hips, lips 'n' tits'.

Who was a pin-up? The Virgin Mary. Venus. Bettie Page, Marilyn Monroe, Jayne Mansfield, Brigitte Bardot. From the latter group, three American women and one French one. The statistics are revealing: the greater part of the twentieth-century 'pin-up' trade was sourced in imagery from the United States. Which is to say imagery that is as slick, commercialized, packaged and undemanding as aphrodisiac Spam. The other quarter was French. Which is to say knowing, sly, artful and a tad more sophisticated.

What is a pin-up? The word comes from the habit of American GIs while on belligerent foreign tours to attach photographs of ideal women to their tent-poles, latrines or mess-hut walls. These images were usually found in Hollywood, but sometimes in air-brushed fictions which used Hollywood as a pattern book. In what complex Homeric way this reminded a young Odysseus from Des Moines of the comforts of home and his duty to return to it we cannot now say. Only one thing is certain: the flawless perfection of pin-up art with its stubble-free legs, sculpted bosom, high-gloss hair, flawless complexion, impossibly long legs and inhuman proportions had only a tangential relationship

with the real Penelope-woman at home in Idaho thumbing the Sears Roebuck catalogue and wistfully dreaming of love as she stirred her instant coffee.

According to Thucydides, Persian cavalry used to insert their hands into mares and then would later introduce the perfume to their own horses in the heat of battle, the better to stimulate them. Perhaps the pin-up helped achieve a similarly encouraging effect on American soldiers in the Rhineland. Sex and war are related, as are love and death. The bomb that dropped from a B-29 and fell on Hiroshima at 8.15 on 6 August 1945 carried upon its murderous shell a picture of Rita Hayworth. Why would a horribly destructive atomic weapon be decorated with a busty starlet? Eros and Thanatos got terribly mixed-up on the way to Hiroshima, adding an unwelcome level of meaning to the expression 'sex bomb'.

The pin-up is only the twentieth-century version of a long history of fanciful images of women which have been deployed across the centuries to meet the differing needs of fashion and taste. The stories of the saints present many lively stories about strong female personalities which may have had their effect on developing female personalities in

Catholic Europe during the early modern period, but it is in Renaissance art that a visual character of woman emerges from what were hitherto psychology-free Byzantine stereotypes. The Renaissance was the re-birth of many things, but especially of the ideal woman who first presented herself as Aphrodite.

According to a conceit familiar to the Goncourt brothers, diarists of Paris' later nineteenth-century art world, medieval convents were used to segregate ugly women from the attractive ones. These '*laiderons*' were (at least reputedly) locked up in their unhappy hundreds of thousands behind convent doors. Thus a special poignancy attaches to images of the Christian Virgin. Imagine a convent full of despised and rejected ugly sisters required to contemplate pictures of a divine Mother whose maternity was fused by a weirdly

inaccessible form of mystical, extra-corporeal sex. For *laiderons*, the dogma of the Immaculate Conception must have been a cruel additional psychological torment to the chilly corporeal privations of convent life.

The appearance of Maria Lactans in art coincided with significant changes in art and manners. It was at the very same moment that fashion separated into styles for men and women that the female breast became a design issue. This was when the nursing Madonna became established as the most potent image in Christian art in the Italian *trecento*, a century later in the north of Europe. The Virgin's pre-sexual breast was a signal that art was beginning to acknowledge observable reality. In this way the Mother of God became beautifully commingled with the vision of a real woman feeding her child.

Above: US servicemen in the Second World War created the 'pin-up', confirming a relationship between war and desire.

Above right: Brigitte Bardot in 1956. The French star's image was professionally designed by her cinematic handlers. Her naturalisme was achieved by hard-won artifice.

Opposite: Rita Hayworth in 1942, the year she made You Were Never Lovelier.

173

Opposite: Eugène Atget (1857–1927), the great photographer of Paris, had a special interest in the city's prostitutes, following a commission to record them from the painter André Dignimont. This is La Villette, rue Asselin, 1921, *showing a* fille publique *taking a break, and is currently exhibited in Musée d'Orsay, Paris. The reality of the prostitute is at odds with the pin-up ideal.*

Above: Before pin-ups, the Christian Virgin was the most familiar image of woman. This Byzantine iconostasis shows that individual psychology played no part in the projection of an ideal: the Queen of Heaven is a cipher.

As the first pin-up, the Virgin is primary evidence of the evolving interpretation of woman. The oldest picture in London's National Gallery is perhaps Margarito d'Arezzo's *Virgin and Child* (1260s). It tells us quite a lot about stereotypes of women in thirteenth-century Italy because here is the Virgin not as an inspirational beatific untouchable beauty, the first thought of God on a brief passage through earth, but as a frumpy sourpuss who might as well be doing laundry in an Umbrian stew as nurturing the Son of God. No happy hours of the Virgin for Margarito d'Arezzo. Here in its way is the start of a realistic treatment of women in art which culminated in Eugène Atget's photographs of Paris' *filles publiques* in the 1920s.

After Christ, the Virgin is the most popular subject in Western art. In his great book *Signs and Symbols in Christian Art* (1954) George Ferguson recognizes, besides the Maria Lactans, or the nursing Madonna, the following types of Virgin:

The Madonna Adoring Christ
Mater Amabilis (The Mother Worthy of Love)
The Madonna of Humility
The Virgin in Glory
The Queen of Heaven
The Majesty of the Madonna
The Madonna della Misericordia, protector of the faithful
The Madonna del Soccorso, carrying a club to chase away the Devil
The Mater Dolorosa
The Virgin of the Immaculate Conception (with sun, moon, lily, rose without thorns, an enclosed garden, a sealed fountain, cedars of Lebanon, Tree of Jesse, closed gates, spotless mirror, Tower of David, Twelve Stars)
The Virgin of the the Rosary
The Madonna del Carmine
The Madonna di Loreto

The Catherine Wheel

St Catherine of Alexandria was an early Christian saint whose identity is preserved in the firework known as a Catherine Wheel. In Italy she is known as Caterina del Ruote and her saint's day is 25 November. The colourful story of this third-century pin-up is as follows. A persecuted Christian, her fragrant presence made her grimy dungeon full of light and angels brought her food. Impressed by her serenity and beauty, the Emperor who imprisoned her proposed marriage, but she indignantly refused. As a result, he ordered her to be bound between four spiked wheels, the better to tear her to death. As the gory punishment was being executed, flames shot from Heaven, setting fire to the wheels and, thus, inspiring the firework. In Michelangelo's *Last Judgement* Saint Catherine was originally shown not only with a wheel, but with an appealingly naked bottom. The attitude of Saint Blaise behind her was said by many to suggest an anticipation of copulation. Accordingly, after The Council of Trent banned nudity in Catholic art, the painter Daniele da Volterra was commissioned to cover-up the offending body parts with drapery.

Tradition might have demanded that painters show the Virgin as the very personification of grace and purity, but just as often paintings of the Virgin show a physically and emotionally flawed mortal woman.

It is a measure of the enlarging modern consciousness to count the number of Virgin paintings created in any given period by serious artists. In the 1380s the subject was a preoccupation. A century later, much less so, being overtaken by history and mythology. Botticelli's *Birth of Venus* was painted in the 1480s. It is not the first, just the most significant, secular painting of a woman. The model may be Simonetta Cattaneo Vespucci, mistress of Giuliano di Piero de'Medici. She may also have been the model for his *Primavera*. It may be assumed Botticelli had an attachment for her: she is blonde, beautiful and frankly nude. She is not sacred-naked, but voluptuously and very provocatively without clothes.

Venus is emerging from the marine foam, protected by a scallop shell which may be a memory of the mandorla with its unambiguous sexual suggestiveness. Her pose is a version of the classical Venus Pudica: one hand holds her long hair in place before the mons veneris, the more prosaic pubic mound which was named for her. Another hand makes a not altogether convincing or successful gesture of covering her breasts. Scholars reckon the erotic verses of Ovid and Politian may be the source for the distinctive iconography:

she is attended by Zephyrs and while her expression is one of blameless innocence, any educated fifteenth-century observer would have known these flying creatures were emblematic of sexual passion.

Botticelli presumably knew the Hellenistic Venus statue which the Medicis owned (now also in the Uffizi). The pose is similar, but Botticelli has made no attempt at a faithful reproduction of anything, let alone a real person. Simonetta Vespucci did not, presumably, have a neck quite as long as the one shown in the painting. And if her left shoulder sloped the way of Venus, then she was deformed. She is certainly profane. The Renaissance pin-up was all of these things.

The pin-up established versions of the ideal woman, or, at least, designs for them. As soon as the design became secularized, first via mythology, later via social portraits, even later via the movies and advertising, then the opportunity to trade on this image became a possibility. So, while prostitution may, as is so often said, be the oldest profession, its recent forms are culturally related to modern business.

The culture of prostitution presents woman as a tradable commodity: a harsh reality, but one sustained by a sort of idealism. And like any other commercially traded commodity, soap, for example, it needed to be designed.

While Americans monopolized the imagery, the French dominated the bureaucracy and the administration.

Left: Her grotesque torture led to a popular firework in the Catherine wheel; in this way the obscure St Catherine of Alexandria entered popular culture. In 1508, Raphael fancied she looked like this.

Right: Botticelli's Birth of Venus, *1485, probably shows Simonetta Vespucci, a Medici mistress. She is very deliberately eroticized, but the painter has made no attempt at accurate description. The proportions of her body are bizarrely exaggerated to create an effect that is artificial, but appears natural.*

Above left: Leonide Leblanc was a prominent insoumise, *the name given to Paris' independent-minded courtesans of the nineteenth century. According to police records she was well-known in the* maisons de rendez-vous *where she was prized for her womanly passion. She became the professional lover of Prince Galitzine and acquired a reputation as a beauty. The cherries are a traditional symbol of wantonness and fecundity.*

Above right: Chez Suzy, rue Gregoire-de-Tours, *a maison close, photographed by Brassaï (1899–1984) in the 1930s, currently exhibited in the Centre Pompidou, Paris.*

Opposite: Marie Duplessis, seen here in Camille-Joseph-Etienne Roqueplan's portrait, circa 1845, was one of Paris' most famous kept women. She was the mistress of Franz Liszt and of Alexandre Dumas fils, *who immortalized her in his novel* La Dame aux Camelias.

If you have the structure, you have the mould. The *cinq-a-sept* is the fabled interlude between the end of the working day and arrival home for dinner when a gentleman might visit his mistress. It was facilitated not only by more relaxed morals, but also the more relaxed underwear coming onto the market in the nineteenth century. Elizabethan whalebone and starched linen stays required more than two hours for such dalliance. The new underwear made commerce of this type more feasible.

With their passion for regulation and hierarchy, the French recognized different sorts of women for sale. *Les Insoumises* were kept by millionaires, dukes or royals. *Les Grandes Horizontales* were the predatory heroines of the demi-monde – Marie Duplessis and La Paiva among the best-known – who entered (and sometimes dominated) society as courtesans. Then there were those *filles publiques* whose frank admission of glorying in the profitable vices added another dimension to conceptions of what a woman should be.

Prostitutes were, at least in France, branded consumer products. Unlike the Greek *hetaerae* whose purpose might (generously) be understood to have been primarily religious, the prostitute of nineteenth-century France was wholly carnal. Her body was a catalogue of delights for sale to men. This was the age of Boucicaut's Bon Marché, the world's first department store, whose material pleasures were described by *Zola in Au Bonheur des Dames*. This was the age too when the new museums put all of civilization on display and labelled it for intellectual consumption. Women too were for sale and consumption.

One stimulus to the development of modern prostitution was the tart's moral contemporary and equivalent: the commercial traveller. They may be seen as a cause and effect. The railways had created a new level of mobility for the businessman. New types of residential hotel appeared. At the same time, the huge international exhibitions held in

Right: Otto Dix Three Girls,
*1926. The German 'Drei
Weiber' carries something of
the suggestion of bitch, or hussy,
rather than juvenile innocence.*

Opposite: La môme Bijou au
Bar de la Lune, Montmartre,
*1932. A famous Montmartre
madame, caught by Brassaï in
the Bar de la Lune, currently
exhibited in the Centre
Pompidou, Paris.*

The Judgement of Paris

The Judgement of Paris is a myth that allowed painters to experiment with versions of the most perfectly desirable woman. Although there have been exceptions: when Charles the Bold entered Lille in 1468, fat Flemish women were employed to play the roles of the Roman goddesses Venus, Juno and Minerva (Aphrodite, Hera and Athena). Still, the story of the Judgement of Paris is a metaphor about female beauty. In fact, it was the first beauty contest. Three goddesses are claiming the Apple of Discord and ask Zeus to arbitrate on who is the most beautiful, so she might claim it.

Zeus delegates to Paris, a hapless Phrygian mortal.

The goddesses bribe Paris. Athena tried to seduce him with wisdom. Hera offered political power. Aphrodite offered sex with Helen of Sparta.

Paris chose sex and it was the Greek expedition to retrieve Helen after this dalliance that was the mythological origin of the Trojan War.

In classical literature there are versions of the story by Homer, Ovid and Lucian. In Western art, Lucas Cranach, Peter Paul Rubens and Renoir have treated the subject.

Paris in 1855, 1867 and 1889 made Walter Benjamin describe the city as 'the capital of the nineteenth century'. Lonely men on the road might seek the comfort of a '*femmes d'attente*', a sort of temporary substitute wife.

Significantly, for many of the male customers using a prostitute was an act of social promotion, rather like eating a gastronomic meal as opposed to home-cooking. Victor Hugo accounted his spending on prostitutes as 'charity'. Commercial records usually disguise money spent on sex in a *maison de rendez-vous* as 'travelling expenses'. It seems that men were not just buying the ancient trinity of erection, entry and emission, so much as buying the sort of woman their social status would never allow them to seduce.

Less auspicious than a *maison de rendez-vous* was the *hotel de passe*. Here a needy customer would take a *fille de brasserie*. These were the serving girls (*verseuses*) who would, dressed in Andalucian, Scottish or Italian costume, drink with their clients. This was something that appealed to all social classes. In a letter to Louise Colet in June 1853 Gustave Flaubert wrote:

'I love prostitution for itself and independently of what it means underneath. I've never been able to see one of these women in their low-cut dresses pass beneath the light of the gas lamp without my heart beating fast.'

— ENID STARKIE FLAUBERT'S LETTERS, 1967

An idealized version of a *fille de brasserie* may be imagined from Manet's *Bar at the Folies-Bergères*. Very much in the spirit of Manet's *fille de brasserie* (with the branded bottles of Bass on the shelves behind), Anton Chekhov wrote in a letter on 25 April 1887 'I was so drunk all the time that I took bottles for girls and girls for bottles.'

And this was the period when sex was scientifically studied for the first time. The sexologist Havelock Ellis was author of the engrossing, repetitive, but pioneering, *Studies in the Psychology of Sex*. His colourful – occasionally obsessional – narrative was strongly tinted by pigments taken from the palettes of Darwin, Mantegazza, Freud and hundreds of less well-known and possibly less reliable sources. He makes several attempts to determine ideas of

Left: The Judgement of Paris *provided painters with a mythologically sanctioned excuse to paint nude women. This is Rubens' interpretation of the story, 1636.*

Right: Manet's Bar at the Folies-Bergères, *1881–2, shows a* fille de brasserie, *a frequent camouflage of Paris prostitutes.*

female beauty, making due allowance for cultural and historical variation. But his every observation is based on the fixed belief that the visual interpretation of beauty is paramount. Eyesight is the main channel by which we receive impressions, he says. From the point of view of sexual selection, vision is the supreme sense. And all the time he believes that his notions of beauty are fundamentally scientific, or, at least functional. The almost universal preferences for finely toned skin, bright eyes and a lively gait suggest health. Choosing a healthy mate is a survival characteristic.

One example of his method concerns the Malay pin-up, as understood circa 1900. It reads like the note books of an astronomer, a meteorologist or the inventory of an international fruit and vegetable merchant. The perfect Malay woman, according to Ellis' source (W.W.Skeat's *Malay Magic* 1900), must have the following equivalent attributes:

brow	=	*a one day old moon*
eyebrows	=	*clouds*
cheeks	=	*mango slices*
nose	=	*jasmine bud*
hair	=	*palm shoots*
waist	=	*plant stalk*
head	=	*must be egg-shaped*
fingers	=	*comparable to porcupine quills*
eyes	=	*c.f. the planet Venus*
lips	=	*the fissures of a pomegranate*

Three centuries before, Arcimboldo had used vegetable iconography in his *trompe-l'oeil* paintings (there is no Italian equivalent expression), but this account of female beauty in terms of fruits and shoots is surely more strange.

Another of Ellis' sources, a W. Dunlop who contributed articles on 'Australian Folklore Studies' to the *Journal of the Anthropological Institute*, has a fine account of aboriginal beauty. At some point in his scientific description he seems to have been disconcertingly seduced by the spectre of savage elegance he so painstakingly describes:

'A beautiful girl who had long, glossy hair hanging around her face and down her shoulders, which were plump and round. Her face was adorned with red clay and her person wrapped in a fine large opossum rug fastened by a pin formed from the small bone of a kangaroo's leg and also by a string attached to a wallet made of rushes neatly plaited of small strips skinned from their outside after they had been for some time exposed to the heat of the fire; which being thrown on her back, the string passing under one arm and across her breast, held the soft

Pioneer sexologists, including Havelock Ellis, were fascinated by interpretations of beauty in different cultures. Above: Asian beauty: a Sea Dyaks girl in a beaded corset completely disguising her breasts; opposite: Kenyah women husking rice, artlessly exposing theirs. The photographs were taken in 1905.

rug in a fanciful position of considerable elegance; and she knew well how to show to advantage her queenlike figure when she walked with her polished yam stick held in one of her small hands and her little feet appearing below the edge of the rug.'
— AUGUST & NOVEMBER, 1898

In 1905 C.H. Stratz published his study *Die Schonheit des Weiblichen Korpers*, often cited by early sexologists. He has no doubt at all what constitutes female beauty. Delicate bones and rounded forms (especially breasts) are necessary. The pelvis must be broad and the hair must be richly abundant and long. The pubic hair should be low and narrow and axillary hair sparse. The body should be hairless, head must be small and round, skin delicate. Optical orbits should be large. Eyebrows must be high and not luxuriant. Transitions from cheek to neck must be smooth. Hands are small with long index fingers. Wrists must be small in circumference. The clavicle must be small and straight while the buttocks must be prominent and domed. Thighs are to be rounded and thick while the pubic arch must be low and obtuse. Ankles slender, knees soft, calves rounded. The second toe must be long and the fifth toe short. The middle incisor teeth must be broad. Stratz' brief for a perfect woman is as detailed as a specification for rolling stock issued by Westphalian State Railways. And as inflexible as its result.

These gripping accounts of colonial, unconscious Kitsch-erotica make a telling contrast to modern science, which has a different view of the ideal. The female shape is determined by three inflection points: the chest, waist and hips. It is the mathematical relationship between them which we find critical.

Above: In Paris the voyageur de commerce, *brought to the capital by the new railways and intent on visiting the great nineteenth-century trade exhibitions, explosively enlarged the market for prostitutes. The lonely commercial traveller had a similar role in England.*

Opposite: Fille dans un Hôtel de passe, rue Quincampoix. *The* Hôtel de passe *was an institution where those desirous of such a thing might enjoy an uncomplicated short-term coupling with a young woman designed to look like a hooker. Brassaï took this photograph in 1932.*

The Culture of Brothels: a Literary Guide

Terence Kilmartin's *Guide to Proust* has a fine entry on 'brothels'. Merely to summarize it is to provide a nice and haunting insight into the period's attitude to women being for sale:

Odette's dealings with procuresses

Swann's visits to brothels

Bloch takes M to a house of assignation

Uninterestingness of women met in brothels

Saint-Loup's enthusiasm for brothels

Luxury brothel at Mainville (mistaken for grand hotel)

The Prince de Guermantes assignation with Morel

Women of the 'closed houses'

M and two laundry girls in a house of assignation

Morel, Albertine and a fisher-girl in a brothel at Couliville

Social gossip in the Mainville brothel

Jupien's brothel in war-time Paris

The Metro in war-time like a Pompeian brothel

Left: A maritime figurehead
from Sweden. Early figureheads
were often men, but all were
designed with some sort of
religious-superstitious aleatoric
function. By the eighteenth
century, women dominated the
type. Almost without exception
they have ample bosoms, to suggest
prosperity and well-being.

Below: Cindy Sherman
exposing a stylised breast,
exactly as a Madonna.

So far as the body is concerned, the shape is determined by the distribution of muscle and fat which, in turn, is a function of the female sex hormone, oestrogen. The presence of oestrogen tends to inhibit the accumulation of fat around the abdomen while stimulating it in the buttocks. (The male sex hormone, testosterone, tends to do the very opposite.) There is no evolutionary basis for thinness being attractive. Since about 25 per cent of a woman's weight is naturally in her thighs, a girl with fashionably skinny legs is against nature.

Devendra Singh, a researcher at the University of Texas at Austin, has made a scientific study of WHR. This stands for 'waist to hips ratio'. Singh's findings suggest that mathematical determinants of the ideal woman's proportions are a 'robust phenomenon', as scientists like to describe ideas they feel to be incontrovertible. Maybe our ideals are not the same as the Malay's or the indigenous Australian's, but Singh insists there is evidence that children tend to gaze longer at adults who are considered conventionally 'attractive'.

Again, the evolutionary psychologist's view would be that the conventional attributes of 'attractiveness' are a certain symmetry, plus well-shaped hips, full lips and a small chin. These suggest the presence of a flourishing stream of good sex hormones, hence positive potential for reproduction. You can't 'read' DNA, but can you can clock a good figure.

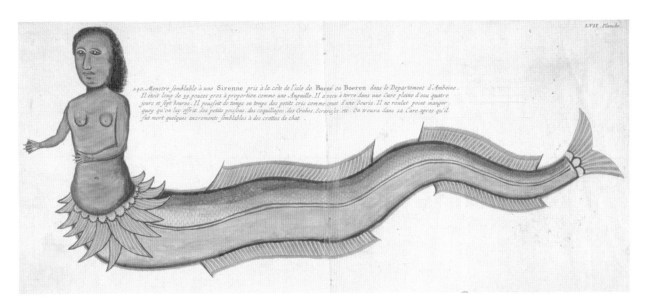

*Opposite: A detail of Fra Angelico's
Cortona Altarpiece, circa 1438,
that shows* The Annunciation.
Mary gracia plenens *(full of
grace) receives the Divine message
and becomes Divine herself.*

The idea of body typing goes back at least as far as the Ayurveda, was taken-up by Nietzsche and firmly established in the 1950s by the behaviourist William H. Sheldon whose *Atlas of Men* (1954) popularized the idea of the endomorph, mesomorph and ectomorph. Or fat, normal and thin. With a nod to now unpopular, if not actually discredited, ideas of eugenics and racial hygiene, Sheldon suggested that character might be interpreted from appearance.

To this Singh has added some observational and statistical data. The crucial WHR is similar in males and females before puberty, but then diverges. A healthy mature woman has a WHR of between 0.67 and 0.8. The evolutionary aspect of this is that a blink of any woman's WHR immediately suggests to a caveman observer whether or not she is pregnant. Since it would be wasteful to spend genetic resources on someone already impregnated by a third party, the wrong sort WHR is rejected.

Singh actually set-up an experiment to test whether this assumption was culturally determined, or had greater relevance. His sample used different ethnic and cultural groups, but the result was: the classic egg-timer figure

Above: Mermaids were projections of ship-bound yearnings. The reality of the mermaid is probably Trichechus manatus latirostris, *or the manatee. The ideal was a topless beauty with a fish tail, as charmingly shown in Louis Renard's* Poissons, Ecrevisses et Crabes, *1754.*

ELVGREN

FRENCH DRESSING

HERE COMES THAT HIGH PRESSURE DIVER AGAIN—

This page: Peruvian artist Joaquin Alberto Vargas y Chávez's influential airbrush technique created an Esperanto of commercial erotica well suited to new lithographic print technologies. Meanwhile, the industrial process sanitized the content as surely as the artistic instinct exaggerated the proportions. School of Vargas adepts included Gil Elvgren, left, and Earl Macpherson, right.

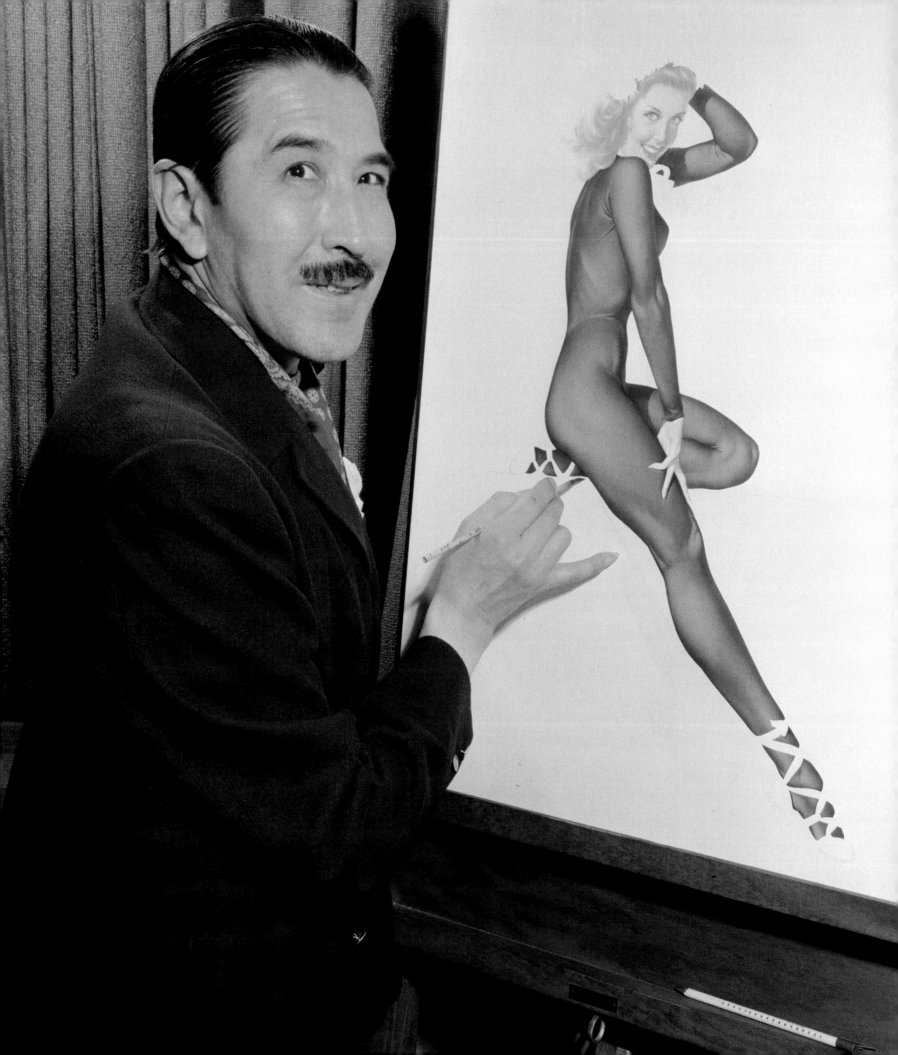

was universally preferred. Of course, this might be an adaptive trait caused by the near-universal acceptance of Western media stereotypes, but Singh believed this response was:

'… programmed in the human mind, because it provides important biological information about a woman's youthfulness, health status and fertility.'
— 'AN EVOLUTIONARY THEORY OF FEMALE PHYSICAL ATTRACTIVENESS' EYE ON PSI CHI VOL.10, NO.3

The Modern Pin-Up was made possible by the new magazines. Among these, *Esquire* was pre-eminent. Its first issue was published by David A. Smart and Arnold Gingrich; high-minded, but masculine as well, it contained stories by Ernest Hemingway and Scott Fitzgerald. But it also included girls. It was art directed by Paul Rand and George Lois. Between 1942 and 1945, 6 million copies of the magazine *Esquire* were sent to US troops to raise their morale. After they had commodified modern woman, Rand went on to design the corporate identity of IBM and Lois became the best-known adman on Madison Avenue in the Sixties.

'Glamour' according to Stuart Berg Flexner, was a term coined in 1941 by Hollywood publicists. 'Pin-up' he says was actually first used in the US armed forces newspaper, *Yank*, on 30 April 1943. There were also 'sweater girls', the young women with hard bras who worked in armaments factories whose busts looked like Howitzer shells. Hard bras and tight sweaters. What a metaphor!

The girls were the airbrushed masterpieces by Peruvian artist, Joaquin Alberto Vargas y Chávez. Vargas became a brand-name for a certain style of female illustration. The son of a professional photographer, it may be that association with the high-sheen photo-chemical processes of the studio influenced his conception of the woman's body. After all, if prints and exposures manipulated, why not with women too?

Vargas first worked for Flo Ziegfeld, whose 1933 movie *The Sin of Nora Moran* features actress Zita Johann becoming ever so nearly Hollywood's very first nude. A vernacular version of his women appeared on the 'nose art' of US Army Air Force bombers flying in the Second World War: girls with spectacular busts (often shamelessly displayed), legs of unlikely length, perfect complexions, abundant high-sheen hair, bright red lips and perfect teeth. These queasy icons of sex and mother, providing simultaneous stimulus and protection, went into battle over Guam and Berlin rather as female figureheads went into naval battles in earlier centuries. The Vargas Girls series began in Esquire in the Fifties, migrating to *Playboy* in the Sixties only to be eventually shaded by ever more artistic and ever more explicit 'glamour' photography. Vargas' technique was so fine that *Airbrush Action Magazine* created the Vargas Awards in his honour. In his iconography of attenuated fingers, toes, nail varnish and breasts we find the equivalent of California's hot-rod cult. Hot rods were ordinary cars, Model-A Fords for example, cut and shut and modified and buffed and chromed almost beyond recognition.

Left: Joaquin Alberto Vargas y Chávez, 1896–1980.

Right: 'Black Widow' nose art on a Consolidated B-24 'Liberator' bomber, 1943. Second World War nose art was often based directly on Vargas' pin-ups. It confirmed a relationship between Eros and Thanatos.

Page 194: 'Passion Wagon' nose art on a North American P-51 'Mustang' fighter. Salvador Dali thought flight was 'the most spectacular expression of the sexual instinct'.

This page: Bettie Page, first with a whip, finally without anything. The successful pin-up artiste was originally seen as a pornographer, but has recently enjoyed re-uptake as a heroine of the feminine.

The hot-rod and the Vargas pin-up shared various essential characteristics, most importantly a high quality of finish and a sense of the ideal. It was the customization of the everyday.

The greatest pin-up of them all was Bettie Page, the daughter of a Nashville *garagiste* who once stole a police car and, later, sexually abused her. Page – or hips, lips 'n' tits as the trade had it – became one of the first *Playboy* centrefolds. Her career had begun with a teaching certificate, although she soon found regular employment boring. She was spotted disporting herself on Coney Island by an amateur photographer in 1949 and soon found her way into specialist magazines. Titles included *Wink*, *Eyeful* and *Titter*. Sadomasochism was her entry into female stereotyping. She was gagged and spreadeagled, actually as well as metaphorically.

Even more than a Flemish Renaissance virgin who would have been the most beautiful person a Brabant peasant had ever seen, for a generation or two, Bettie Page was the first woman young men had actually seen nude. Her WHR was extraordinary. At 36-23-36 she challenged the norms.

In an interview published in her *Los Angeles Times* obituary, Hugh Hefner said in Bettie Page he found 'a combination of wholesome innocence and fetish-oriented poses that is at once retro and very modern'.

In the first half of the Fifties she posed for amateur photographers. Often she was nude, otherwise in bikinis, high heels and bondage gear. She acquired various identities: Nurse Bettie, Jungle Bettie, Voodoo Bettie, Banned in Boston Bettie, Maid Bettie and Crackers in Bed Bettie.

It was in 1955 that Bettie Page became properly commodified. This was the year professional photographer Bunny Yeager photographed her, somewhat like Venus, splashing in the breakers. In January 1955 *Playboy* published her as a centrefold (partially) dressed as Father Christmas.

Page is now seen as a heroine of the sexual revolution, but was thought in her pomp to be a pornographer and was subpoenaed to testify before a Congressional hearing (she claimed federal agents pursued her waving nude photographs of herself), but never actually appeared.

In 1982, after a series of disastrous marriages, Bettie Page was sentenced to ten years in San Bernardino County's Patton State Hospital after she attacked her landlady with a kitchen knife. By the time of her release, she had become the object of a massive ironic re-uptake. Her website, for

example, claims 600 million hits in the five years before her death, although in latter years she declined to be photographed since she wanted to be remembered as the version of perfection she presented in the Fifties. Hefner said 'She was a remarkable lady, an iconic figure in pop culture who influenced sexuality, taste in fashion, someone who had a tremendous impact on our society.' She told a 2006 interviewer: 'I want to be remembered as the woman who changed people's perspectives concerning nudity in its natural form.'

'Natural nudity' is an interesting concept. George Lucas specified that the droid in *Star Wars: Revenge of the Sith* should be like an automated Bettie Page. It became known as a Bettybot. The *Los Angeles Times* obituary reported that not only was she immortalized in the 2005 movie *The Notorious Bettie Page*, but she was also available in shot glasses, Zippo lighters and playing cards. Artist Olivia de Berardinis said:

'I always paint Bettie Page. But truth be told, it took me years to understand what I was looking at in the old photographs of her. Now I get it. There was a passion play unfolding in her mind. What some see as a bad-girl image was, in fact, a certain sensual freedom and play-acting – it was part of the fun of being a woman.'

A detail of the Mona Lisa and Kate Moss. Leonardo's famous portrait of circa 1503 is sometimes known as La Gioconda *because of her smile (Italian* gioconda = *cheerful, merry), but it is more enigmatic than jocose. Kate Moss' allure is also partly founded on an ambivalent sexuality and inscrutable expressions.*

The CMG agency which controls the image of Bettie Page also controls the rights to the images of Marilyn Monroe and Princess Diana. But now there are different stereotypes. The model Kate Moss has been compared to Mona Lisa in her influence on perceptions of woman. Each shares a severe smile and an enigmatic sexuality which is very appealing. Walter Pater said of all ancient pictures, she has chilled the least. And was more famously quoted in saying: 'She is older than the rocks among which she sits; like the vampire, she has been dead many times and learned the secrets of the grave.'

In 2005 Christies' sold Lucien Freud's naked portrait of Kate Moss for £3.9m. What else do they have in common? George Sand said Leonardo's mystery woman had '*la laide seduisante*' which might be translated by some as captivating ugliness. Kate Moss' particularities are very different. Of La Gioconda's legs we know nothing – nor her *poignées d'amour* – but cannot in any case imagine her in tight boots or even tighter trousers. Nor can we imagine her hair, a fundamental part of the Kate Moss corporate identity.

And the image of Moss is everywhere – billboards, magazines – although she is not a conventional pin-up in the Vargas sense. She is sexually ambiguous. Dan Brown, author of *The Da Vinci Code*, said Leonardo painted an androgynous self-portrait. Moss' gamine looks have a similar sexual ambivalence. If these are universal women, there is something weirdly fluctuating about the conventions of desire. Kate Moss is at one end of Sheldon's Somatypes and has a WHR which is also an extreme.

As a media version of a modern woman, Moss makes a telling contrast to Pamela Anderson whose WHR is also an extreme, but at the mountainous – not the plateau – end of the similes. Moss dabbles with fine art; Anderson with pornography.

Kate Moss and the Madonna Lisa ('Mona' is a diminutive) have, however, a great deal in common. One of Andy Warhol's first commentaries on the mystery of fame and its relationship to mass-production was a 1963 silkscreen print of Mona Lisa called *Thirty Are Better Than One*. Kate Moss has spun her Warholian fifteen minutes into more than ten years. Madonna Lisa has managed five centuries.

The image of each has been captured and exploited. In 1915 an Italian laxative manufacturer launched Gioconda Aqua Purgativa.Her mysterious dignity somehow survived. Perhaps her strange smile – 'Gioconda' means 'smiling', as in 'jocund' – had a gastro-intestinal source.

Opposite and above: The extremes of acceptable womanly proportions are represented by Kate Moss and Pamela Anderson. The Waist-to-Hips-Ratio calculation is a reliable indicator of sex hormones, but no guide to 'attractiveness'.

The range of possible womanly shapes is huge: researchers at North Carolina State University found that percentage shapes of women are: 46 per cent banana, 20 per cent pear, 14 per cent apple and 8 per cent hourglass.

201

Page 202: Photographer David Montgomery recruited the sitters for Jimi Hendrix' 1968 Electric Ladyland *album from Chelsea pubs and cafes. It was* de facto *a sociological experiment: women from many backgrounds made this symbolic masterpiece of the sexual revolution.*

Below: Soon after the paint had dried on Leonardo's masterpiece, pirate versions showed La Gioconda *nude. Something about her mystery invites violation, none more subversive than Marcel Duchamp's LHOOQ of 1919. The artist has added an incongruous moustache and goatee while the letters, pronounced in French, are a homophone for 'she's got a hot arse'.*

Opposite: The singer Dolly Parton maintains 'it costs a lot of money to look this trashy'.

204

L. H. O. O. Q.

What else could explain Marcel Duchamp's famous travesty of the Smiling One? His 1919 version of Leonardo bears the inscription LHOOQ. Pronounced in French, this sounds like '*elle a chaud au cu*' or 'she's got a hot arse'.

Sigmund Freud was fascinated by Leonardo in whom he found rich veins of psycho-sexual disturbance to mine. His rambling 1910 essay about Leonardo, female phalluses, bird's tails and by no means wholly successfully repressed homosexuality was, in fact, based on a mistranslation of an account of a Leonardo dream. Freud acknowledged this in 1923, but this did nothing to diminish the mysteries. Rather, it added to the effect. Since Giorgio Vasari, Mona Lisa has excited unusual speculation. Vasari was the Florentine gossip who wrote *The Lives of the Artists*. He never actually saw the original painting, but this did not stop him insisting that if you examined it very intensely, you could feel the pulse in the neck.

Lucien Freud, Sigmund's grandson, has given us closer access to Kate Moss' body. Examine it very closely and see that small fold of flesh just below the waist. Perhaps you can feel the pulse. There is a strong erotic connection along the Mona Lisa–Moss axis. She sat for Leonardo for four years. During this exceptionally long time Leonardo arranged for tumblers, jugglers and musicians to keep her entertained so as to avoid 'the melancholy painters usually give to portraits', in Vasari's words. This may, of course, account for her extraordinary expression, described by Angus Trimble in *A Brief History of the Smile* (2004) as 'the single most famous representation of smiling in our culture'.

Within a century of Leonardo, various pirate versions of Mona Lisa showed her nude. Kate Moss has been photographed nude by Herb Ritts and Bruce Weber, something of a heresy for an international supermodel. The Renaissance historian Jules Michelet spoke of Mona Lisa's diabolical power. His son-in-law, the critic Alfred Dumesnil, described 'the treacherous attraction of a sick soul… a soft look, that, like the sea, devours'. Aphrodite came out of the sea; Leonardo's Mona Lisa, the smiling one, may be calling us back into it. Meanwhile, Lucien Freud treats Kate Moss as green meat. Every age gets a pin-up that is a reflection of itself.

PLAYBOY

ENTERTAINMENT FOR

playboy.com • JANUARY 2007

HOLIDAY
ANNIVERSARY
ISSUE

FEATURING
12
STELLAR
PLAYMATES
VYING
FOR YOUR
ATTENTION
PLUS
AN OIL-RICH
T. BOONE PICKENS
INTERVIEW, AN
ANATOMICAL
20Q WITH ELLEN
POMPEO, JIMMY
BRESLIN ON
IMMIGRATION,
ROBERT STONE
ON STARTING
OUT AND NEAL
GABLER ON
OUR COVER MODEL

THE
PASSION
OF PAM
FEEL THE
HEAT

KEITH
OLBERMANN
DAN
PATRICK
CHRIS
BERMAN

AN ORAL
HISTORY OF
SPORTS
CENTER

KINKY NEW FICTION
BY WALTER MOSLEY

$6.99

0 130095 35270 8

01>

This page: Playboy, Titter,
Fiesta *and* Loaded. *The
iconography of woman in
'glamour' magazines is
essentially conservative.*

STEREOTYPES
IN
MOVIES,
PHOTOGRAPHY
&
ADVERTISING

The Camera Always Lies

Opposite: A detail of
Adele Bloch-Bauer by
Gustav Klimt, 1907.
The most expensive painting
ever sold is of a woman…
and she is reduced to a flat pattern.

The most expensive painting in the world is of a woman. And it is not the Virgin Mary. It is a portrait of a rich Viennese socialite called Adele Bloch-Bauer. It was painted by Gustav Klimt in 1907 and was bought by cosmetics tycoon Ronald Lauder for $135m in 2006. Thus a voracious circle of desire and acquisition was neatly squared. The Estée Lauder company had become a leading cosmetics manufacturer, selling designs for concept-women all over the planet. The riches accrued from this global quest for the ideal via unguents allowed Ronald Lauder to acquire one of art's great designs on women.

Klimt's image has such force because it is essentially a graphic diagram of a woman, not a realistic nor even a psychologically true portrait. Its force comes from pattern and flatness, not from contour and texture; the artist simplified, then exaggerated. The result is, to use for once a mis-used word entirely correctly, an icon.

Every kind of cliché has already been written about Gustav Klimt's Vienna. Yes, obviously, this was a city of experimentation in the arts. Sex, as Freud discovered after a lot of looking, was everywhere and sometimes in rather surprising places. Extreme emotions were commonplace; God was dead; architectural decoration was fanatical and then it was deemed a crime, at least by architect Adolf Loos. It was a secular age, but it is important to know that Klimt's culture was industrial as well as artistic: the Wittgenstein family, for example, made its money from manufacturing, not from logical positivism. It was an industrial inheritance that allowed Ludwig Wittgenstein to become a philosopher.

Vienna was not all depravity, hysteria and perversion. It was also electricity and drop-forging, electric light and mains gas. And while it is easy for art historians to trace Klimt's aesthetic legacy from Aubrey Beardsley and Charles Rennie Macintosh, his psychological one from Freud and tormented playwright Karl Kraus, it is at least as important to appreciate that he was working when the mass-production of images was becoming a commercial reality. While Klimt was pattern-making with women, the very first photographic agencies were being set-up. Art itself was being commodified by photography. Art replied by making itself available as a commodity.

METRO-GOLDWYN-MAYER PRESENTS

ELIZABETH TAYLOR
LAURENCE HARVEY
EDDIE FISHER

IN JOHN O'HARA'S
BUTTERFIELD 8

The most desirable woman in town—and the easiest to find....Just dial BUTTerfield 8

Left: The cinema created new designs for women, with criteria different to painting and sculpture. New lighting techniques allowed different effects. Mass-communication undermined hierarchies of tastes. This is Gloria Swanson in 1929.

Above: Butterfield 8 *was the 1960 movie starring Elizabeth Taylor as Gloria Wandrous, an 'actress' seeking sympathy. Based on a novel by John O'Hara, it won Taylor an Oscar and led to her being cast as* Cleopatra, *one of the greatest womanly stereotypes of them all.*

And Klimt's Vienna was full of advertisements. Most of the first collectors of his work were Jewish entrepreneurs; his very greatest patrons were August and Serena Lederer, a Jewish couple enjoying the success of a manufacturing business. If social promotion through art was the aim, it was achieved by Klimt designing paintings as flat patterns specially adaptable to mechanical reproduction: it is not the craftsmanship of Adele Bloch-Bauer that is captivating, it the reproducible *design*. A generation later the Frankfurt School sociologist Walter Benjamin would write about 'The Work of Art in the Age of Mechanical Reproduction' and speculate on this very issue. If you can readily reproduce a perfectly reliable image (of the Mona Lisa or Frau Bloch-Blauer), what special value does the 'original' retain? Just the mystical contact of the artist's hand… or something?

It was the Viennese art dealer Otto Kallir who first introduced the paintings of Gustav Klimt to the United States in 1940, perhaps sensing that a culture that was wholly devoted to mass-production, mass-consumption and mass-media might be specially receptive to glamorous images that might be easily reproduced. To stimulate interest and then demand, initially Kallir gave away original art… as if it were soap sold with coupons. This adventure was not without its perils.

In this America Hollywood still demanded observation of the 1930 Motion Picture Production Code (always known as the Hays Code). This required that in bedroom scenes a woman must have one foot on the floor so as to make an advanced sexual proposition impossible, a requirement that indicated as much as anything else a profound lack of imagination on the behalf of Hollywood's moral guardians. In so puritanical a context, Klimt's images were originally denounced as perverted excess and pornography. This is extraordinary as to our eyes they appear elegantly reticent. Any disturbing suggestion of a simmering sexuality is – surely – a matter of the observer's imagination. Be that as it may, because of their facile translation into print, Klimt's images eventually became one of the most popular commercial poster images of all. Accurate figures are nowhere kept, but Frau Bloch-Blauer is not only the most expensive woman ever painted, she is the most popular poster girl, possibly exceeding even Mona Lisa in mass-media heft. The art critic Edwin Mullins asked 'Imagine Adele Bloch-Bauer as a man'. It can't be done.

It was the movies that taught us to move and dance. Jean Cocteau remarked at the 1959 Cannes Film Festival that the cinema was a 'Temple of Sex, with its Goddesses, its Guardians and its Victims'. Or, if they did not actually teach

Opposite: Elizabeth Taylor, 'La Liz'. After Bettie Page and before the age of Pop, the world's most influential image of woman.

the disciplines of dance and movement, they made them an expectation. And with this expectation of graceful, meaningful movement came another re-design. After about 1920 the influence of the movies where – if a restatement of the obvious is allowed – the actresses had to move… required a version of dress that allowed them to do so. From the Twenties onwards there was a dramatic reduction in the bulk, weight and sheer volume of women's clothing. Additionally, thinness suited the movies. Thinness also suits the fashion catwalks: clothes simply hang better and look better on thin women.

'Healthy innocence, sexual restlessness, creative zest, practical competence, even morbid but poetic obsessiveness and intelligence – all seemed appropriate to size 10.'
— ANNE HOLLANDER, SEEING THROUGH CLOTHES, 1978

And these were the qualities the first movie actresses exploited. The movies allowed, for the first time in history, women to achieve a sort of dominance over men. The idea of the *femme fatale* does not originate in Hollywood, but was made overwhelmingly powerful by it.

One of the pioneering movie stars, Gloria Swanson, explained the power she was sensing:

'I have gone through a long apprenticeship. I have gone through enough of being a nobody. I have decided that when I am a star I will be every inch and every moment the star. Everyone from the studio gateman to the highest executive will know it.'
—ALEXANDER WALKER, SEX IN THE MOVIES, 1968

Alexander Walker pointed out that had the movies been 'born talking' they might never have become so popular.

This is because the first audiences were predominantly working-class Americans and for the majority of these, English was not the first language. Silent movies allowed *images* of women to dominate the perceptions of viewers, uncontaminated by the complexities of language. Hollywood is as much a state of mind as a Los Angeles suburb and this state of mind passed into national, then international, consciousness. And with this state of mind came powerful images: the design of twentieth-century woman. It was, for a while, known as the star system.

The first actress to be designed for the star system was Theodosia Goodman, an immigrant Jewish tailor's daughter from Cincinnati. First phase of the design was re-branding, so Theodosia Goodman became Theda Bara. Her designer was William Fox, an independent producer and cinema owner (whose company was eventually incorporated into Twentieth Century Fox). Publicity shots showed her as a Sphinx-like creature with bizarre spider's webs as bra cups (although at this stage the design did not include nipples). Theda Bara was taken on publicity tours where she struck poses as erotic as they were enigmatic. Her eyes are dark in gloomy sockets, her skin pale. She sat in canopied structures suffocating with incense. With no real acting credentials, her image became so strong that Fox was able to tell Upton Sinclair that he had discovered the world's greatest actress.

Eventually, with iconography most critics think was adapted from Philip Burne-Jones' 1897 painting *The Vampire* (which was shown at Knoedler's in New York in 1902), Bara portrayed a series of historical and mythological vamps: Salome, Cleopatra, Carmen. Each featured sultry looks and luxurious accoutrements. Cecil B. DeMille would later move the *femme fatale's* theatre of operations to the modern bathroom and bedroom, away from the vamp's batcave, acknowledging cinema's progress in treating the sexual nature of modern woman in a modern environment.

The First World War had the effect of familiarizing the middle-classes with the movies as a source of 'escapism' from routine horrors. Paramount told DeMille in 1918 that he was to get away from all that Biblical stuff and concentrate instead on movies featuring clothes, lavish modern sets and, by extension, modern women. And in the next five years DeMille made a series of films whose titles alone suggest a new sexual liberation: *Old Wives for New* (1918), *Don't Change Your Husband* (1919), *Male and Female* (1919),

Right: Gloria Swanson and Ted Shawn in Cecil B. DeMille's Don't Change Your Husband, *1918. Early Hollywood movies suggested (and illustrated) infidelity, as if the medium that liberated the body also liberated the morals.*

Opposite: Theda Bara in Cleopatra, *1917. J. Gordon Edwards' production was one of the most lavish Hollywood movies to date. Filmed in Long Beach, California, the historical role allowed the very camp Bara to strike magnificent poses and expose her breasts.*

217

Left: Clara Bow. Her 1924 movie about a woman's rejuvenation through the injection of animal hormones was a landmark in woman's self-perception. Her sultry aspect was widely copied.

Above: Elinor Glyn (1864–1943), the English erotic novelist who coined the expression 'It' to mean that curiously attractive quality, not dependent on looks or intelligence. She was originally writing about a man. The tiger-skin rug which she was reputed to use as a romantic prop is clearly visible in the foreground.

Why Change Your Wife? (1920) and *Adam's Rib* (1923). Each suggested a bracingly heterodox attitude to monogamy.

An unlikely, but nonetheless profound, influence on the emerging Hollywood woman was an aristocratic Englishwoman called Elinor Glyn. She liked to be known as Madame Glyn and wrote racy love stories which were amazingly anachronistic, becoming famous for inviting all-comers to enjoy sex on a tigerskin rug (or, she offered as an alternative, 'to err on some other fur'). She gave well-paid seminars on sex and wrote self-help books including *This Passion Called Love* in which she argued that to maintain a husband's primitive hunter-gatherer instincts, a modern wife must be mysterious, elusive and unpredictable. Accordingly, she was invited to become an advisor and scriptwriter in Hollywood. Glyn joined Paramount in 1920, moving to MGM three years later. In an article published in *Cosmopolitan* in 1927 Glyn coined the expression 'It' to mean that undefinable, but always detectable, quality which combined style with sexual appeal.

Glyn chose the actress Clara Bow to be the first 'It Girl'. There were various factors in the choice. One was that Glyn had had red hair, thought to be rather common for a woman of her class in her day. So, Clara Bow was a red-head. Although this chromatic option was lost in black and white movies, a compensating point had been made to studio bosses and 'red-head' became an eponym for raunchy. But if the audiences could not immediately imitate Clara Bow's hair colour, millions of them imitated the touchy-feely gestures which characterized her screen roles. And when in 1924 she made a film about rejuvenation achieved through the injection of animal hormones, another stage in the re-design of woman had been passed.

Marilyn Monroe came out of a Californian orphanage with a sense of destiny. Her name was designed: she was born Norma Jean Mortenson. Like Jean Harlow (who rubbed her nipples with ice cubes before press conferences so the thermal shock would cause the erectile tissue to simulate sexual excitement, an effect not lost on her predominantly male audience), Monroe often chose not to wear underwear on set.

Mae West

Sometimes known as The Statue of Libido, Mae West (1893–1980) was Hollywood's first self-designed, stage-managed sex symbol. Taking full authority from the generation that had begun to accept Freud's insights into the erotic, she emphasized her hips with padding, an effect occasionally enhanced by wearing Colt .45 revolvers. And she was a platinum blonde. West handled the transition from vaudeville to silent movies to the talkies and it was in the latter that she excelled with her (often self-scripted) innuendoes and double-entendres and extravagantly exaggerated appearance. Her mother was known as Champagne Lil and Mae West's 1928 movie *Diamond Lil* was her defining early masterpiece: the Mother transfigured into a sexually aware consumer. In 1934, under the lowering influence of the Depression, that Catholic Legion of Decency imposed censorship and Mae West's film *It Ain't No Sin* had to be re-titled *Belle of the Nineties*. Despite, or perhaps because, she projected a successful image of a smart, sexually ambitious, witty individual, Mae West was never popular with female audiences. Alfred Hitchcock explained that this was because women dislike other women stealing their men.

Above: Some Like it Hot, *1959. The plot features cross-dressing and gender stereotyping. Marilyn Monroe was an ironic dizzy blonde; Tony Curtis said kissing her was like kissing Hitler.*

Opposite: Monroe in a publicity still from Some Like It Hot.

Page 222: Marilyn Monroe in a publicity still for the Hollywood adaptation of Howard Hawks' Gentlemen Prefer Blondes, *1953. Jane Russell also starred.*

Page 223: Marilyn Monroe in 1953, the year she became Playboy's *first centrefold.*

She dyed her hair; she slimmed; she worked-out; she had voice coaching. The process was so intense that, eventually, she looked more like an air-brushed pin-up than an air-brushed pin-up. If the great adventure of mid-century America was a mixture of industrial chemicals, industrial design and mass media, here was the American adventure in a woman.

Some Like It Hot appeared in 1959, near the peak of American industrial power and economic prosperity. The '59 Cadillac was a similarly magnificent, yet elegiac creation, as insanely desirable, as powerfully symbolic, as ridiculous and as ultimately doomed as Monroe herself. After all, her husband Arthur Miller's best-known play was *Death of a Salesman* (1949) where the sad anti-hero deplores the tragic ephemerality of consumer goods. The washing machine promises to improve your life, then it breaks and ruins it instead. Marilyn was such a thing. It was in France that another, more lasting design of cinema woman was created.

Brigitte Bardot was designed by Roger Vadim. Her showroom was the 1956 movie *Et Dieu Crea la Femme.*

Bardot was not so much God's creation as Vadim's. The film is an erotic romp of no great cinematic distinction, but Bardot's style is epochal. Her clothes, her figure, her face and her hair became stereotypes. The young and the beautiful! Besides creating Bardot, Vadim's film popularized the bikini and started the cult of St Tropez. Bardot in a wet dress lolling on the beach may be the image containing the very first (ghost of a) nipple in mainstream cinema. The movie magazine *Cinemonde* calculated that, following the publication of 29,345 press images of Bardot in the year the film opened, she was the subject of no less than 47 per cent of all French conversations.

A product of the Fifties, Brigitte Bardot became famous at just the moment new sensibilities about women's identities were beginning to enter political thoughts and cultural life. One of the leading thinkers of what became 'Women's Liberation' (a term first coined in the November–December edition of *The New Left Review* in 1966) was Simone de Beauvoir.

WOMAN AS DESIGN

This page: Brigitte Bardot in
Et Dieu Crea la Femme, 1956.
A magazine calculated that
Bardot was the subject of
47 per cent of all French
conversations that year.

Entirely unaware of how odd it would read to celebrate such an artefact of male consciousness 50 years on, de Beauvoir wrote a perceptive little appreciation of Bardot in 1959. Hilariously, without anticipating that this was the objectification of a woman's body that Sixties feminists would so deplore, de Beauvoir says that in 1959 box office receipts from the US run of *Et Dieu Crea la Femme* were, at $4m, equivalent to the export value of 2,500 Renault Dauphines.

In the film Bardot plays Juliette, a feisty young girl who is a competition for men. There is sleeping around, an amazingly sexy dance scene and, throughout, Bardot's fabulously sculpted breasts dominate. Andrea Dworkin was perhaps not thinking of Bardot's amazing WHR when she wrote 'the skin is a line of demarcation, a periphery, the fence, the form, the shape, the first clue to identity in a society' (*Intercourse*, 1987), but that is what Bardot as feral, eroticized woman represented. When the film was shown in Angers, the local press reported that youth had been spontaneously perverted.

To what extent he was conscious of the power of his creation while writing the specification we will never know, but Vadim's design established a female type as telling of its age as Margarito d'Arezzo's Virgin told us about his. Bardot was a stylized version of the Earth Mother, just as the Renault Dauphine was a stylized version of the Renault 4cv.

'Femininity triumphs in her delightful bosom,' de Beauvoir wrote. Her hair is negligently undressed. Her feet are bare. Her lips pout. She is not only Modernized Universal Woman, she is an 'ambiguous nymph'. And while many would agree, de Beauvoir also says that from behind Bardot/Juliette is androgynous, but this might only be in comparison to Bardot/Juliette from the front, who is unambiguously womanly.

And if youth is venerated in the Bardot design this might even trespass into the idea of the child-woman. This was also the age of Vladimir Nabokov's *Lolita* (1955) and Arthur Miller's *View from the Bridge* (1955). Nabokov's heroine was jailbait, Miller's only just beyond puberty. In this context it may be specially useful to record that 'Lolita' is a diminutive of Lola which in turn is a diminutive of Dolores. Which in Spanish means 'sad'.

Bardot herself said 'When I'm in front of the camera, I'm simply myself.' This seems a bit of an over-simplification, but Vadim later described Bardot as an innocent. At the age of 18 she thought that mice laid eggs. He said her eroticism was 'not magical, but aggressive'. Significantly, Latin American audiences of *Et Dieu Crea la Femme* found it just too cerebral.

Stereotypes of woman in the movies have their equivalents in photography and advertising. Or 'fictions beheld by the eye and facts about which we are in the dark' according to critic Harold Rosenberg. For US *Vogue* magazine Irving Penn created ensemble treatments of models in the late Forties still being imitated by Annie Leibovitz 50 years later. His predecessors included Edward Steichen, Baron Adolphe de Meyer, Erwin Blumenfeld, Horst, George Hoyningen-Huene and Cecil Beaton. Penn's contemporaries included William Klein and Richard Avedon. His successors are Helmut Newton, Steven Meisel, Patrick Demarchelier and Bruce Weber. In Susan Sontag's own words they are imprisoning reality.

In advertising, the mid-Fifties woman was trapped in the nightmare of a 'dream' kitchen which may, or

226

Right: In 1959 Simone de Beauvoir calculated that Brigitte Bardot's financial importance to the French Republic was similar to the export value of the Renault Dauphine.

Opposite: In 1962 Stanley Kubrick made Vladimir Nabokov's transgressive Lolita *into a movie. Critics said its most erotic scene was a pedicure.*

Left: Olivetti was the first office equipment manufacturer to sell its goods on the basis of visual appeal. Women – often in seductive poses – contributed to the persuasive semantics of the advertising.

Right: George Lois art directed a famous cover for Esquire March 1965 which showed a woman shaving. The lesbian singer K.D. Lang picked-up the disturbing

motif for a Vanity Fair cover in August 1993.

Page 230: 'How to Undress in front of your Husband' was a classic feature from Nova, May 1971, Britain's most influential style magazine of the later Sixties and early Seventies. Art director David Hillman and photographer Duffy turned striptease into a slickly designed domestic ritual.

may not, have been a reality to American women. The limits of a woman's scope were, the ads suggested, determined by the size of fridge or the acreage of easy-wipe laminate surface available to her. A decade later, choices were emerging. In March 1965 art director George Lois (who created the Olivetti Girl, a suited and bobbed figure empowered by her choice of office equipment) produced a cover for *Esquire* magazine. This was the same *Esquire* that had made its reputation 20 years before with conventional pin-ups.

The cover showed a Marilyn-style blonde woman shaving her foam-covered face with a razor, evidently also with full make-up. This sexually ambivalent image was, as Lois explained, pre-Friedan, pre-Millet, pre-Greer, pre-Steinem, pre-Abzug. Pre any feminist you could mention. Already, a wider idea of woman was becoming available. Was there a point, Lois mused, where sexual equality would end and confusion begin? Might hormones, treatments, therapies and new forms of consciousness create not just a new sort of woman, but a hybrid gender?

A new generation of neuro-aestheticians is claiming technical insights into all matters of choice, from preferences in art to sexual direction. Neuro-aesthetics brings together

the biometrics of MRI scanning with the critical opinions of the connoisseur and thus makes claims to having a biological answer to the question 'What do Theda Bara, Clara Bow, Marilyn and BB have in common?' By identifying neural colonies in the brain and monitoring their responses to measured inputs, the neuro-aestheticians may – just may – have removed fuzzy logic from desire. They can count the neurons responding favourably to the wiggle of Mae West's hips or the pout of Clara Bow's lips or the curve of Marilyn's bust.

The latest tentative advances in neuro-aesthetics leave the discipline still more in the area of alchemy than reproducible, peer-monitored science, but they are more advanced than the first attempts to measure aesthetic response from more than 20 years ago. Modern neuro-aesthetics was preceded by an electro-mechanical study of the internal circuits which evolved in the brain by natural selection, or so it was supposed. One pioneer was Victor Johnson of New Mexico State University who put electrodes on scalps to test the physiological responses to various forms of 'beauty'. In the researchers' language he found a 'high correlation of Late Positive Component in event-related potentials'.

What this means in English is that our response to stimuli (Mae West's hips, Clara Bow's lips, Marilyn's bust) is by no means wholly determined by local social or culturally historic factors, but may to a surprising degree be built into the architecture of our brains. So while it is evident that the stereotypes of women presented in movies, photography and advertising were often willed into existence, they also reflect something profound. To a surprising degree the *femmes fatales*, the stars and sex bombs of the movies were 'designed'. So does the camera lie? Yes, maybe. But as Jean Cocteau observed, I lie to tell the truth.

232

If I Have One Life,
Let Me Live it as a Blonde

Opposite: The quintessential blonde. Evolutionary biologists have agonized about the troubling status of blondes. The cosmetics industries have always been more clear: blonde is the ultimate in desirability.

On evidence from Egyptian mummies, King Tut moisturized. We may, with some imaginative liberty, imagine Queen Tut did too. Ancient Egyptians had their vanities. We have ours too, all maintained and enhanced by new technologies while pitilessly projected by global communications. What should I look like? Who knows?

Our existence is amidst a delirium of options for temporary body-modification, involving chemicals, surgical knives, dyes, mutilations and decorations. There always has been, but now there is ever more, substantial scope for altering 'natural' appearance. Of course, the definition of 'natural' in this competitive context is by no means uncontroversial. Why would a naturally naked human want to modify herself? In even thinking around the edges of answering that question you encounter some of the most obdurate obstacles in the path to clear understanding of human values.

Americans in the early twenty-first century spend more on 'beauty' products than on education. They are intent on an escape from Nature, even as temporary fashions demand a 'natural look. Other cultures ape the American example, even if their reach exceeds their economic grasp. It seems that where bodies are concerned, a search for corporeal perfection is as universal (and as hopelessly misguided) as a taste for ornamentation. And this perfection is sought even in defiance of rationality. The women of Kalahari bushmen, for example, use nutritious animal fats to moisturize their skin even in conditions of famine or drought where such fats might have a more vitally functional purpose as food. Here is vanity above survival.

The quest for beauty promulgated by the global cosmetics industries is often described as corrupting. To what end, the conventional feminist critique argues, should a woman imitate or obey the possibly smutty whims of an advertising art director with millions of cosmetics marketing dollars to spend on 48 sheet posters and 60 second slots? Why not be feral, fat and smelly? To go further, is the very idea of beauty a sinister (male) conspiracy? Is the beauty industry as intent on cruelly subjugating the female as a caveman who tugs his mate's hair, yanks her arse-backwards and brutally mounts her for a few grunts of intromittent pleasure? On the other hand, as Nancy Etcoff asked in *The Survival of*

Is it true... blondes have more fun?

Just for the fun of it, be a blonde and see...a Lady Clairol blonde with shining, silken hair! You'll love the life in it! The soft touch and tone of it! The lovely ladylike way it lights up your looks. With *amazingly gentle* new Instant Whip Lady Clairol, it's so easy! Why, it takes only minutes!

And New Lady Clairol feels deliciously cool going on, leaves hair in wonderful condition—lovelier, livelier than ever. So if your hair is dull blonde or mousey brown, why hesitate? Hair responds to Lady Clairol like a man responds to blondes —and darling, *that's* a beautiful advantage! Try it and see!

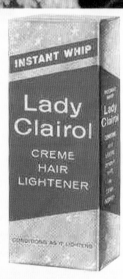

INSTANT WHIP

Lady Clairol

CREME HAIR LIGHTENER

← GARAGE

• Mandatory fake Beauty mark.

• Hair DYED TO cover some grey.

OOPS. BAD HAIR

• FALSE EYELASHES.

• Eyebrows penciled in Higher

• Hair set in hot ROLLERS for important CURLS But this creates dry + split ends.

• EXTRA PINK CHEEKS USING BLUSH

• Fetish powder BLUE EYE SHADOW →

• Red lipstick

• CHOKER IS REALLY CHOKING ME

• BODY MAKE-UP

• Breasts ARE NATURAL BORN BUT SAG. BRA LIFTS Breasts.

• Bra is a FULL SIZE TOO SMALL to make breasts look bigger.

• LUNGS RESTRICTED. I CAN'T BREATHE

• CORSET MAKES MY WAIST 4½" SMALLER BUT I CAN'T BREATHE

• CORSET HIDES A VERY BIG Belly.

• Hemorrhoids DON'T SHOW IN THIS POSE THANKFULLY.

• I need ASSISTANCE TO HOOK ALL THESE GARTERS and to LACE THE BACK OF CORSET.

• I never WEAR gloves except in pin-up photos.

• Gloves cover tattoos for a more all-American girl EFFECT. BORROWED from MISTRESS ANTIONETTE.

• EXTRA TALL STOCKINGS MAKE legs look longer

• BLACK STOCKINGS MAKE THIGHS LOOK THINNER

• BOOTS TAKE 19 MINUTES TO LACE. I need assistance because I can't Bend over IN THE CORSET.

• PLEXIGLASS SQUARE KEEPS WHITE PAPER FROM SMUDGING

I can't walk and can Barely hobble.

• THESE HEELS ARE EXCRUCIATING HIGH.

Boots are 1½ sizes too small. Borrowed + worn only for this photo.

• my feet are killing me.
★ (In spite of it all, I'm sexually excited + feeling great!)

Anatomy of A 1980's Pin Up   1984/2006 Annie Sprinkle 1/20

the *Prettiest* (1999) 'Isn't it possible that women cultivate beauty and use the beauty industry to optimize the power that beauty brings?'

Maybe. In the matter of preferences, some things seem fixed beyond fashion and taste; blonde hair for example. 'Golden hair was ever in great account' we read in Robert Burton's *Anatomy of Melancholy*. Burton was writing more than 400 years ago, but reliable options for women wanting to change their hair colour and become blonde had to wait until 1907 when L'Oreal's modern synthetic hair dye appeared. Thereafter mouse-coloured women could re-design themselves. While the first generation of Hollywood vamps was black-eyed and dark and campily spooky, the second was blonde flappers (possibly turbocharged by L'Oreal chemicals). Blonde was indisputably best.

So it was in 1925 that a Hollywood screenwriter called Anita Loos published *Gentlemen Prefer Blondes*, one of those rare books which seems to be known even by people who have not read it. Loos had begun with epic and ascended to cosmetic. She worked for D.W. Griffith at the American Mutograph and Biograph Company, but soon moved to more potent trivia. Her comic masterpiece about arguments in favour of golden hair began as a series of articles in *Harper's Bazaar*.

Hollywood and Loos made the powerful suggestion to a powerlessly suggestible audience that to be blonde was to enjoy more of life's privileges, especially the frivolous sort. But is it actually true that blondes have more fun? Very possibly, according to the consciousness of mid-century America. Thus, very perturbing for the brown and dark.

235

Left: Annie Sprinkle marks-up a fashion shoot and art directs herself into a form of perfection.

Right: The actress Ruth Taylor reading Anita Loos' Gentlemen Prefer Blondes *in the 1928 film of the book. Taylor's Lorelei Lee character was later made famous by Marilyn Monroe.*

Page 236: Carla Bruni-Sarkozy. Women over 28 should not wear make-up, it ages them. She says.

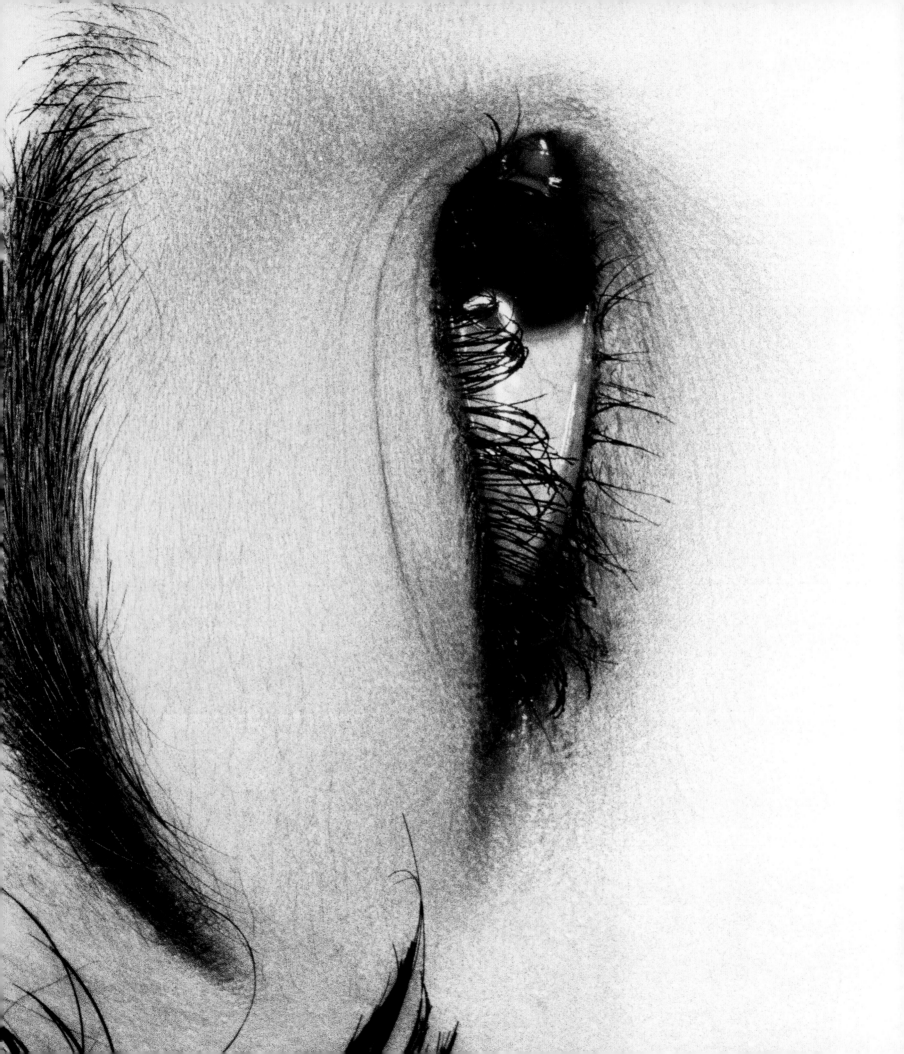

Page 238: Nobuyoshi Araki enjoys the ambiguity of the body. Rotating an eye by 90 degrees transforms its meaning.

Page 239: Barbara Cartland (1901–2000) was an admirer of Elinor Glyn. A life-long bottle blonde, she published more than 600 novels mostly concerned with a retardataire *interpretation of romantic love. She was a champion of anti-wrinkle cream and an advocate of heavy make-up, but late in life repudiated all artifice and was buried in a cardboard coffin.*

Page 242: The storyline of the 1956 movie Blonde Bait *concerns a woman escaping a stifling existence. Blondeness was presented as an instrument of freedom.*

241

Left: 'Is it true blondes have more fun?': Shirley Polykoff's copylines for Clairol hair-dye exploited international doubts and fears about the blonde.

Right: Edouard Manet's Dejeuner sur l'Herbe *scandalized Paris when it was shown at the Salon of 1863. Its unambiguous depiction of a sexually aware woman predicted motifs which dominated cosmetic advertising in the later twentieth century.*

The proposition that blondes have more fun was the substance of an advertising copy line written by Shirley Polykoff. Another was 'If I have one life, let me live it as a blonde.' These were both propaganda in the service of Clairol hair-dye, a cynically brilliant and exploitative exercise in mass-market cosmetic yearning. Clairol's chemicals could turn you blonde and Polykoff could explain why such a re-design might be desirable. Shirley Polykoff used to sit in the offices of the Foote Cone and Belding ad agency on the 36th floor of Manhattan's Pan-Am Building where she was vice-president, associate creative director and copy group supervisor. Here she supervised and directed the frustrated yearnings of middle American woman.

Another Polykoff-written ad for Clairol hair-dye was the 1955 'Does she . . . or doesn't she? Only her hairdresser knows for sure.' *Life* magazine would not run this ad because it was felt to be sexually suggestive, but it was voted the eighth most effective copy line of all time and conferred on its author the honour of being only the fifth woman to be elected to the Advertising Hall of Fame. Asked the secret of her success, Polykoff said 'I'm a girl first and an advertising woman second.' She was a Clairol blonde herself. On creativity she said 'You generate better when you think you're gorgeous.' And she wrote 'The closer he gets, the better you look', a line that cruelly fed on timeless womanly insecurities. And 'The girl with the beautiful mouth has it made.' In the mid-Fifties (at least on Madison Avenue) the use of an anatomically frank word such as 'mouth' (still less any other orifice!) was a shocking taboo.

But Polykoff also took inspiration from art galleries, where she sought out blonde archetypes. A stimulus to her advocacy of re-configuring the colouring of American Woman was a reluctance to acknowledge the reality of her own brown hair. Mice have brown hair, so this is scarcely ideal material for imitation. No one (apart from Hitler who thought it a 'very German colour' has ever rhapsodized about brown. Titian, on the other hand, presented the world with the most lascivious imaginable flame-headed nude temptresses.

"I DON'T NEED A GUN TO CAT[C]

BLONDE

The

"...CH A MAN!"

BAIT

...ind of mistake a man can make only once!

Above: Two portraits of Lana Turner (1920–95) was the original 'Sweater Girl'. This was a euphemism for melodramatic emphasis of the breasts brought about by new bra technology and teasingly enhanced by clinging outerwear.

Opposite: Marilyn Monroe in 1956. 'I intend to remain in pictures,' she said, 'But I'm looking forward to being a housewife, too.'

Marilyn Monroe was, perhaps, the greatest blonde of them all. From 'The Most Advertised Girl in the World' in 1945, she advanced through *Playboy's* first centrefold in 1953 to international fantasy figure. She was not just a cheerful nude, but a subject of serious literary speculation for Norman Mailer, Joyce Carol Oates, Jean-Paul Sartre, Simone de Beauvoir, Roland Barthes, Truman Capote, Diana Trilling and Ayn Rand.

Until the myths were meticulously deconstructed by Sarah Churchwell in 2004, most biographers said Monroe was a masterpiece of self-invention and of self-design who was 'not really beautiful'. Instead, she relied on the fiction of cosmetics… as if this were unusual. Be that as it may, of Marilyn's many anxieties, hair colour was perhaps pre-eminent. Changing her hair colour was her own way of saying 'Goodbye, Norma Jean'. She dyed her hair obsessively: under that platinum helmet of fetishist's perfection was an angry, red, raw scalp.

Blondes had a distinctive role in history even before the movies: they were the '*rubios*' of Spanish romances, heroines with a version of whiteness that had an important symbolic link to notions of purity. For different reasons, perhaps those

understood by Shirley Polykoff, Ernest Hemingway made his fourth wife, Mary Welsh, change her natural red hair to unnatural blonde. To Andrea Dworkin this was a pitiable example of male objectification. Mrs Hemingway herself, however, viewed it differently :

'Deeply rooted in his field of aesthetics was some mystical devotion to blondness, the blonder the lovelier. I never learned why. He would have been ecstatic in a world of women dandelions.'
— MARY WELSH HEMINGWAY HOW IT WAS, 1976

Today French pharmacies still claim that a firm (therefore, the theory goes, attractive) body may be retained by rubbing in lotions and unguents. In-store display cards attest to this alchemy. This culturally specific notion may be traceable to a source such as Jean Liebault's *Trois Livres pour l'Embellissement du Corps Humain* (1582) in which he suggests a pulp of cumin seeds may be applied to the breasts to achieve a pleasing firmness. So circummortal purity may remain symmetrical and vibration-free.

Cosmetics are the medicine of beauty and a history of civilization could be written in their terms.

*Cinema blondes. Left: Tippi
Hedren, in Alfred Hitchcock's*
The Birds, *1963. Right: Anita
Ekberg in Federico Fellini's* La
Dolce Vita, *1960. Below right:
Brigitte Bardot in Roger Vadim's*
Et Dieu Crea la Femme, *1956.*

247

Essentially, cosmetics concern colour and early ingredients were elemental, often lethally poisonous. Kohl was used to blacken the orbits of the eyes, lending a sense of mystery. Kohl is made of lead, copper, almonds and soot. It has a startling effect: the Egyptians thought this form of eye make-up might be a preventative against the evil eye, although it possibly had some functional basis in controlling glare in harsh sunlight. Thus, the Bronze Age had its equivalent of dark glasses.

Edward Gorey was an illustrator and poetaster of idiosyncratically dark tastes who acquired a reputation for being Modern Gothic. So much so that many admirers thought him British, while he was born in Chicago. He had a little verse about kohl that catches the mixed messages of submission, subversion and sex its wearing implies:

*'The Wanton, though she knows its danger
Must needs smear kohl about her eyes
And catch the attention of a stranger
With drawn-out, hoarse erotic sighs.'*

Although some Islamic fundamentalists reject cosmetics, Mohammed's habit was to retire at night with kohl around his eyes. Indeed, much of the science of cosmetics was established by Arab scholars who spoke of Adwiyat al-Zinah, or the 'medicine of beauty'. In pre-Modern Europe, kohl was unknown and a pale skin was an indicator of high social standing since it suggested an inclination and ability to spend time indoors rather than in the raw blasts of the fields. Access to cosmetics was restricted to the same privileged caste who chose to whiten their skin or apply (often lethal lead-based) powders to maintain or even exaggerate a paleness which indicated a leisurely rather than a laborious life.

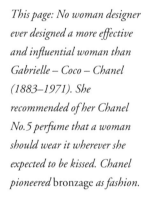

This page: No woman designer ever designed a more effective and influential woman than Gabrielle – Coco – Chanel (1883–1971). She recommended of her Chanel No.5 perfume that a woman should wear it wherever she expected to be kissed. Chanel pioneered bronzage *as fashion.*

Opposite: Marlene Dietrich applying lipstick in the 1941 movie Manpower.

This assumption about skin colour only changed in the early twentieth century when Coco Chanel invented the suntan, sexualizing skin. Various influences on Chanel may be identified. First, her interest in simplifying women's fashion by learning from male military uniforms. Second, her chance to study and then imitate the dark-brown deck hands on the Mediterranean yacht of her lover, the Duke of Westminster. Third, the growing cults of heliotherapy, callisthenics and diet-based well-being which all suggested a 'natural' existence (even if only available on a high budget) was superior. And natural meant brown and thin.

So a semantic inversion took place: by about 1930 a pale skin indicated a person lacking the wherewithal to travel somewhere hot for leisure. And tanned skin suggested cosmopolitanism. It was only after 1945 that colour photography in print and in film fully popularized Chanel's radically simple body modification. But that Eugene Schueller, founder of l'Oreal, saw the commercial opportunity to produce the very first sunscreen in 1936 suggests Chanel's sunbathing was something of an established cult by the mid-Thirties. Women learnt to suffer to be beautiful.

Cosmetics do not merely enhance the positives with colour, they also diminish the negatives. In most Islamic cultures it is established tradition for women to deforest their Mountain of Venus, although the fashion came later to Europe: a book called *Natural Magic* by John Baptista Porta was published in London in 1658 (a century after it first appeared in Naples). It includes recipes for depilatory lotions which does not exclude the possibility that they might be applied to the pubic region, although this was probably rare in Europe before the late twentieth century. From the beginning of reliable records when erotic photography began in the mid-nineteenth century, depilation of the pubic mound was a very rare occurrence.

The olfactory sense is also susceptible to direction and improvement so therefore may also be 'designed'. Smell has a primitive evolutionary basis: one unsavoury theory maintains that pubic hair exists only to trap the sexual pheromones essential, eventually, to trapping sexually inclined males. Heavy scents (one eighteenth-century authority suggested an alarming mixture of vinegar, sulphur and gunpowder) were often used to disguise body odour. Thus, 250 years ago, heavy scents carried the suspicion of unhygienic practices. In compensation, lighter – often floral – scents arrived in history at the same time as the delicacies of the toilette. Mains plumbing soon followed.

The artificial control of body odour – whether by disguise or by annihilation – provides a gloss on civilization and its changing values. When it appeared in Philadelphia, Mum became the first trademarked deodorant. Delivery technologies improved with time: the roll-on deodorant became available in 1952, the aerosol in 1965. It is not only a woman's shape that can be designed, but her colour and smell too.

Jewellery is another means of temporary body modification. I once asked an actress about her tongue-piercing. She gave me an old-fashioned look and said 'It's just another place to put jewellery.' So, when you have run out of fingers, wrists, necks, ankles and ears, do not despair: jewellery extends the limited possibilities of Nature. Consider those neck rings of the Padaung: is this aesthetic distortion or elective disability?

Darwin said a desire for body ornament was universal. And if was sourced in self-harm then that was the price to be paid. Thus bracelets are cultural descendants of the weals and wounds inflicted on themselves by drunken maenads. A pierced tongue combines the those twin senses of the transgressive and the assertive which define jewellery in all cultures. Apparently chaste Victorian women sometimes enjoyed a pierced nipple, usually camouflaged with the French expression *anneauxs des seins*. (Queen Victoria's own husband, Prince Albert of Saxe-Coburg-Gotha had his foreskin pierced, the better to manipulate himself when wearing tight military trousers. This form of jewelled perforation actually became known, at least in the perforation trade, as an 'Prince Albert'.)

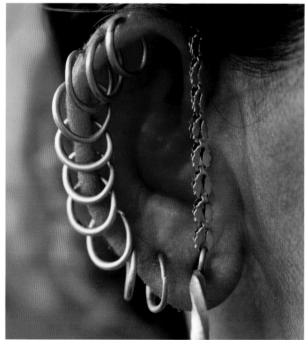

Western body modification through unguents and applicators is simply a temporary version of more enduring types of body modifications favoured by tribal women.

Whether a piercing or an austere platinum band – or possibly even a Frederick's of Hollywood diamanté anklet – jewellery is a form of body modification and enhancement that separates woman from beast as clearly and indisputable as opposable thumbs and electric pepper mills.

The origins of jewellery may have been largely functional: the metal clasp needed to keep a woad-stained and malodorous hemp cloak in place was a convenient way of transporting wealth. While we have instantaneous global cash transfer, in the dinosaur era your net worth could travel with you from cave to cave. Long before diamonds became a girl's best friend, jewellery was an eloquent symbol of other status relationships. Soon, these symbolic factors made this functional attribute more subtle and complex.

Precious metals and gemstones have acquired their own mythologies. Pliny believed that pearls were formed when drops of rain fell into oysters on the half shell. It is pleasing to note that the presumably mad Roman emperor Caligula gave his horse a pearl necklace. This in itself may not be evidence of insanity, but that he fed the same horse wine and made it a consul does rather tend to confirm the diagnosis. It is a wonderful gloss on the complexities of cultural history to note that Truman Capote's Holly Golightly and the ineffably English girl-with-pearls are connected to depraved Romans and French barrow boys. The latter because when Louis-Francois Cartier opened his shop on rue Montorgeuil in 1847 it had only just ceased being the most important Paris market for *coquillages*.

The value of precious metals and gemstones may be semantically transferred to the wearer, but the semantic possibilities of new materials continuously evolve. Confucius said better a diamond with a flaw than a pebble without, but value systems evolve. A revolution in taste begun by Queen Victoria when she started wearing jet black jewellery after the death of Albert may yet be continued with jewellery made of steel and complex thermo-plastics. Anything can become a 'jewel'; even the once despised 'paste' has become collectible. The questions of value transferred to the wearer are, of course, non-linear and ambiguous. The interpreter of signs may want to ask questions about value. Whether voluptuous or austere, jewellery is an accelerator of *bella figura*. When Mae West said a diamond received as a gift shined rather better than one you bought yourself, an essential truth about jewellery and its wearers was revealed.

Cosmetics and jewellery allow the wearer to give her one life a variety of different designs.

253

Left: Audrey Hepburn (1929–93) in Blake Edwards' 1961 Hollywood version of Truman Capote's Breakfast at Tiffany's. *Hepburn's Holly Golightly character hopes – like the* Playboy *covergirl (right) – the value of her diamonds gets semantically transferred to her personality. Her agent says 'She's a phoney, all right, but a real phoney.'*

Top right: Voluntary mutilation in the service of trade. It is the custom of the Ethiopian Surma tribe to insert progressively larger clay plates into the perforated lips of brides-to-be. The size of the plate is an indication of how many cattle she is worth. This is of more interest to her suitors than her naked breasts. This photograph was taken in 1990.

Page 254–5: Chanel lipstick and Saint-Laurent mascara. Marketing research shows that women attribute the greatest value to branded products used on orifices.

HOW
FASHION
DISTORTS
AND
EXAGGERATES

Hemlines and Heels

Above: The novelist Restif de la Bretonne assumed all men shared his erotic fascination with shoes. He gave his name to 'Retifism', or shoe fetishism. To the retifist, a shoe (a warm, intimate container) is both a symbol of sex and an assistant to it.

Opposite: The Mainbocher Corset by Horst (1906–99) is one of the twentieth century's great photographic images. The German–American photographer studied under architect Le Corbusier and the architectural influence is obvious in this dramatic design. The photograph was taken during the afternoon of 11 August 1939 in Vogue's Paris studio.

Fashion may well be buying things we don't need with money we don't have to impress people we don't like, but it is nonetheless a preoccupation of our culture. We seem to need its periodic distortions and its exaggerations, it spurious dynamics and its frivolously wasteful cycles of desire and redundancy. In either the breach or the observance, it defines women. There's no such thing as saying 'I don't care about fashion, I just wear jeans and a T-shirt.' Jeans and a T-shirt are a form of fashion; they create an image for the personality and a shape for the body. We design clothes and they design us.

Yet fashion is not a universal in all cultures. The idea of tailored clothes changing both with the short seasons and evolving over longer historic cycles is specifically Western, unknown in pre-industrial cultures. And specifically it is a part of industrial civilization.

Clothes begin where bodies end, but the two are in continuous transaction. Changes in fashion design do not just alter the clothes, they have an affect on the body. Always wise, Robert Burton, in his *Anatomy of Melancholy* says 'the greatest provocations of lust are from our apparel'. As any heterosexual male amateur of even the mildest erotica

knows, absolute nudity is by no means more *necessarily* interesting than the partial sort. Clothes, or, at least, clothes of a certain sort, emphasize gender. They do not disguise woman, they advertise her. Clothes are what Yale art historian George Hersey called 'genital maps'. Hersey describes a woman in a late Victorian ballgown:

'[it] borrows her attractor complex from the bisexual yet feminine world of flowers. The cone of her straight solid skirt forms a plinth for her breasts, which emerge like a gadrooned vase from her narrow belted waist. As for primary genital expression, she carries a loose, ribboned bouquet of roses in front of her groin. The roses = organs motif is continued in the embroidery around her bosom and the puffed sleeves, which thus suggest more roses and also additional breasts.'
— THE EVOLUTION OF ALLURE, 1996

The adventure of twentieth-century fashion was an escape from Victorian conventions, the restrictions of class, caste and wealth as described by cloth and its cutting. And the elaborate navigational system necessary to understand them. In this adventure, Coco Chanel was a great navigator.

An untutored provincial from Puy-le-Dome, Chanel became the greatest fashion designer of all. Placed in an orphanage run by tough and cheerless nuns, her diminished status was made explicit by a pauper's smock. Her friend the psychoanalyst Claude Delay-Tubiana explained to *Vanity Fair* the effects of this privation: 'Her revenge was to put all women in a uniform – a luxurious uniform.'

Chanel was not just a great woman designer, she was a great designer of women. She told the writer Paul Morand, a life-long confidant, as she talked into the evenings in a St Moritz hotel in the days after the end of the Second World War, that she had 'lived the life of the century and was the first to do so'. She dictated the memories, confessions and opinions that became her second best testament after her style, in a voice 'like lava' and with words that 'crackled like dried vines'.

From the orphanage, Chanel started work as a seamstress. This was another experience from which she designed other amazing vectors of escape. Chanel remembered 'I was working for women whose lady's maids had to pass them their stockings.' But as her career evolved, 'I now had customers who were busy women; a busy woman needs to be comfortable in her clothes. You need to be able to pull-up your sleeves.' Thus the invention of the 'sports dress', much influenced by her lover, Arthur 'Boy' Capel, the English polo-playing banker, who set her up in 1910 in the shop in the rue Cambon which is still the centre of a vast fashion empire.

The sports attire this Englishman wore on the field – *le style anglais* – was tailored and re-invented by Chanel for the international woman. She also put women in men's trousers. They were called slacks. The Chanel style was both a matter

of taste and a psychic projection of early privations, plus – very possibly – a need to distance herself from the frou-frou of the cocottes kept also by the men who kept her. She wore mannish open-necked shirts and gave instructions for women to ride horses as if they had balls: leaning well back to avoid crush injuries. Alexander Liberman of US *Vogue* said she got her entire sense of elegance from looking at men, an astonishing psychological insight. One of the boys, she actually raided men's wardrobes rather as, in an earlier age, the Chevalier d'Eon might have done with women's. Certainly, in terms of style it was sexually ambiguous: 'Cut my head off and I look like an adolescent boy,' Chanel claimed. This was cross-dressing *haut de gamme*.

However, many of Chanel's technical innovations in fashion were created to disguise what she felt were the shortcomings of her own less than voluptuous figure. The great *ancien-régime* couturier Paul Poiret called it '*miserablisme de luxe*'. Paris dandy Boni de Castellane told *Vanity Fair* that because of Chanel's formal innovations 'women no longer exist'. Instead, we had feminized boys.

Chanel was in St Moritz after her voluntary exile to Switzerland after the liberation of Paris in 1945. Since 1939 she had been living with an elegant German diplomat-spy called Hans-Günther von Dincklage in a suite at Paris Ritz (whose back door was conveniently nearly opposite her premises on the rue Cambon). Von Dincklage's position *vis-à-vis* the Nazis was slightly compromised since he had an English mother and had previously been married to a woman with sufficient Jewish relatives to excite suspicion of philo-Semitic sympathies.

259

Far left: Coco Chanel in sailor's trousers on the Lido, Venice, 1930. In appropriating men's clothing for women, Chanel became what photographer Horst called 'the queen of them all'.

Left: Mid-Sixties swimwear by Cole of California, the manufacturer who commercialized the bikini in the United States.

Right: Miss Universe, 1953, Long Beach, California. While leaders of fashion, especially Coco Chanel, were striving for simplicity, the lowbrow beauty pageant required the paraphernalia of sceptres, robes, sash and crown.

Still, Chanel was assumed to be a *collabo horizontale* by the Free French and was arrested by an *epuration* (purification) squad. This horrified her, not so much for the scandal and inconvenience as the *horreur* of the two young men wearing sports shirts and sandals in fashionable Paris. Worst of all, they addressed the Ritz doorman as '*tu*'. To someone as aware of social gradients as Coco Chanel, such familiarity was barbaric.

Exile first in an ugly house in Lausanne meant Chanel had to sit out the frustration of seeing Dior's 1947 New Look reported globally as a symbol of post-War freedoms. But there was an amazing second act in the Chanel drama. If exile had been a career setback, it was evidence of truth in that French saying *reculer pour mieux avancer*. After re-financing with her backers, the Wertheimer brothers, by about 1953 Chanel was ready to show the old school of Balenciaga, Dior, Fath, Lanvin and Givenchy just where they were wrong in terms of the design of modern woman. Their fashion was unworldly fantasy; Coco Chanel was interested in reality. At least as she saw it.

The vehicle was the 1954 launch of the Chanel suit, described by one fashion editor as 'a perverse schoolgirl uniform'. There were pockets for cigarettes. Since Chanel thought knees looked like cannonballs, knees were covered, although skirts were relatively short so as to aid the movements required of the modern woman. Heavy chains were sown into hems so jackets would hang properly. Quilted linings maintained the specified shape. The famous Chanel pumps had flat heels because these were better for walking, but included significant perceptual sophistications too: the black patent toecap had the effect of making the foot look smaller, while the immaterial pale main body of the shoe flattered the shape and length of the wearer's leg. Coco Chanel sculpted modern woman. 'I like fashion to go down into the streets, but I can't accept that it should originate there,' she told biographer Edmonde-Charles Roux.

In his Proustian magnum opus, *Der Mann ohne Eigenschaften* (The Man Without Qualities 1930–42) the Austrian modernist novelist Robert Musil has this passage about fashion:

'Clothes… in their monstrous life on the human body, are weird sheaths… perfectly compatible with the nose jewel and the lip ring… in a well-cut garment we see proof of their ability to interpret the invisible everyday.'

Right: Rudi Gernreich's Monokini inspired many imitators. This is a fashion shoot of a Ruben Torres topless swimsuit, 1964.

*Opposite A Padaung woman
shows the extremes of body
modification. The Padaung are
ethnic Mongolians settled in
Myanmar. Successive rings are
fitted to the necks (and
sometimes limbs) of girls born on
Wednesday. The number of rings
is both disabling and a status
symbol. Like high heels, a
compromise between masochism
and narcissism.*

Left: Madonna's 1990 Blonde
Ambition *tour featured the
singer in a Jean-Paul Gaultier
bullet-bra corset.*

In designing the essence of modern woman, that is what Coco Chanel achieved. *Life* magazine gave 'the Chanel Look' four whole pages. Someone told her she was her own best logo. Her own best logo was, of course, the fabulous Chanel No 5 perfume. Indeed. Long before such forms of brand-extension were routine in business, there had been talk of a Chanel toothpaste. A wholly modern woman could be completely sculpted, designed, packaged, branded. Chanel prepared woman for the modern world and she was the first to do so. All fashion has since followed.

1968 was the year of the Paris *evenements* when pretty girls in pleated skirts and cashmere V-necks, normally at their *etudes in SciPo*, threw cobblestones at Parisian *flics*. It was also when the Miss America 'beauty pageant' was held in Atlantic City, a depressed resort near Philadelphia (incidentally the source for the street names on the original game of Monopoly). At the beauty pageant feminists encouraged protesters to throw bras, corsets, high heels, lipsticks, what-have-you into rubbish bins (branded a 'Freedom Trash Can'). So on the one hand you had one version of modern woman in a ballgown or a swimsuit and another ferociously discarding all the attributes of 'woman' which culture and design had laboured for centuries to acquire. It was not in its way unlike the contest between naked and nude or, if you prefer, between the raw and the cooked, to use Levi-Strauss' phrase in a way he certainly never intended.

The feminists were objecting to the distortions and exaggerations of the fashion and cosmetic businesses. An organization called New York Radical Women originated the protest. They were joined by sisters from six other US cities and all were united in the conviction that 'beauty' competitions degrade women. Their other target was 'male chauvinism, commercialization of beauty, racism and oppression'.

Their protest included the ironic crowning of an ewe as an alternative Miss America. An impromptu chorus sang 'Ain't she sweet, making profits off her meat'. When the Women's Liberationists threatened to set fire to the highly flammable contents of the Freedom Trash Can (mostly derived, as beauty products were in those days, from petroleum by-products), the police intervened to protect the nearby landmark wooden boardwalk.

When you think of body modification, an image comes to mind of, say, the Padaung, a tribe of Mongolian origins now domiciled in Myanmar, famous from smiling studies in *National Geographic*. The Padaung enjoy a culture of stretching the necks of their women by up to 25cm (10in), through accumulation of constraining rings.

Right: Sculptor-turned-designer Flaminio Bertoni's Citroen DS19 of 1955 is routinely cited as the greatest car of all time. Bertoni's tectonic language is unambiguously feminine.

Opposite: The formalities of Elizabethan dress. A structure is imposed on the woman's shape by whalebone and starch. This portrait of an unknown sitter is by John de Critz the Elder.

264

Victorian Lady Travellers

The feminists of the later twentieth century were not the first to reject the imposition of degrading and unfunctional costumes (often designed by homosexual men). The extraordinary phenomenon of the Victorian Lady Travellers is an illuminating moment in the history of female self-identity. For example, the predominant psychology of the type may be inferred from indefatigable botanical artist Marianne North, who began travelling when her father died because she had 'lost the one strong emotional attachment' in her life. On fashion, Kate Marsden was eloquent. Marsden wrote On *Sledge and Horseback to Outcast Siberian Lepers* (1892). She was inspired by chastity, self-sacrifice and religious mania. At Verhoyansk she experienced the world's greatest temperature variation: from minus 94° Fahrenheit to plus 98° Fahrenheit. For this permafrost and scorching ordeal she chose to wear Gustav Jaeger's new liberal undervests (which promoted, in the theory of the day, healthy circulation), three topcoats, an eiderdown Ulster, full length sheepskins, reindeer skin coats, long-haired hunting stockings and felt boots. She said 'I rather shrink from giving a description of my costume because it was so inelegant.'

This wilful deformation of the neck was originally designed to deter slave traders, but the number of rings used and the amount of distortion ultimately achieved began to acquire a high status in Padaung society. With awful symbolism, adultery by women Padaung is punished by the forced removal of the neck-rings, leaving the guilty woman physically helpless.

But body modification began with clothes. In terms of pure function, in protecting the body from heat, cold, wet, dirt, damp and danger, the majority of clothing is demonstrably inefficient. But practical function is a very insignificant part of fashion. The true function of clothing is to send messages.

In medieval Europe, for example, wearing shoes a *la poulaine*, which is to say in the form of a (chicken's) beak or claw, advertised the wearer as a scandalous libertine. Certainly, shoes have ever since had an emphatic erotic character, perhaps because, as Casanova believed, men are attracted to feet. The Chinese lotus foot, horribly distorted by the practice of *chanzu*, or foot-binding, in fact replaced the primary sexual organs as a source of male erotic curiosity; in pre-Communist China, a woman would only expose her feet to a lover. Literary records suggest that *chanzu* began in Nanjing about 1,000 years ago.

The process is richly illustrative of the privations willingly suffered in the service of sex or fashion (when they are not the same thing). In *chanzu* a young girl's feet were ritually broken, slashed and bound in 3m (10ft) of tape soaked in animal blood and aromatic herbs. The resulting 'lotus foot' led to the 'lotus step', an unstable mincing gait found to be

Above: The ritual distortion of the Lotus Foot, *achieved by breaking bones and binding the feet was still practised in the early twentieth century. Dynastic sex manuals make it clear that the malodorous and deformed foot was an object of intense erotic fascination to Chinese men.*

attractive to men at court. Significantly, there was a social aspect of *chanzu*: peasant women who were required to hump loads of rice in the paddies needed properly functioning feet. It was privileged aristocrats who enjoyed interfering with nature's design of woman.

Modern foot and shoe fetishism takes a different shape, although the philosophical imperative is the same. When China became economically more free, women sought out shoes with unfeasibly high heels. With spike high heels, the woman is temporarily disabled: a curious compromise between narcissism and masochism. The stress put upon the tendons of the leg creates a posture which, in making the buttocks more prominent, invites sexual curiosity. Vivienne Westwood explained:

'The shoe is theatrical, beautiful, and clothes and accessories have the effect of giving one a role to play. To walk in very high heels with an in-built platform you need to draw the body up straight and centred. One can't help but feel powerful, beautiful, when wearing them.'
— THE TIMES 13 DECEMBER, 2008

An Italian urologist is said to have found a connection between high heels and the 'pleasure muscles' linked to orgasm.

So, as the buttocks took on a junior sexual role in pre-historic quadruped woman (being replaced by the more visible breasts), fashion made its re-adjustments to the ancient order. Charming to think of Charles Jourdain or Jimmy Choo as anthropological investigators of the dark matter of human evolution. Their shoes are not protecting the wearer's feet, but emphasizing other parts of the wearer's body.

268

Right: Hussein Chalayan's irreverent treatment of the burqa *is a reminder of experiences recounted by early Western travellers in Arabia. Women surprised swimming naked would, in their embarrassment, spontaneously cover their… faces.*

Opposite: A shoe designed by Manolo Blahnik as a 'Tribute to Sicily', 2000. Inspired by Lampedusa's great novel of memory, The Leopard, *1958, Blahnik's shoe is a tribute to the woman hobbled for style.*

This page: De-sexualized naked breasts and bottom in an Alexander McQueen fashion show. In contrast, melodramatically sexualized breasts (covered in latex) from a Pirelli calendar shoot by Duffy (opposite). Between 1964 and 1974 a promotional device for a tyre and rubber goods company provided the high-concept iconography of the Sexual Revolution.

272

Right: Mary Quant's Sixties fashions were as neat and crisp and colourful and consumable as contemporary injection-moulded plastic kitchen accessories.

Greek temple prostitutes used to announce themselves by the noise their shoes made on the Parian marble.

Just as there is a theory that fashions, facial hair and hemlines may be indicators of broader social and economic activities, so the height of high heels seems in some way not yet scientifically determined, but nonetheless often the subject of comment, also related to the spirit of the age.

Germaine Greer says wearing high heels means you are also wearing a complex set of sexual implications (which she does not, incidentally, disdain). But crucially, high heels also signal that the wearer is living (or wants to live) a life of leisure and, therefore, pleasure. Since nothing functional by way of ambulation can be achieved in high heels, they advertise an inclination to indulgence. Moreover, the very specific muscular tensions imposed by the wearing of them may in itself have a sexually stimulating character.

Nylons went on sale on 15 May 1940. They were surrounded by some science-fiction speculation. Customers asked for the new 'steel stockings' and *The New York Times* described them as 'Time Defying Hosiery'. Supplies of steel stockings were soon frustrated after the US entered the Second World War, when nylon was required for glider tow-ropes and to reinforce the sidewalls of aircraft tyres. But in 1946 there were nylon riots in US department stores.

In 1959 Glen Raven Mills of North Carolina, a business with a long history in cotton – it was owned by the Gant family whose fortune was based on selling duck for the US Army's tents – introduced a product called Panti-Legs. Design is sometimes attributed to the CEO's wife who is said ingeniously to have combined the functions of nylon stockings and a garter belt into a single garment. It was so radical an innovation that instructions had to be included in packs of the first 'pairs' sold.

These were the tights that miniskirts made an essential guarantee of modesty. Mary Quant's miniskirt moved the erogenous zone to the legs. And Sixties photographers, including David Bailey and Terence Donovan, used to enjoy exaggerating the legginess of the models by photographing their legs from a worm's eye view. (Today it is a trick often employed by fashion photographers to make models stand on their heads when taking pictures of their legs because some mystery of blood circulation makes legs look 'better' this way.)

273

Above: Soviet Socialist Realist painting attributed hitherto masculine attributes of muscularity and heroism to women. This is Aleksandr Deineka's The Russian People in the Great Patriotic War, *1944.*

Right: The reality of Socialist Realism was women in uniform. This is an Aeroflot hostess at Tashkent, 1958.

Opposite and right: In the United States, air hostesses were treated as an element in progressive corporate identities. In 1966 Lockheed was proposing an SST (Supersonic Transport) and Braniff hostesses used a mock-up as a stage to present their new Emilio Pucci uniforms. Pucci also proposed that hostesses should wear transparent visors. Braniff's women were designed and packaged as if a lunch tray or a bag of peanuts.

The miniskirt also made underwear a subject of speculation and curiosity, if not absolute advertisement. In fact, with her adroit marketing of co-ordinated bras and knickers in bright colours and confident spots or stripes, Mary Quant did for women's underwear exactly what Terence Conran had done for the kitchen. Conran had, incidentally, designed Quant's first shop, Bazaar on Chelsea's King's Road, and was a friend of Quant's husband, Alexander Plunkett-Greene. So, just as Conran's Habitat was aestheticizing the kitchen and its utensils (bringing into colourful and optimistic display what used to be hidden understairs), so Quant made underwear polite and stylish.

As if to confirm the Sixties Zeitgeist, the US flag that flew on the surface of the Moon in 1969 was made of a Gant fabric. In her book *What we Wore* (1984) Ellen Melinkoff said 'Pantyhose edited legs. They hid the hair, the blotches, the cellulite.'

The technology of re-shaping was powerfully enhanced by the invention of Lycra in Waynesboro, Virginia in 1957 which was later commercialized in 1962. Lycra is DuPont's brand name for a rubberized nylon which helps improve on Nature (which was, incidentally, Voltaire's definition of 'Art'). It is a petroleum-based synthetic with special morphological characteristics: its 500 per cent capacity for stretch and recovery allows rolling plains of ugly lard to be turned into smooth plains of desire. Lycra enabled the redistribution of girth: when you think about it, the very expression '500 per cent stretch' seems in itself a perfect metric encapsulation of the ambitions of body modifiers.

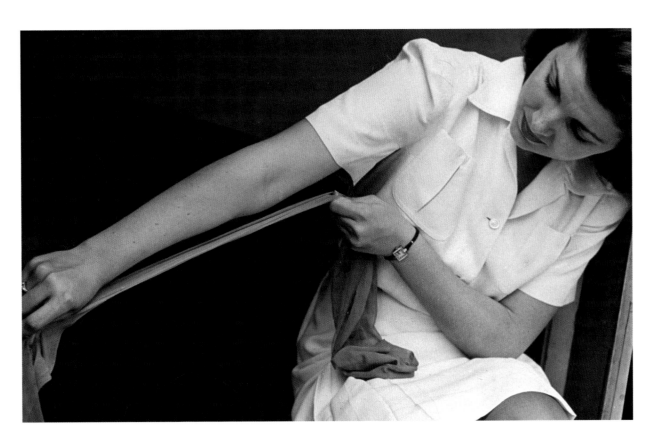

This page: Nylon was the consumer sensation of 1939. This new synthetic allowed women a new freedom in laundry routines, but also gave their legs a machine-like finish which was felt to be very modern.

This English scientist (opposite) c.1955 is examining samples for signs of wear. (Significantly, fashion photographers who specialize in legs like to photograph their subjects upside-down since the inverted blood flow flatters the shape of the leg.)

Page 278–9: The name Lycra appeared in 1959. Combining the elastic qualities of rubber with the strength of nylon, it presented a number of interesting new options in directing and controlling women's shapes.

In 1961 Warner Bros introduced 'the future of hosiery' – a Lycra undergarment called 'The Birthday Suit' whose deceitful purpose was to suggest total nudity beneath the outer garments.

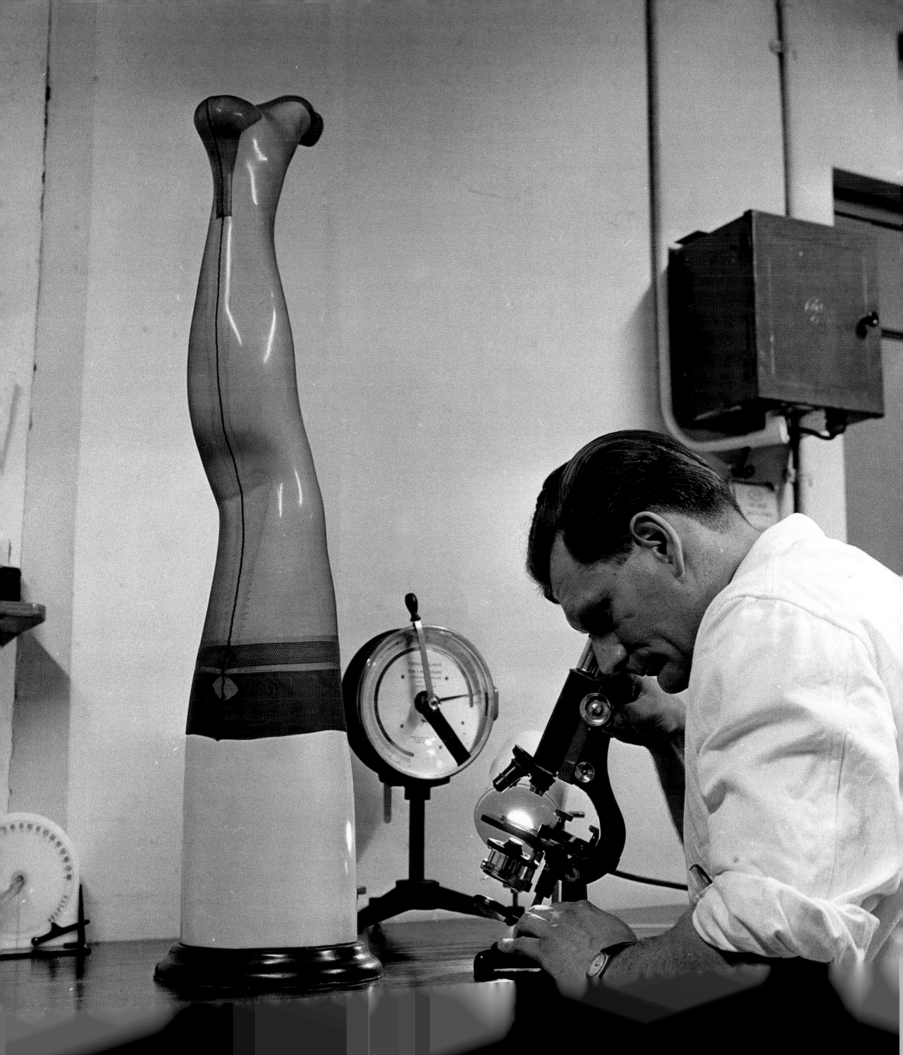

LYCRA® 3D
The Future of Hosiery

Sensuous, smooth, gently caressing in every direction, cradling legs in sublime comfort and elegance. Women, captivated, rushing to buy. Magazine advertising that motivates, impresses, persuades. Stockings and tights that disappear off the shelves as fast as you put them there. LYCRA 3D. It really knows how to move. Join the movement. It's the future of hosiery.

Photography by Tyen

® DuPont registered trademark

LYCRA 3D
ONLY BY DUPONT

Nothing Moves Like LYCRA.

Featured garment:
Wolford stay-ups.

SOME CLOTHES LOVE YOU BACK

LYCRA
BRAND

The Calipygian Curve

HOW
DESIGN
APPROPRIATED
THE
FEMALE
FORM

Above: The oyster is a bivalve mollusc whose reputation as an aphrodisiac may be based on its vaguely gynaecological appearance.

Opposite: The Caryatid, or a column in the form of a woman, is one of the basic elements in Classical architecture. The Erechtheion porch, Akropolis, Athens, late fifth century BC.

Page 282: The calipygian curve is a recurrent motif in architecture and design.

Callipygos is – literally – Greek for beautiful (usually female) bottom, but has come to suggest the appropriation of womanly curves, whatever their precise anatomical source, into designed objects.

The voluptuous curves of Aphrodite's bottom and other parts have been through several cultural and industrial transformations. They have, for example, appeared as structural elements in architecture, furniture, cars and soft-drink bottles. That the pioneer industrial designer Raymond Loewy chose to cite the shapely goddess in his often repeated appreciations of the Coca-Cola bottle is evidence, if nothing else, of the great sophistication of the French educational system. (Loewy was born in Paris in 1893 before shipping himself to New York in 1919. It seems unlikely that, had he been born in New York, he would have been tutored to make so fine a classical reference in the context of pop culture.)

Coca-Cola was launched in 1886 and by the beginning of the First World War it had become so successful that it was inspiring all sorts of knock-offs, including Koca-Nola, Gay-Ola and Cold-Cola. By about 1910 the nationwide bottlers and

gazifiers of the industrially produced syrup in Atlanta were looking for a distinctive new package 'which a person will recognize' rather as a female bottom 'even when he feels it in the dark'. Approaches were made to bottle manufacturers, including the Root Glass Company of Terre Haute, Indiana. There the chief engineer, an immigrant Swede called Alex Samuelson, had the happy conceit of looking at Coca-Cola's primary ingredients for inspiration. So he looked at the coca leaf and the kola nut. It is in fact the curves and grooves of the nut, not the cleft of the buttocks of the Goddess of Love, that inspired the world's most famous package design.

The Coke bottle became such a symbol of successful American consumerism that Loewy, always keen to identify with the most positive and glossiest aspects of his adopted American Dream, found himself brooding 'a good deal about the callipygian Coca-Cola bottle' or so he told journalist John Kobler in a career-defining interview in *Life* magazine published in May 1949. Loewy never actually claimed to have designed the bottle, but also never bothered later to correct anyone who misinterpreted his enthusiasm and erroneously propagated a delusion.

284

Life magazine went on using semantically significant language:

'Though in full retreat from streamline principles, [the Coke bottle] remains the queen of the soft-drink container. But then, Loewy points out, its shape is aggressively female – a quality that in merchandise as in life, sometimes transcends functionalism.'

In 1962 Loewy adapted the 'Coke-bottle look' to the hipline of his sensational Studebaker Avanti automobile. Two years later, Ford and General Motors took that same curve mass-market with the Mustang and the Chevrolet Camaro. In 1970 The Coca-Cola Company created its own 'dynamic contour curve' as a wordless global logo. In strange combination, Callipygos and the kola nut went global.

There are earlier examples of design appropriating the female profile. In Greek architecture, a caryatid is a column in the form of a woman: the caryatid porch of the Erechtheion on the Acropolis is only the most famous example. But architecture's absorption of the female body was not so much a literal as a metaphorical one. In *De Architectura*, known in English as *The Ten Books on Architecture*, the Roman military engineer and architectural theorist Vitruvius explains the classical orders of architecture in terms of the human body. The tough and solid and stout and simply decorated Doric is, he says, male. The decorative, delicate and elegant Ionic order is female. This may be the absolute origin, in design terms, of the equation of femininity and delicacy.

There are yet more occult influences of the woman's body in architectural design. The plan of European Romanesque churches, themselves derived from Roman basilicas which had their own source in an architecture of pre-history, may be an emblematic diagram of the female reproductive system. The circular plan of the very earliest pre-Christian temples may suggest the endless continuum of sex and life: Sanskrit suggests this in the imagery of its language. The *yoni*, or the symbolic vulva, is the 'door' of life or a sacred channel. This transformation is confirmed in *The Kama Sutra* where the architectural yoni morphs into the sexual vagina.

The passage through a Christian church from porch to nave to altar with its sacraments is, some imaginative authorities have maintained, almost a parody of the sequence of erection/entry/emission.

Top: The Roman architect Vitruvius believed the classical orders had a sexual character, or, at least, a gender identity. This is from Cesare Cesariano's 1521 translation of De Architectura.

Above: And the sense in which architecture is inspired by gynaecology is revealed in primitive buildings whose yoni *plan suggests a channel and a womb. These are the second-century caves at Karnataka, India.*

Opposite: Even the highly sophisticated plans of Christian churches – this is the late twelfth century Cistercian Abbey of Le Thoronet in the Var – may be explicit diagrams of the woman's sexual system.

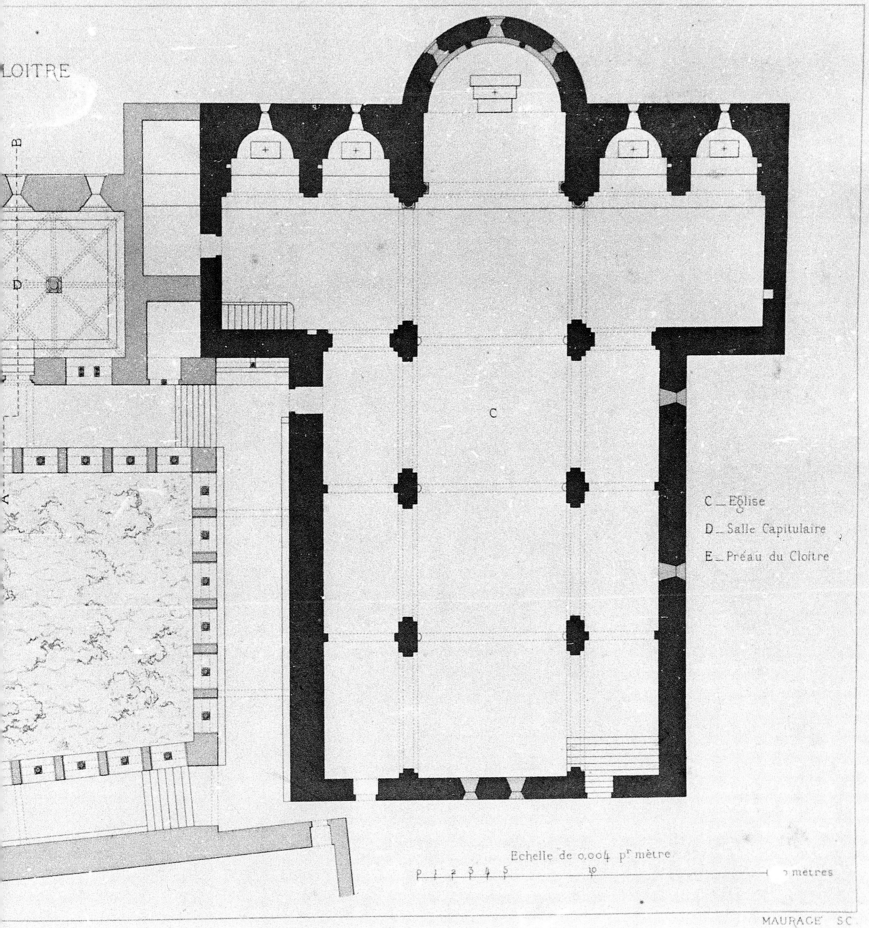

LOITRE

C _ Église
D _ Salle Capitulaire
E _ Préau du Cloître

C

Echelle de 0,004 p.r mètre

0 1 2 3 4 5   10   5 mètres

MAURAGE SC

ABBAYE DU THORONET.

VAR

And the architectural progress can be understood in terms of female anatomy. Specifically :

The double doors	=	*labia maiora*
Vestibule	=	*vestibula*
Inner doors	=	*labia minora*
Auditorium	=	*vagina*
Altar	=	*womb*
Apse	=	*Fallopian tubes*
Fontwater	=	*amniotic fluid*

A window in Dunblane Abbey was considered by John Ruskin to be one of the most beautiful in Britain. Ruskin, never adroit at sexual matters, may have been unaware of its sexual symbolism. In his *History of Sex Worship* (1940), Cutner claims the design of the window makes explicit reference to the labia and the clitoris.

Henri II's personal drinking goblet was reputedly modelled on the breast of his mistress, Diane de Poitiers. Alas, no precise notes have been retained to explain the technology involved in this process. Be that as it may, not necessarily consciously, the French king was following a classical tradition which maintained that the breast of Helen of Troy was the model for the very first wine glass. Helen's face may have launched a thousand ships; her breasts did the equivalent for drinking.

At Rambouillet, Marie-Antoinette, in a delirium of noblesse *campagnarde*, had a personal dairy staffed by prettily frocked maids and visited, from time to time, by gentlemen who took an interest in the staff.

Above: Marie-Antoinette's champagne coupe – le 'bol sein' – was made in 1788 by Jean-Jacque Lagrenée (1739–1821) as part of the fitting out of the laiterie *at Rambouillet (now exhibited in the Musée National de Céramique-Sèvres). It is reputed to be moulded from one of her breasts.*

Right: Louis XVI gave the Rambouillet dairy to Marie-Antoinette as a gift in 1786. It was the most extreme example of the aristocratic cult of the laiterie d'agrément *(the pleasure dairy). The association between cows, milk, milkmaids, breasts and carnality was absolutely clear even in the days before Freud.*

Her breasts served as a model for the prototype champagne bowl. If this is so, Marie-Antoinette's breasts were a very strange shape: semi-circular, symmetrical and flat.

In our own age the Brazilian architect Oscar Niemeyer, a disciple of Le Corbusier, filled sketchbook after sketchbook with drawings of girls on Rio de Janeiro's beaches, the better to stimulate his formal inventiveness. Le Corbusier himself used an androgynous, although rather curvaceous, human figure to explain his system of proportions known as Le Modulor, his own attempt to bring Leonardo's Vitruvian Man up to date. And then, of course, there were the Surrealists whose frequent subconscious and, indeed, very often explicit, fantasies were powered by a preoccupation with the female body. To the Surrealists, the woman's body was not just of aesthetic significance in the way it had been

to, say, painters of the eighteenth century. It was much, much more. It was used as a laboratory: an imaginative sourcebook for art and design. In his novel *L'Amour Fou* (1937), André Breton found the female body a route to the 'marvellous'.

In 1920 the Surrealist photographer Man Ray made a coat-stand (now in the Boymans Museum in Rotterdam) with a life-size cut-out photo of a naked woman. The Proust of Surrealism was Marcel Duchamp who used a sort of dream logic in his subversive art: the Volkswagen car he latterly drove gave rise, on phonetic grounds, to a suite of prints known as the '*faux vagin*', a nice coming together of the automobile and the erotic. False vagina is how it sounds if you pronounce the name Volkswagen abbreviation VW in a surreally mangled version of French and German.

Opposite and above: Oscar Niemeyer's Niteroi Popular Theatre, Rio de Janeiro, 2007. Niemeyer says his sinuous architectural forms were influenced by sketches of girls on Ipanema beach.

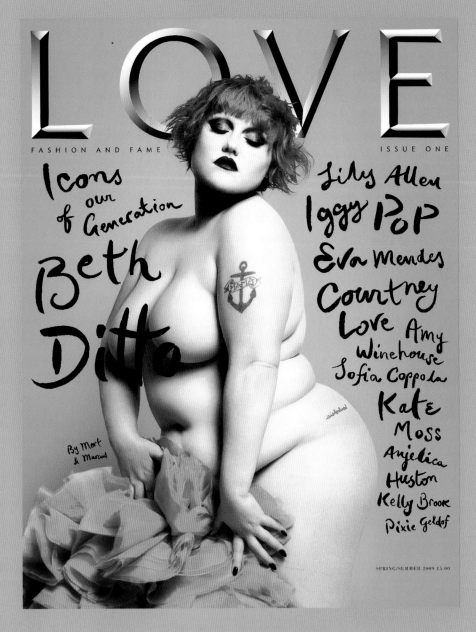

The Curve is back

There's an obscure, but rather marvellous, theory in economics known as Kondratieff's Waves, named after Nikolai Kondratieff, briefly director of Stalin's Institute for the Study of Business, before he was sent to the Gulag. The theory is that all business-cultural-political activity is on very long sinusoidal supercycles lasting about seventy-five years. So we go from sweet to sour, from fascism to liberal democracy… And with women, from thin to fat.

It's not that the shape of women is changing, it's just that our preferences are. With the recession of the early twenty-first century, curves are back in favour. The cinema and catwalk fashion shows demanded thin women because they move better, or, at least, in a way that suited the camera. Now, different media are liberating our choices.

Of course, there's an argument about the contrarian chic of having a voluptuous figure in an age of economic restraint, but the truth is actually rather different. Men have always preferred the shapely and inviting callipygian curve; the mother-whore dichotomy has timeless relevance. Each needs a generous body.

This page: The conceptual artist Yves Klein was interested in nothing and in women. In 1958 a show called Le Vide (The Void) opened at Paris' Galerie Iris Clert. In 1960 a series of events called Anthropometries de l'Epoque bleue *saw the artist trailing naked paint-soaked women across canvases. 'Yves le Monochrome's' audacious adaptation of the nude body made his IKB colour (International Klein Blue) famous.*

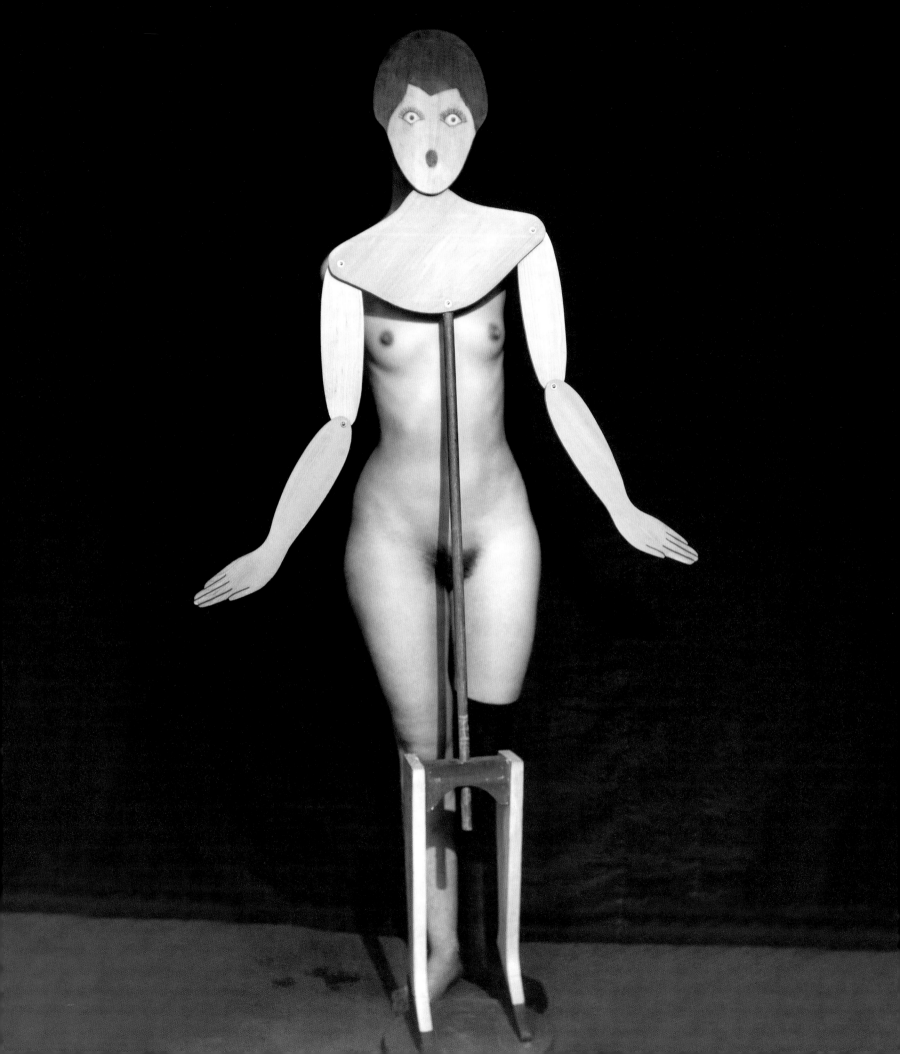

Women surrealists were not innocent of objectifying the female body. Ghislaine Wood explained in a booklet for the Victoria and Albert Museum: 'For many women artists, the boundaries of the self were not limited by the image, but spread to the object, home and body.' (2007) The woman's body and its (usually erotic) associations became a sourcebook. Meret Oppenheim's fur-covered cup and saucer of 1936 was originally called *Objet* and later named by André Breton as *Le dejeuner en fourrure*. The fur is a reference both to Edward von Sacher-Masoch's *Venus in Furs* (a Surrealist favourite in the perversion category), but also explicitly to pubic hair. Furthermore, the title also alludes to the *fête champêtre* paintings of Gorgione and Manet, in which gorgeous, nude women mix incongruously with clothed men. Texture, sensation and transgression were part of the adventure of navigating the female body and these could all be applied to the design of objects and furniture.

It was Edward James, the reclusive, eccentric English patron of the arts, who first involved Salvador Dali in furniture design. This was after some experimentation with Surreal fashion when James asked Dali to design frocks (subsequently made practicable by Elsa – Shocking Pink – Schiaparelli) which one exhausted wearer described as 'startling and crazy'. Dali's Shocking Pink sofa in the form of the cupid's bow of Mae West's lips was first seen in the incongruous setting of James' London townhouse on dignified Wimpole Street. (It was in the study here that James also had Dali's lobster telephone.)

For the Coney Island site of New York World's Fair of 1939 (the very same international expo where nylon was introduced to avid women customers seeking new legs),

Opposite: This 1920 composition by Man Ray has a real nude body behind a cardboard mask, a visual pun about sexual identity.

Right: Salvador Dali's lobster telephone, 1936. For Dali, surrealism was 'a dreamed itinerary of paranoiac phenomena'. And the lobster was an unambiguous symbol of womanhood.

Page 294: Salvador Dali's sofa was inspired by Mae West's lips. It appeared in 1937 in the Wimpole Street townhouse of the collector and patron Edward James.

Below: At the 1939 New York World's Fair Salvador Dali introduced the American public to nudity in his frankly mad Dream of Venus pavilion. Outraged at some artistic compromises required by the organisers, Dali published a self-defence pamphlet titled Declaration of the Independence of the Imagination and the Rights of Man to His Own Madness.

Right: A Dali mermaid, preparing to milk a submerged cow, applying make-up. Dali believed that hair is the only thing about an elegant woman that must be healthy. Here it is disguised by a spiky head-dress

296

This page: Over fifteen years Audi's design language has evolved from bold surfaces and a frankly masculine refusal of detail towards a more feminized treatment of a car's profile. Curves are more delicate, details more exquisite. Top to bottom: 1995, 2004, 2009.

Salvador Dali built his Dream of Venus pavilion. A cut-out of Botticelli's Venus stood over the doorway in full irony. This doorway was framed by 'columns' which clearly suggest the legs of a woman sitting with a generous gap between her knees. To enter Dali's pavilion was a parody of birth and sex. Meanwhile, real women in swimsuits sat on deck chairs above this bizarre feature, also embellished with voluptuous semi-abstract ceramic nudes and submarine tendrils in plaster.

It was Dali's New York dealer, Julien Levy, who had introduced him to the prospects of World's Fair. In a 1938 letter to Levy, Dali explained that he had in mind to build:

'An intrauterine room portable, with heated saliva inside flowing down the hairy walls. When one is distressed by anything at all, one mounts this apparatus and enters in, as one would the belly of the Mother.'

This ambitious concept was not fully realized in the Dream of Venus, but the watery theme inside was – at least to Dali – pleasantly suggestive of the beckoning womb. Two huge water tanks contained incongruous elements including a cow and a grand piano. Between these, 17 topless girls posed as mermaids and presented the United States with one of its first public displays of nudity. The mermaids (who represented a 'pre-natal chateau' in Dali's delightfully mad language) milked the underwater cow. Outside the water tanks there were features including a Venus Dream Chamber which gave male visitors an opportunity to ogle a prostrate nude while listening to the voice of Venus played over a Tannoy who says 'In the fever of love, I lie upon my bed. A bed eternally long, and I dream my burning dreams – the longest dreams ever dreamed without beginning and without end.'

Above: Chris Bangle was inspired by the curve and cleft of a woman's bottom when designing the headlamp lens of the 1993 Fiat Coupe.

Above right: Carlo Mollino, mirror for Casa Miller, 1936.

Opposite: Reclining chair plus ottoman, 1947. Carlo Mollino (1905–73) applied his erotomaniac obsessions to furniture and cutlery design (see page 304).

Ideas for 'costumes' worn by the (mostly nude) exhibits included a woman with a lobster where her fig leaf should be.

No methodology exists to calculate the influence Dali's Dream of Venus had on the American imagination, but in his convergence of the physical body with psychological states, the Surreal Woman created a standard of psycho-sexual ambiguity, of fetishization of body parts, of stylized, high-finish breasts and lips that became a staple of advertising. For example, Horst's famous photograph *Girl with Mainbocher Corset*, 1939 (see page 257)was conceived as a Surrealist work of art. To us it looks like a high-concept ad. After all, one of Salvador Dali's biggest clients was not a collector, but the Bonwit Teller department store.

Salvador Dali's megalomaniac obsessions certainly had their influence on mass-media, but the woman's body was also a preoccupation of more sober (if not very much more sober) designers. Carlo Mollino was one of the twentieth century's Renaissance men. Architect, designer, racing-driver, pamphleteer, photographer, erotomaniac and self-publicist. Mollino's astonishing furniture designs are routinely called biomorphic, which is to say their shape and profile is inspired by callipygian curves. His inspiration was the massive archive of photographs, latterly Polaroids, which he took of local Turin whores and, indeed, of women of social standing, sufficiently lacking inhibitions who he lured to nocturnal shoots in one or other of his libidinously designed studio lairs. The Polaroids were occasionally used by Mollino as greetings cards, but their primary purpose was to be a morphological database for his architecture and design. They were eventually collected and published in book form 12 years after his death.

WOMAN AS DESIGN

This page and opposite:
Carlo Mollino lured all classes of
Torinese women to his love-nest
and took Polaroid photographs
of them. He never published the
photographs, but used them as
formal inspiration in his
architecture and design.

Both Carlo Mollino and Oscar Niemeyer had links with Surrealism. And their architecture and design has direct links with the most prominent architects of the early twenty-first century, Rem Koolhaas, Zaha Hadid and Frank Gehry among them. Now that fashion dictates architectural form, headline architecture is infatuated with dramatic, neophiliac, attention-getting designs often of female form. The architect's task, it seems, is to conceptualize shapes which photograph well. The conceptual link between the present-day and Carlo Mollino is ever more apparent. His Teatro Regio in Turin was completed only in the year of his death; it can be seen as an investigation of his id, and, perhaps ours as well. The critic Herbert Muschamp was inspired into a reverie of erotic speculation by Teatro Regio, unusual for a civic building. Even stepping into the theatre is like being swallowed. It is, Muschamp wrote in the *Sunday New York Times* in 2006 'a place for falling in love at first sight with an elusive stranger. She will have vanished by the time you've made your way through this spatial labyrinth without walls… the auditorium is unphotographable. And it should probably be X-rated.' Describing a vast oval room illuminated by transparent rods, Muschamp was given the 'unmistakable impression of spermatozoa penetrating an egg'.

Magnificently and compulsively odd as he may be, Carlo Molllino (who died in 1973) was out of time. For so long as major architecture was defined in terms of corporate identity and shareholder responsibility – as it was in the last decades of the twentieth century – there was no place for fantasy. Callipygian curves did not communicate the sober values of debt swapping. Goldman Sachs did not, perhaps, see the value in a corporate HQ whose atrium might remind visitors of spermatozoa entering an egg. What the bankers wanted was a Global Corporate Vernacular Glass Box that would advertise the qualities of rectitude efficiency, probity and seriousness that we now know they so conspicuously lacked.

The idiosyncratic designer Gaetano Pesce has railed against the sameness of Global Corporate Vernacular Glass Box Architecture. Pesce enjoys biomorphic form and has designed a house made of rubber in Brazil. He told an *International Herald Tribune* reporter (6 October 2004) that 'The elasticity of feminine thought is extremely coherent with our era. The masculine is typical of other eras when the world sought other ideologies. Our time is multidisciplinary and elastic.' He looked at a boring building and said 'Had that project been done with feminine values, it would have been more human, more sensual, more joyous.' And with a more-or-less conscious sexual image Pesce added 'Tomorrow we'll find materials that bounce.'

Page 302: Carlo Mollino's bodywork for the OSCA 1100 that competed in the 1954 Vingt-Quatre Heures du Mans. The morphology is clearly based on female form.

Left: Carlo Mollino, 1959, competition design for cutlery.

Right: Carlo Mollino's last project, Teatro Reggio, Turin, was completed in 1973. Some critics thought the details of the atrium were inspired by spermatozoa entering an egg.

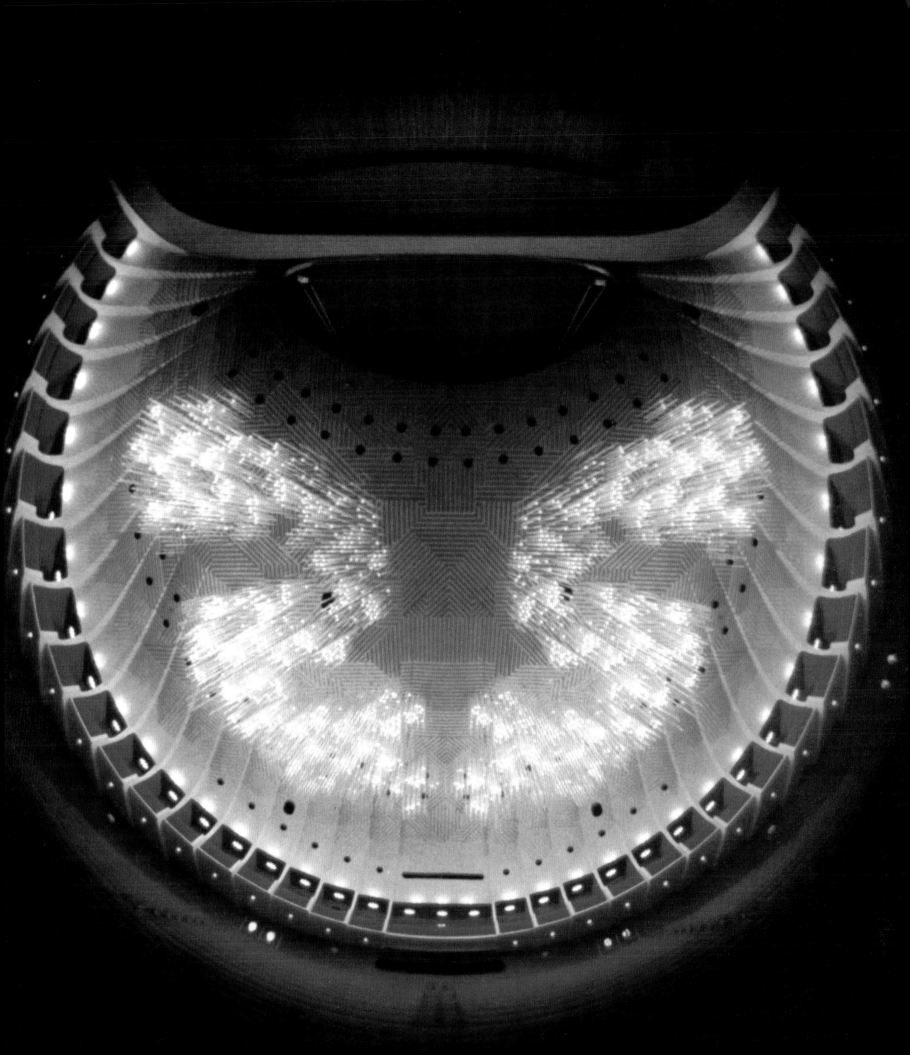

Right: Gaetano Pesce's own house in Bahia, Brazil, 2006. It's not that the colourful resin tile cladding is superficially 'feminate', but Pesce consciously invests his designs with external womanly form. This, in his view, politicises architecture and design just as it sexualizes it. Of his 1969 'Up' chair he said, 'It resembles the female body with ball and chain'. In Bahia, the ball and chain were removed.

Opposite: Zaha Hadid's Bridge-Pavilion at the 2008 Zaragoza Expo. Hadid's signature bio-morphic form adapted to a serious dual role. Notions of encirclement and womb-like containment within an organic structure have obvious feminine associations.

THE CALLIPYGIAN CURVE

In modern architecture there has been a tradition of comment about the overt sexual character of some architects' drawings and even buildings. But more often the association is male. In his unrealized ideal city (imaginative fragments of which were actually built at Arc-et-Senans near Besançon where his Salines Royales are now a World Heritage site) the neo-classical architect Claude-Nicolas Ledoux proposed an *oikema*. This was a novel institution, part polytechnic and part brothel, where youth was instructed on how best to manage felicitous sexual relations. These were revolutionary times and Ledoux did not hesitate to make the plan of his *oikema* unambiguously phallic.

More recently, some commentators have remarked on the voluptuous (and largely phallic) sexual fantasies they see in the drawings of Piranesi and Sant'Elia. And even in Hugh Ferriss, the influential architectural illustrator of ragtime New York. Ferriss certainly drew with a sensual style and describes buildings whose stone and concrete looks as plushy as skin. He exploits *chiaroscuro* and makes tall buildings dramatic and glamorous, but – equally – when he draws a Manhattan subway, the sinuous tube has reminded imaginative observers of the vaginal canal.

But it is facile to make morphological associations between buildings and a woman's body, even if wordy feminists sometimes find themselves wont to discuss 'the renegotiation of gendered space'. It is the elasticity of feminine thought that is the significant influence, not the tracing of callipygian curves. And so, as the

aesthetic desirability of a shapely bottom gives way to a female view of the Universe, there is a perfect metaphor of a civilization whose values are maturing from heavy things you can weight to buildings (and, indeed, ideas, that bounce).

The female influence in modern architecture is occult. It is manners rather than style. And the personal histories of two remarkable architects show how very substantial even occult influences may be. Edward Durrell Stone, a near contemporary of the illustrator Hugh Ferriss and another New York architectural legend, was the designer (with Philip L. Goodwin) of New York's Museum of Modern Art (1939). The famous MoMA is a pure exercise in the International Style (a term for the popularization of Bauhaus principles which was coined for a MoMA exhibition.) Which is to say, rectilinear and undecorated. But Stone's style changed after marriage to a colourful and feisty – and possibly bouncy – Latin woman, Maria Elena Torchio. Now Stone's style became delicate and lacy. Critics said it was more like pastry-cutting than building design. Stone's US Embassy in Delhi has decorative concrete screens like a vast diplomatic *zenana*. And, continuing the exotic references, his Huntington Hartford Gallery of Modern Art completed at Columbus Circle in 1965 was, in dramatic contrast to the chaste MoMA, described as a sleazy 'Persian whorehouse'.

An exactly similar transformation overtook the architectural style of Norman Foster as a more feminine psychology came to bear on his ambitions. The thrusting technology of Foster's HSBC Building in Hong Kong suggests a very masculine sort of energy. In contrast, the smoothly sculpted Swiss Re Building in the City of London indicates a

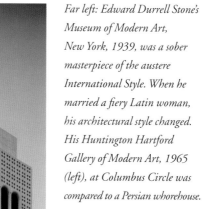

Far left: Edward Durrell Stone's Museum of Modern Art, New York, 1939, was a sober masterpiece of the austere International Style. When he married a fiery Latin woman, his architectural style changed. His Huntington Hartford Gallery of Modern Art, 1965 (left), at Columbus Circle was compared to a Persian whorehouse.

This page: Norman Foster's architectural style was strictly technocratic: his HSBC HQ in Hong Kong of 1979–85 (above left) is a masterpiece of hard-edge machine-age severity. After marrying a Spanish sex therapist, other forces appears to have influenced his style which became much more ovoid, sensuous and feminine. Swiss Re, London, 2000–2004 (above right). Albion Riverside, London, 1998–2003 (opposite).

different attitude to building, perhaps reflecting an underlying change in personality. But the most dramatic contrast in Foster's building styles can be seen side by side on the banks of the Thames in London's Battersea. In 1990 Foster built an apartment block in Global Vernacular Glass style; it houses his vast design studio on the ground floor. In 2002 he built, right next door, another apartment block called Albion Riverside. This is curvaceous and globular, a design in rank contradiction of what went before. In design terms, unless we accept that frivolous changes of direction are no enemy of good architecture, if one is right, the other must be wrong. The significant point is that in between HSBC and Swiss Re, in between his 1990 apartment block and Albion Riverside, Foster married a dashing Spanish woman who once ran a Barcelona radio-therapy show called 'Dr Sex'.

If the first subject of art was a woman, the first subject of twenty-first century architecture is also a woman. This is Zaha Hadid. Here is a woman who designs buildings that look as though they may bounce. Hadid also designs furniture of spectacular biomorphic aspect, so baffling to

construe that press releases created for the product launch have to contain explanatory passages on whether it is a chair or a table. Hadid rejects formalism of the rectilinear sort and insists on replacing it with formalism of the biomorphic kind. It would be artless and crass to suggest that in this type of absurd rejection of hard-edge masculine 'function' there is something typically feminine, but there is surely something essentially womanly in Hadid's formal language which (even as it relies on advanced computer-modelling for its invention and realization), calls up in the imagination primitive ideas of oviparous mammals, of nurturing, of womb-like spaces, of warmth, touch, sensibility. These are not just buildings that look as though they might bounce, they also suggest Eliot's pneumatic bliss. Looking at Zaha Hadid's back-catalogue, it is remarkable how her design has so quickly gestated. Twenty years ago she was doing hard-edged zig-zags. Her evolution into a delirium of ovoid shape-making is evidence both of the progressively advancing computer technology which makes it possible, but also of an enlarging taste everywhere for a woman's values in design. Warm callipygian curves are more pleasing in stressful times than cold razor edges.

Left: Tom Wesselmann Great
American Nude Number 44,
1963.

It would be impossible to catalogue the full extent of
callipygian curvaceous influence in recent art and design.
In the Sixties American Pop artist Tom Wesselman created
his series *The Great American Nude* which turned folds of
flesh into flash-card graphics. His friend Allen Jones quite
literally adapted the female form into memorably odd
one-off furniture.

In the more mass-market area of furniture sales,
Olivier Mourgue's Sixties chairs and sofas exploited
biomorphic form. It is perhaps more than just coincidence
and of some psychological note that callipygian *chaises
longues* by Mourgue found their way into the womb-like
environment of the spaceship in Stanley Kubrick's *2001
A Space Odyssey* (1968).

The language of car design maintains a primitive sexism.
Indeed, the 1993 Fiat Coupe had a front headlamp lens that
with no subtlety whatsoever was inspired by a woman's
bottom, cleft and all. The same designer, American Chris
Bangle, went onto to radicalize BMW. Hitherto conservative
in style, under Bangle's creative influence, BMW's shapes
became more complex, more sculptural, more wilful, subtle,
irrational and demanding. We will not say more 'feminine'.

Yet car designers talk often of creating feminine curves
and they know that such a curve can be distinguished from
its masculine counterparts by just a matter of a few
millimetres in the radius. There is no science here, only art
and feeling, but by common consent among car designers,
the most handsome machines are ones that somehow
combine feminine elegance with masculine strength.

The vocabulary used by Jean-Pierre Ploué in the Citroën design centre at Vélizy just outside Paris is revealing and frankly erotic. The Chef du Design talks freely of forms being '*lisse*' (slippery and soft). These same forms, he says, must have '*fluidité*'. And the managing intelligence uses '*asperité*' in a battle between '*controle*' and '*tension*'. Designing a car's shape seems to be not dissimilar to a sexual encounter. Ploué says, in terms of formal inspiration, he likes dolphins, but a conversation with him about car design sounds like a transcript of an intimate tête-à-tête with Aphrodite Callipygos herself.

Either explicit or occult, the influence of woman in architecture and design is ever present. This does not mean that all architecture and design always has an erotic character. But often it does. In a similar way, oysters are an aphrodisiac not in a bio-chemical sense, but in one of associations. I asked the chef Eric Chavot if there was sexual symbolism in food. He went 'Pah! A langoustine! You make stupid joke. You treat your girl like shellfish?' But then he conceded that, especially in the heat of a masculine kitchen, 'everything is sexual'.

Chavot says 'Everything I touch is sensual. I get excited by an apple. Mother Nature made it. A nice piece of fish? Your mind starts wandering. Is it, perhaps, a mermaid?' Then I asked him very specifically about the notorious oyster. He thought and replied "It can wake up the senses, certainly.' Then he beamed and went on an imaginative wander in his mind: 'Oysters equals beach equals ladies equals bikinis.'

In these, and all the foregoing, connections is the sweet mystery of life.

314

Opposite, bottom left:
Forniphilia *is a recent coinage describing fetishised, eroticised furniture. Olivier Morgue's 1965* Djinn *recliner is suggestively biomorphic in inspiration; it was used by Stanley Kubrick in the rotating Hilton space-station in* 2001: A Space Odyssey *1965.*

Opposite left, top left and this page: Allen Jones's 'furniture' is not suggestive, but frankly explicit. He began his series of tables, chairs and cocktail cabinets using female mannequins in 1969. Kubrick, again, borrowed the idea for his 1971 version of Anthiny Burgess' A Clockwork Orange.
Jones outrages feminists. In 1973 Lisa Tickner saids his treatment of women relied on passivity, availability, narcissism, exhibitionism, physicality and mindlessness. Jones insists his furniture is morally neutral, exploiting women only as a formal, aesthetic device.

316

Opposite: Jean-Pierre Ploué's
Citroën C6, 2006, has a hip-
line and a callipygian rump that
are incontrovertibly womanly,

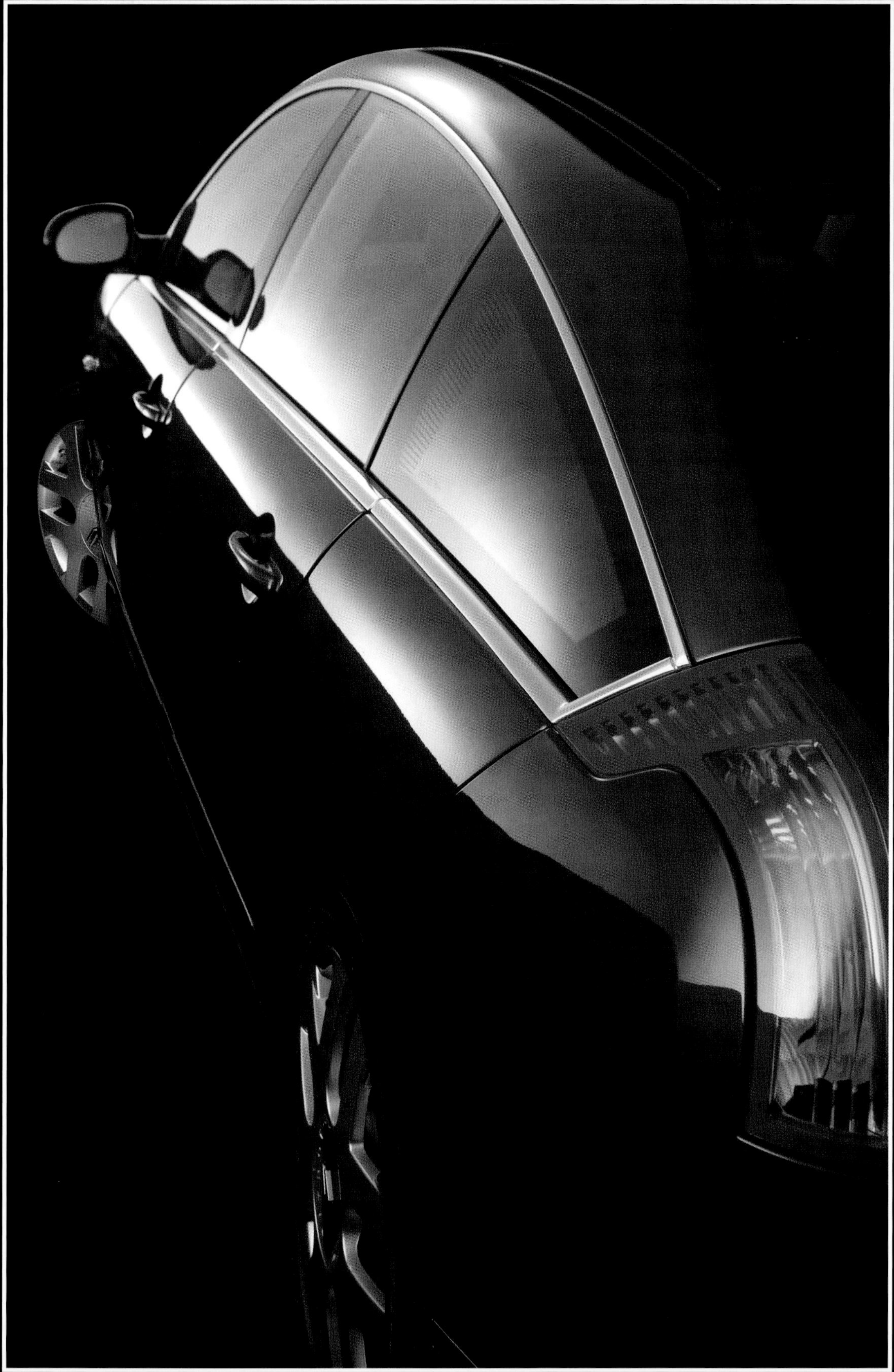

SURGERY,
TELEMATICS,
ORGASMOTRONS,
SMART
DRUGS,
EX-UTERO
FOETAL
DEVELOPMENT,
MEN
BECOME
REDUNDANT

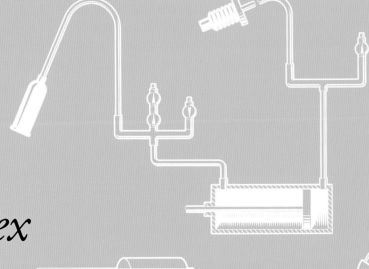

The Future of Sex

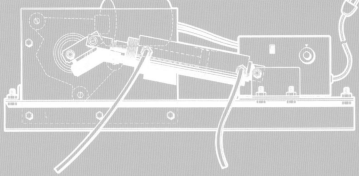

Above: In the later nineteenth century new technologies were enlisted to soothe the 'hysteria' diagnosed in early modern women. The engineering drawings are a metaphor of the slowly revealed psychology of sex.

Opposite: Gianlorenzo Bernini The Ecstasy of Santa Teresa, 1647–52, Santa Maria della Vittoria, Rome. Saint Teresa of Avila was a mystic Discalced Carmelite. In one mystical vision an angel carrying a dart pierced her 'causing intense bodily pain, but much spiritual joy and calm'. This is clearly an occult description of orgasm, whose 'little death' Bernini captures in marble.

Any even informal history of Western art shows that the favoured shape of women changes with time. Aesthetic bones have no strict relationship with the anatomical ones: here you have a pronounced clavicle, there a jawbone disappears. Thigh bones are improbably lengthened according to taste, everyday proportions adapted to fashionable aesthetic need. Thus, Rubens and Klimt. Real skeletons might only evolve slowly, but our ideal view of them changes almost with the rise and fall of hemlines or the sinusoidal fashions of bosom-profile. The early nineteenth-century ideal, at least as expressed by, say, the sculptor Canova, showed a female shoulder line that could not have contained bones: it sloped in frank denial of real human mechanics. If in the Renaissance breasts were symmetrical and mounted high on the ribcage, as Simonetta Vespucci's are in Botticelli's *Venus*, later they assumed different shapes. For Ms Vespucci, Botticelli clearly used a geometrical compass to describe perfect – although perfectly unlikely – hemispheres. Since then, breasts have been on many different morphological adventures: pert or pendulous, ample or mean. They have yet to disappear entirely, but since they

were willed into existence in relatively recent evolutionary time, that possibility cannot be altogether excluded. Medical and technological progress, to say nothing of more sophisticated sexual practices, may yet make breasts redundant.

So, art will cause other versions of woman to be designed and in synch with the spirit of the age, this design might be inspired not by corporeal lust or tactile or aesthetic delight, but by digital technologies. We have seen fat and thin, curves and flat lines. There are other possibilities, limited only by the imagination. Indeed, one possibility is to speculate that the body itself may be a thing of the past. After 27,000 years of interpreting the woman's body, after 3,000 years of exploiting that body for inspiration in architecture and design, maybe that very same body is evolving into extinction. The woman's body was designed in response to specific evolutionary demands, usually driven by men's sexual preferences. Then desire took over and, in turn, it became symbol, inspiration and commodity.

In truth, it became the very greatest symbol, inspiration and commodity. But what of the woman in future? Since the evolutionary role of sexual reproduction has no functional or

scientific basis, it is reasonable to assume that sex is a wholly contrived artificial pleasure. The kiss, for example, is as much an invention of culture as the 96-piece floral pattern dinner service. And if sexual reproduction has been designed, it may, like other designed objects and systems, become redundant. It may yet be replaced by technological alternatives. And so what use would a female human be?

Historically, foot-binding, waist-binding and breast manipulation have helped design woman. Whalebone starch, wire and Spandex have enhanced, or, at least, re-directed, Nature. Presently, silicone, collagen, laser resurfacing and botox play their part in our search for the ideal, or, at least, in our escape from reality. In future, however, electronics may first change bodies then, to depart on a slightly mad speculation, make them obsolescent. If this happens, we will – inevitably – care rather less about their appearance.

So it is entirely reasonable to surmise that the design of women might change in future. Certainly, there are emergent technologies that might encourage this. After all, sexual stereotypes are not constants. In Edo Japan, for example, notions of homosexual and heterosexual were as fluid as the floating world the geishas and shoguns inhabited. Heterosexuality might in future be understood as an involuntary condition maintained only by primitive technology.

There is, for example, no Darwinian explanation for sexual reproduction. In evolutionary terms it doesn't make sense since in Darwin's version, Nature is a stern economist and as conventional sexual reproduction only lets the parent give half his or her genes to the child, that is an inefficient system. In his book *What Remains to be Discovered* (1998) Sir John Maddox, a strict rationalist and one-time editor of the science journal *Nature*, says 'The advantages of sexual reproduction are not obvious… the metabolic cost of maintaining this system is huge.'

One of the costs involved in maintaining this system is keeping bodies 'attractive'. A vast catalogue of design options and sculptural improvements is now available to customers for cosmetic surgeons who specialize in UTES, which stands for Upper Thorax Enhancement Surgery. What artists laboured to express can now be achieved on a credit card. There are specialists too in the Delta of Venus. The 'designer vagina' has recently been aggressively marketed by cosmetic surgeons, sometimes to the alarm of professional in the area of uro-gynaecology because the demand is driven not for reasons of health, but for reasons of aesthetics.

A procedure called hymenorraphy restores (or appears to restore for those not too forensically, intellectually or aesthetically inquisitive) a state of virginity. Some women have collagen injected into the vagina wall, the better to amplify responses from the G-spot. There is demand too for labial reduction surgery, calling up memories of the Hottentot Apron and how distended vaginal lips may have unwelcome associations of primitivism. It is a routine in pornographic photography for the labia to be tucked away so as to present a pudendal cleft that appears as flawless and smooth as an industrial injection moulding.

Right: Breast enhancement surgery in the Lebanon, 2007. Lebanon has become a Middle-Eastern hub of beauty tourism: Arab women from less tolerant countries arrive at cosmetic surgeries with photographs of exemplars they wish to imitate. Elegiacally, as many seek reduction as enlargement.

Opposite: The May–Irwin Kiss, 1896. The very first time osculation had been shown in cinema.

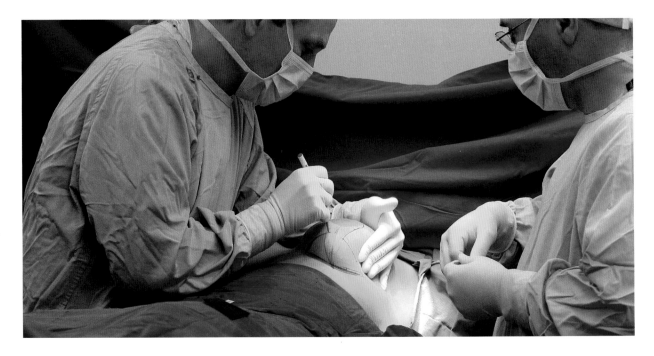

The History of the Kiss

The kiss has its equivalents in the animal republic: both Charles Darwin and Cesare Lombroso
made detailed studies of it. Guillemots nibble each other's feet. Snails rub their antennae (the
vagina is in the snail's head). The human kiss is prehistoric in origin, but its development has
been influenced by culture. In short: the kiss was designed. Very small children tend to put
anything in their mouths. And they lick a lot, as do most mammals. This fundamental animal
impulse is stimulated in modern adults by sexual arousal. However, there are few references
to kissing in the Greek classics. During his travels in Japan, Lafcadio Hearn noted 'kisses and
embraces are simply unknown… as tokens of affection.' Under the influence of Western
models, the Japanese have learnt to kiss. Havelock Ellis claimed 'among nearly all of the black
races of Africa lovers never kiss' and when they do, it was because they learnt it from the
Arabs. In The Perfumed Garden the kiss is given great significance. In the European middle
ages the lower classes – the churls – did not kiss; it was more a mark of knightly distinction.
The olfactory kiss (preserved today in the mwah-mwah of air-kissing) is much more
widespread than the European tactile kiss with its directly sexual implications. The first
cinema kiss was on a twenty second loop made in 1896 by Edison's Kinetoscope. Actress
May Irwin nuzzled and pecked rather like a guillemot.

Amid this flurry of surgical cuts, hormone therapies and chemical injections, the celebrity geneticist Steve Jones of London's University College argues that 'evolution is over' because of declining numbers of mature male parents. The older a father is, the more likely he is to pass on the mutations that are essential to human 'progress'. The reason for this is that cell division increases with age and it is cell division that creates the mutations that drive change.

The social aspects of sexual behaviour are, however, changing. We have fewer mature male candidates for parenthood. Jones cites the example of Moulay Ismail Ibn Sharif, the celebrated Alaouite sultan of Morocco who, as well as claiming descent from Mohammed, made Meknes the Versailles of the Maghreb. Here he kept a harem of 500 women and by some accounts fathered 888 children. It has been estimated that Moulay must have enjoyed an average of 1.2 women a day for 60 years to achieve this record of virile fecundity. Such behaviour is nowadays rare.

Additionally, natural selection is having a less significant influence on evolution. Improvements in healthcare mean, at least in the West, that the vast majority of children survive beyond twenty-one. In history, only the most fortunate and privileged would have done so. Thus, mutation is in decline and natural selection no longer a factor. In the past, the argument goes, small isolated populations might evolve as genes were lost, but in our connected world everything is tending towards a uniform standard. The connoisseurship of breasts and bottoms which has been the subject of this book may soon seem quaint when more profound pleasures can be revealed elsewhere.

In 1973 Woody Allen released *The Sleeper* and introduced the world to the idea of an electronic device that created orgasms without the need to trouble a partner. That seemed fanciful until in 1987 a product called Sybian ('proudly made in the USA') came to market. Californian sexologist and syndicated agony aunt Isadora Alman was so impressed by Sybian's effectiveness, she declared it an 'orgasmatron'. Then in 2004 an anaesthesiologist from Winston-Salem called Stuart Meloy introduced a product actually branded thus. Meloy's research into alleviating lower back pain led him to discover a part of the spinal cord which,

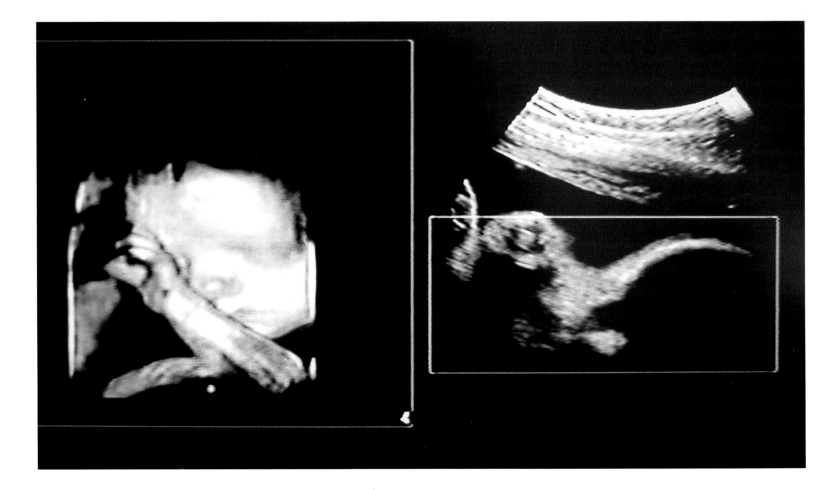

Her breasts served as a model for the prototype champagne bowl. If this is so, Marie-Antoinette's breasts were a very strange shape: semi-circular, symmetrical and flat.

In our own age the Brazilian architect Oscar Niemeyer, a disciple of Le Corbusier, filled sketchbook after sketchbook with drawings of girls on Rio de Janeiro's beaches, the better to stimulate his formal inventiveness. Le Corbusier himself used an androgynous, although rather curvaceous, human figure to explain his system of proportions known as Le Modulor, his own attempt to bring Leonardo's Vitruvian Man up to date. And then, of course, there were the Surrealists whose frequent subconscious and, indeed, very often explicit, fantasies were powered by a preoccupation with the female body. To the Surrealists, the woman's body was not just of aesthetic significance in the way it had been

to, say, painters of the eighteenth century. It was much, much more. It was used as a laboratory: an imaginative sourcebook for art and design. In his novel *L'Amour Fou* (1937), André Breton found the female body a route to the 'marvellous'.

In 1920 the Surrealist photographer Man Ray made a coat-stand (now in the Boymans Museum in Rotterdam) with a life-size cut-out photo of a naked woman. The Proust of Surrealism was Marcel Duchamp who used a sort of dream logic in his subversive art: the Volkswagen car he latterly drove gave rise, on phonetic grounds, to a suite of prints known as the '*faux vagin*', a nice coming together of the automobile and the erotic. False vagina is how it sounds if you pronounce the name Volkswagen abbreviation VW in a surreally mangled version of French and German.

Opposite and above: Oscar Niemeyer's Niteroi Popular Theatre, Rio de Janeiro, 2007. Niemeyer says his sinuous architectural forms were influenced by sketches of girls on Ipanema beach.

The Curve is back

There's an obscure, but rather marvellous, theory in economics known as Kondratieff's Waves, named after Nikolai Kondratieff, briefly director of Stalin's Institute for the Study of Business, before he was sent to the Gulag. The theory is that all business-cultural-political activity is on very long sinusoidal supercycles lasting about seventy-five years. So we go from sweet to sour, from fascism to liberal democracy… And with women, from thin to fat.

It's not that the shape of women is changing, it's just that our preferences are. With the recession of the early twenty-first century, curves are back in favour. The cinema and catwalk fashion shows demanded thin women because they move better, or, at least, in a way that suited the camera. Now, different media are liberating our choices.

Of course, there's an argument about the contrarian chic of having a voluptuous figure in an age of economic restraint, but the truth is actually rather different. Men have always preferred the shapely and inviting callipygian curve; the mother-whore dichotomy has timeless relevance. Each needs a generous body.

when electrically stimulated, creates in women a perfect simulacrum of an orgasm, including pleasantly voluptuous pre-orgasmic muscle spasms.

On sale at $12,000, the Orgasmotron is available with a remote control device. One patient asked Meloy 'Would it be adultery if I gave the remote control to someone other than my husband?' It works on men too. Male patients with erectile dysfunction have reported pleasing results from electronic intervention.

There are neurochemical options too: increasingly, the landscape of desire is being mapped not by artists, but by specialists in brain chemistry. You can, for example, take a pill and have sex with some complex hydro-carbons. What was once described by Titian or Goya is now determined by melanocortin PT-141, a synthetic peptide analogue of alpha-MSH. The so-called melanocortin agonist family of drugs cuts-out the social and cultural aspects of sex (as well as the intromittent or vibratory physical ones) and works directly on the central nervous system.

Insofar as the woman's body was designed as a way to and means of the satisfactions of erotic love, what's the point of that body if you can take a pill and replace the agreeable involuntary muscular contractions of the lower pelvic region with a neurochemical event which releases endorphins and creates euphoria without the mess or effort?

At the same time, ex-utero foetal development may become an attractive option for women who can do without the fatigue and inconvenience of pregnancy. When sex and birth are designed out of the woman's body, then other changes in anatomy and behaviour may be imminent.

The year after *The Sleeper* Theodor Nelson coined the term 'dildonics'. Nelson is a Fellow of Wadham College, Oxford, and an IT pioneer. He coined the term 'hypertext' in 1963 and was one of the first to sell the original Apple computer to geeks in California. Nelson's dildonics referred to sonically generated sexual gratification, but virtual reality makes the idea more, as it were, accessible. In a dildonic set-up you will wear 3-D goggles and climb into an all-enveloping body suit covered with intelligent receptors. The idea is that, fully kitted-up, you might enjoy sex with a remote stranger across the Universe. No foreplay. You just log on.

Left: Ultra-sound of a foetus.

Above: In the Islamic Republic of Iran the mandatory hijab *covers the body leaving only face and hands exposed. As a result, a disproportionate amount of interest is focussed on the face: in* relatively cosmopolitan Tehran, *there had recently been an extreme rise in cosmetic nose jobs.*

Right: Jocelyne Wildenstein in 2006. When Mrs Wildenstein found her husband in flagrante *she began a course of cosmetic* surgery to ensure his fidelity *and her inheritance. The calamitous results led to her becoming known as The Bride of Wildenstein, a reference to the 1935 Boris Karloff horror movie,* The Bride of Frankenstein.

Pornography

– PORNOGRAPHY: a composite word using the Greek words 'prostitute' and 'writing'. Thus, something pornographic is an expression of a prostitute's imagination.

– The difference between pornography and erotica is the lighting.

– 'Pornography is the theory, and rape the practice.' — ROBIN MORGAN, 1977.

325

Right: Fernand Fonssagrives
Perspective Pointille, *1954–58.*
Fonssagrives, first husband of the
model Lisa, became one of New
York's highest-paid photographers
working for Town and Country
and Harper's Bazaar, *although*
he reckoned himself a sculptor.
His highly stylized photographs
use the devices of gallery art to
turn a woman's body into a
decorative composition.

That was science fiction, but there is now talk of neuromacrosensing. This involves sending streams of nanobots (ultra-miniature nanotechnology robotic devices) around the human system, so all your nerves – and not just the sensitive receptors in the old-fashioned erogenous zones – can have sex. In this expanding definition of sex, the weighty, lardy, fleshy, hairy, gravity-dependent body seems a thing of the past. Transhumans will have a different aesthetic. Designers have long argued that the future is to design experiences, not products. This future may arrive with the design of sex before it arrives with the design of chairs.

If advanced transducer and feedback technologies can give us a virtual sex slave, if nanotechnology allows us to have fabulous sex with ourselves, what is the future of woman's body? Or, indeed, of the redundant man? Might we design something rather different? It is certain that the grounds of generation and pleasure are shifting. No-one today would, even if the resources were available, design an erotic dairy

with costumed maids as Marie-Antoinette did at Rambouillet. Richard Kadrey, San Francisco novelist, author of *Kamikaze L'Amour* and an editor of the short-lived little magazine *Future Sex,* says virtual sex 'will not resemble ordinary sex at all… it will be an entirely different form of sexuality, with its own pleasures and pitfalls, fans and adversaries, fetishists and posers. Whether you think this is a good thing or not depends on how you view sexual and body experimentation.'

And talking of mysteries, when sex and birth are out-sourced, what of the future of love? The romantic love that began with the Troubadours made real people into fantasies. Then the glamour industries with their technologies of improvement and enhancement promised to make fantasies accessible to real people. Let me escape from the limits of here-and-now and design myself a better future! Why else buy a 1951 inflatable bra?

Perhaps we will one day come to see the design of the woman's body as the most complete and perfect fantasy of them all.

326

Angier, Nathalie, *Woman: An intimate geography*,
   New York: Houghton Mifflin, 1999

Bell, Graham, *The Mysteries of Nature: the evolution of genetic
   sexuality*, Cambridge: Cambridge University Press, 1982

Killoren Bensimmon, Kelly, *The Bikini Book*,
   London: Thames & Hudson, 2006

Borkowski, Mark, *The Fame Formula – how Hollywood's fixers,
   fakers and star makers created the celebrity industry*,
   London: Sidgwick & Jackson, 2008

Charles-Roux, Edmonde, *Chanel*,
   London: Jonathan Cape, 1976

Churchwell, Sarah, *The Many Lives of Marilyn Monroe*,
   London: Granta, 2004

Clark, Kenneth, *The Nude – a study in ideal form*,
   New Jersey: Princeton University Press, 1956

Corbin, Alain, *Women for Hire*,
   Boston: Harvard University Press, 1998

Corbin, Alain, *The Foul and the Fragrant – odor and the French
   social imagination*, Boston: Harvard University Press, 1986

Cowles, Fleur, *The Case of Salvador Dali*, London: Heinemann, 1959

Drenth, Jelto, *The Origin of the World – science and fiction of the
   vagina*, London: Reaktion Books, 2005

Dworkin, Andrea, *Pornography: men possessing women*,
   London: The Women's Press, 1981

Ellis, Havelock, *Studies in the Psychology of Sex*, Philadelphia:
   F. A. Davis, 1910–18

Etcoff, Nancy, *Survival of the Prettiest – the science of beauty*,
   London: Little Brown, 1999

Fischer, Lucy, *Designing Women: cinema, art deco and the
   female form*, New York: Columbia University Press, 2005

Frazer, James, *The Golden Bough – a study of magic and religion*,
   London: Macmillan, 1890

Freud, Sigmund, 'Delusion and Dream in W. Jensen's Gradiva' *The
   Standard Edition of the Complete Psychological Works*, London:
   Hogarth Press and The Institute of Psychoanalysis, 1953–74

Hollander, Anne, *Seeing Through Clothes*,
   New York: Viking Press, 1978

Hansen, Dian, (ed.), *The Big Book of Breasts*, London: Taschen, 2008

Hersey, George L., *The Evolution of Allure – sexual selection
   from the Medici Venus to the Incredible Hulk*, Cambridge:
   Massachusetts Institute of Technology, 1996

Johns, Catherine, *Sex or Symbol – erotic images of Greece and
   Rome*, London: British Museum Press, 1982

Kilmartin, Terence, *A Guide to Proust*, London:
   Chatto & Windus, 1983

Kraus, Linda, et al *Amour Fou*, Washington DC:
   Abbeville Press, 1985

Legman, Gershon, *The Rationale of the Dirty Joke – an analysis
   of sexual humour*, London: Jonathan Cape, 1969

Levins, Hoag, *American Sex Machines – the hidden history of
   sex at the US Patent Office* Adams Media Corporation,
   Massachusetts: Holbrook, 1996

Maines, Rachel P., *The Technology of Orgasm*, Baltimore:
    Johns Hopkins University Press, 1999
Middleton, Dorothy, *Victorian Lady Travellers*, London:
    Routledge, 1965
Morand, Paul, *L' Allure de Chanel*, Paris: Hermann, 1976
Neumann, Erich, *The Great Mother*, New Jersey: Princeton
    University Press, 1955
Pearsall, R., *The Worm in the Bud: the world of Victorian
    sexuality*, London: Weidenfeld and Nicolson, 1969
Penny, Nicholas & Haskell, Francis, *Taste and the Antique – the lure
    of classical sculpture*, London: Yale University Press, 1982
Roberts, Nickie, *Whores in History – prostitution in Western
    society*, London: HarperCollins, 1992
Rounding, Virginia, *Grandes Horizontales – the lives and legends
    of four nineteenth-century courtesans*, London:
    Bloomsbury, 2003
St George, Andrew, *The Descent of Manners*, London:
    Chatto & Windus, 1993
Schienbinger, Londa, *Nature's Body: gender in the making of
    modern science*, Boston: Beacon Press, 1993
Schwartz, Kit, *The Female Member – being a compendium of
    facts, figures, foibles and anecdotes about the loving organ*,
    New York: St Martin's Press, 1988
Sevely, Josephine Lowndes, *Eve's Secret – a revolutionary
    perspective on human sexuality*, London: Bloomsbury, 1987
Sheldon, William H., *Atlas of Man*, New York: Harper, 1954

Stern, Jane and Michael, *The Encyclopaedia of Bad Taste*,
    New York: HarperCollins, 1990
Tiger, Lionel, *The Pursuit of Pleasure Little*, New York: Brown, 1992
Thompson, C. J. S., *Mysteries of Sex*, London: Hutchinson, n.d.
Walker, Alexander, *Sex in the Movies*, London: Penguin, 1968
Warner, Marina, *Alone of All Her Sex*, London: Vintage, 1976
Webster, Richard, *Why Freud Was Wrong – sin, science and
    psychoanalysis*, London: HarperCollins, 1995
Wurtzel, Elizabeth, *Bitch – in praise of difficult women*,
    New York: Doubleday, 1998
Yalom, Marilyn, *A History of the Breast*, London: Pandora, 1998

INDEX

ACKNOWLEDGEMENTS

334

† indicates that a detail of the picture has been shown

2–3† Roger Mavity; 4–5† Galleria degli Uffizi, Florence, Italy/The Bridgeman Art Library; 8 ©Lee Miller Archives, England 2009. All rights reserved; 10–11 Erich Lessing/akg-images; 12 Geoffrey Kidd/Alamy; 13† akg-images; 14† Leni Riefenstahl/akg-images; 16–21 Ronald King; 22 Freud Museum, London, UK/The Bridgeman Art Library; 23 Thyssen-Bornemisza Collection, Madrid, Spain ©Salvador Dali, Gala-Salvador Dali Foundation ©DACS, London 2009; 24 Thurston Hopkins/Picture Post/Getty Images; 25 above Alinari Archives-Brogi Archive, Florence; below TopFoto; 26† Bob Thomas/Popperfoto/Getty Images; 27 Image courtesy of The Advertising Archives; 28† State Hermitage, St Petersburg/akg-images; 29 Dmitri Kessel/Time Life Pictures/Getty Images; 30–31 Courtesy of Allen Jones; 33† Menil Collection, Houston, Texas, USA/Giraudon/The Bridgeman Art Library ©ADAGP, Paris & DACS, London 2009; 34 The Natural History Museum, London; 35 Naturhistorisches Museum, Vienna, Austria/Ali Meter/The Bridgeman Art Library; 36† Hammer/The Kobal Collection; 37 The Natural History Museum, London; 38 Courtesy of Catherine Johns; 39† Erich Lessing/akg-images; 40† Louvre, Paris, France/Lauros/Giraudon/The Bridgeman Art Library; 41† akg-images; 42 Museo Archeologico Nazionale, Naples, Italy/Alinari/The Bridgeman Art Library; 43† Leni Riefenstahl Production; 44–45 Tristan Lafranchis/akg-images; 46–47 Dean Conger/Corbis; 48 © Bowness, Hepworth Estate/Tate, London 2009; 49 akg-images; 50† Memling Museum, Bruges, Belgium/Giraudon/The Bridgeman Art Library; 51 Musee de la Chartreuse, Douai, France/Giraudon/The Bridgeman Art Library; 52 Hamburger Kunsthalle, Hamburg, Germany/The Bridgeman Art Library; 53 akg-images; 54–55† Galleria

Palatina, Palazzo Pitti, Florence, Italy/The Bridgeman Art Library; 57† akg-images; 58 Chapel of the Cemetery, Monterchi, Italy/The Bridgeman Art Library; 59 Jan Bengtsson/Etsa/Corbis; 61† Jeanloup Sieff; 62† ©Tate, London 2009; 63† Museo Archeologico Nazionale, Naples, Italy/Alinari/The Bridgeman Art Library; 64† Bob Thomas/Popperfoto/Getty Images; 65† Royal Geographical Society; 66 © The National Gallery, London 2009; 67 left† ©The National Gallery, London 2009; 67 right† St. Bavo Cathedral, Ghent, Belgium/Giraudon/The Bridgeman Art Library; 68 Araldo de Luca/Corbis; 69 ©Man Ray Trust/ADAGP, Paris & DACS, London 2009. 70 Musee National d'Art Moderne – Centre Georges Pompidou, Paris © Photo CNAC/MNAM, Dist. RMN/Philippe Migeat ©ADAGP, Paris & DACS, London 2009; 71 Private Collection/The Bridgeman Art Library © Salvador Dali, Gala-Salvador Dali Foundation, DACS, London 2009; 72–73† Musee National d'Art Moderne – Centre Georges Pompidou, Paris © Photo CNAC/MNAM, Dist. RMN/Jacques Faujour ©Estate Brassai – RMN. All Rights Reserved; 74† Harry Todd/Fox Photos/Getty Images; 75 Martin Elliot; 76 Image courtesy of The Advertising Archives; 77† Jeanloup Sieff; 78–79† Imagno/Getty Images; 80–81† Louvre, Paris, France/Giraudon/The Bridgeman Art Library; 83† Pushkin Museum, Moscow, Russia/The Bridgeman Art Library; 84 © China Hamilton; 85† Bettmann/Corbis; 86 Courtesy of Phillips; 87 a Rob Walls/Alamy; b ICP/Alamy; c Sian Irvine/Bon Appetit/Alamy; d H. Reinhard/Arco Images GmbH/Alamy; e H. Reinhard/Arco Images GmbH/Alamy; f fotoshoot/Alamy; g Martin Baumgartner/Bon Appetit/Alamy; h O. Diez/Arco Images GmbH/Alamy; i Wildlife GmbH/Alamy; 88† Thomas Fisher Rare Book Library, University of Toronto, Canada; 89† Wellcome Library, London;

90 left† akg-images; 90 right Indianapolis Museum of Art, USA/Martha Delzell Memorial Fund/The Bridgeman Art Library; 91 Musee d'Orsay, Paris, France/Giraudon/The Bridgeman Art Library; 92† Bibliotheque des Arts Decoratifs, Paris, France/Archives Charmet/The Bridgeman Art Library; 93 Wellcome Library, London; 94† Denise Bellon/akg-images; 95 ©Trustees of the British Museum, London; 96 Hulton Archive/Getty Images; 97† Image courtesy of The Advertising Archives; 98† Linnean Society, London; 99 left† Phil Talbot/Alamy; 99 right† Alfred Eisenstadt/Time Life Pictures/Getty Images; 100–101 Heather Watson/Alamy; 102† Louvre, Paris, France/Giraudon/The Bridgeman Art Library; 103 Courtesy of Dr Annie Sprinkle; 104 Louvre, Paris, France/The Bridgeman Art Library; 105† Imagno/Getty Images; 106† Private Collection/Giraudon/The Bridgeman Art Library; 107 Erich Lessing/akg-images; 108 Koninklijk Museum voor Schone Kunsten, Antwerp, Belgium/Giraudon/The Bridgeman Art Library; 109 Kevin Terrell/WireImage; 110 Courtesy of Harri Pecchinoti & David Hillman; 111 Steve Sant; 112 above† Keystone Features/Getty Images; 112 below Mary Evans Picture Library; 113 Image courtesy of The Advertising Archives; 114 left† Julian Wasser/Time Life Pictures/Getty Images; 114 right Image courtesy of the Advertising Archives; 115† George Hurrell/John Kobal Foundation/Getty Images; 116† Bettmann/Corbis; 117† AP/PA Photos; 118† Keystone/Getty Images; 119 Allied Artists/The Kobal Collection; 120 left Tony Korody/Sygma/ Corbis; 120 right Bettmann/Corbis; 121 PA Photos; 122–123 Heloise Acher/Conran Octopus; 124† Richard Bickel/Corbis; 125 Philadelphia Museum of Art; Purchased with the Gertrud A. White Memorial Fund, 1995. © ADAGP, Paris and DACS, London 2009; 126† Popperfoto/Getty Images; 127† Danjaq/Eon/UA/

The Kobal Collection; 128–129† Jagdish Agarwal/SCPhotos/Alamy; 130 City of Westminster Archive Centre, London/The Bridgeman Art Library; 131† Musee d'Orsay, Dist RMN/Patrice Schmidt © ADAGP, Paris & DACS, London 2009; 132–133† Private Collection/The Stapleton Collection/The Bridgeman Art Library; 134 Popperfoto/Getty Images; 135† General Photographic Agency/Getty Images; 136† Daily Express Hulton Archive/Getty Images; 137† Mary Evans Picture Library; 138–139† Erich Lessing/akg-images; 140–141† Johann Spanner/New York Times/Redux/eyevine; 142 left† Private Collection/The Bridgeman Art Library; 142 right Eugene Atget/George Eastman House/Getty Images; 143† Private Collection/The Bridgeman Art Library; 144 Scrovegni Chapel, Padua, Italy/Alinari/The Bridgeman Art Library; 145† National Gallery London/The Bridgeman Art Library; 146† & 147† Prado, Madrid, Spain/Giraudon/The Bridgeman Art Library; 148–149† Louvre, Paris, France/Giraudon/The Bridgeman Art Library; 150–151† Musee d'Art Moderne de la Ville de Paris, France/ Lauros/ Giraudon/The Bridgeman Art Library © ADAGP, Paris & DACS, London 2009; 152† Russell-Cotes Art Gallery & Museum, Bournemouth, UK/The Bridgeman Art Library; 153 © Judy Chicago 1979 Collection of the Brooklyn Museum, New York, USA. Photo © Donald Woodman © ARS, NY & DACS, London 2009; 154 Alfred Stieglitz Collection/Ph Malcom Varon/The Metropolitan Museum of Art/Art Resource/Scala, Florence; 155 Fundacion Dolores Olmedo/Photo Art Resource/Scala, Florence; 156–157† & 158† Private Collection/The Bridgeman Art Library; 159† Fratelli Alinari/Musuem of the History of Photography/Wanda Wulz Archive, Florence; 160 a-d & f Wellcome Library, London; 160 e ©Trustees of the British Museum, London; 161 & 162† Wellcome

Library, London; 163 Tom Dixon; 164–165† Wellcome Library, London; 167 © Estate of Tom Wesselmann/ DACS, London & VAGA, NY 2009; 169† Archive Photos/ Getty Images; 170 left† Paul Popper/ Popperfoto/Getty Images; 170 right† RDA/Getty Images; 171† Underwood &Underwood/Corbis; 172† © Eugene Atget/Paris Musee d'Orsay © RMN (Museed'Orsay)/ Gerard Blot; 173† ©The National Gallery, London; 174† National Gallery, London, UK/The Bridgeman Art Library; 175 Galleria degli Uffizi, Florence, Italy/ Giraudon/The Bridgeman Art Library; 176 left† adoc-photos; 176 right† ©Musee National d'Art Moderne – Centre Georges Pompidou, Paris © Photo CNAC/MNAM, Dist. RMN/Adam Rzepka © Estate Brassai – RMN. All Rights Reserved; 177† Musee de la Ville de Paris/Musee Carnavalet, Paris, France/Lauros/Giraudon/The Bridgeman Art Library; 178 Kunstmuseum Stuttgart; 179† © Musee National d'Art Moderne – Centre Georges Pompidou, Paris © Photo CNAC/MNAM, Dist. RMN/Jacques Faujour © Estate Brassai – RMN. All Rights Reserved; 180 akg-images; 181 The Samuel Courtauld Trust, Courtauld Gallery, London; 183† & 184† Royal Geographical Society; 184 John Chillingworth/Picture Post/ Getty Images; 185 ©Photo RMN/Jean-Gilles Berizzi © Estate Brassai – RMN. All Rights Reserved; 186 Statens Sjohistoriska Museum, Stockholm, Sweden/The Bridgeman Art Library; 187 Courtesy the artist & Metro Pictures; 188† Museo Diocesano, Cortona, Italy/The Bridgeman Art Library; 189 above† The Natural History Museum, London; 189 below Brian J Skerry/National Geographic Stock; 190† & 191† Private Collection/DaTo Images/The Bridgeman Art Library; 192† Bettmann/Corbis; 193† Thomas L Shafer/Bettmann/Corbis; 194–195† Jim Sugar/Corbis; 196 left Archive Photos/ Getty Images; 196 right Michael Ochs Archives/Getty Images;

197 left Weegee/International Center of Photography/Getty Images; 197 right Michael Ochs Archives/Getty Images; 198† Louvre, Paris, France/ Giraudon/The Bridgeman Art Library; 199† & 200 Vic Singh Studio/Alamy; 201† Andrew H Walker/Getty Images; 202–203† David Montgomery; 204† Private Collection/Boltin Picture Library/The Bridgeman Art Library © Succession Marcel Duchamp/ADAGP, Paris & DACS, London 2009; 205 DMI/ Time Life Pictures/Getty Images; 206 & 207 Images courtesy of The Advertising Archives; 209† & 210† akg-images; 211† & 212–213 MGM/The Kobal Collection; 214† Paramount/The Kobal Collection; 215† Fox Films/Album/ akg-images; 216† E.R Richee/Album/ akg-images; 217† Fox Photos/Getty Images; 219 John Kobal Foundation/ Getty Images; 220 United Artists/The Kobal Collection; 221 United Artists/ Album/akg-images; 222 Ed Clark/Time Life Pictures/Getty Images; 223† Michael Ochs Archives/Getty Images; 224–225† Sipa Press/Rex Features; 225† Bettmann/Corbis; 226† Keystone-France/Camera Press London; 227† MGM/Album/akg-images; 228 Archivio Storico Olivetti, Ivrea, Italy; 229 Art Director: George Lois/Ph Carl Fischer; 230–231 Courtesy of David Hillman; 233† Clairol; 234 Courtesy of Dr Annie Sprinkle; 235† George Hommel/John Kobal Foundation/Getty Images; 236† Nic Bothma/EPA/Corbis; 237† BDV/Corbis; 238† © Nobuyoshi Araki/Courtesy Yoshiko Isshiki Office; 239† Norman Parkinson Limited/Corbis; 240† Clairol; 241 Musee d'Orsay, Paris, France/Giraudon/The Bridgeman Art Library; 242–243† Associated Film Releasing Corp/The Kobal Collection; 244 left† akg-images; 244 right† John Kobal Foundation/Getty Images; 245† Michael Ochs Archives/Getty Images; 246† Universal/The Kobal Collection; 247 above† Riama-Pathe/ The Kobal Collection; 247 below IENA/ UCIL/Cocinor/The Kobal Collection;

248 Image courtesy of The Advertising Archives; 249† Warner Bros/The Kobal Collection; 250 left† Image courtesy of The Advertising Archives; 250 right Peter Rayner/Axiom Photographic Agency/Getty Images; 251 above† Leni Riefenstahl Production; 251 below† Image courtesy of The Advertising Archives; 252† Paramount Pictures/Getty Images; 253 above Carol Beckwith/Angela Fisher/The Image Bank/Getty Images; 253 below Image courtesy of The Advertising Archives; 254 & 255† Images courtesy of The Advertising Archives; 256 Christian Dior; 257† © Horst P. Horst/Art+ Commerce; 258 left† Time Life Pictures/ Getty Images; 258 right Conde Nast Archive/Corbis; 259† Hulton Archive/ Getty Images; 260–261 Paul Schutzer/ Time Life Pictures/Getty Images; 262† Three Lions/ Getty Images; 263 Kevin Winter/DMI/Time Life Pictures/Getty Images; 264 ©M Rousseau/Citroen; 265† Private Collection/Photo © Bonhams, London, UK/The Bridgeman Art Library; 266† ©The Board of Trustees of the Royal Botanic Gardens, Kew; 267† Mark Ralston/AFP/Getty Images; 268† Chris Moore/Catwalking; 269 Courtesy of Manolo Blahnik; 270 Chris Moore/ Catwalking; 271 Duffy/Getty Images; 272 John Young/Camera Press London; 273 left† State Russian Museum, St Petersburg, Russia/The Bridgeman Art Library © DACS 2009; 273 right Howard Sochurek/Time Life Pictures/Getty Images; 274† & 275† Bettmann/Corbis; 276† Walter Sanders/Time Life Pictures/ Getty Images; 277† Popperfoto/Getty Images; 278 Image courtesy of The Advertising Archives; 279† Courtesy of Lycra ®; 280 Tim Hill/Alamy; 281 Allan Baxter/The Image Bank/Getty Images; 282 Erich Lessing/akg-images; 282–283 Conran Octopus; 283 Martin Lee/Mediablitzimages(UK)Ltd/Alamy; 284 above† RIBA Library Photographs Collection; 284 below Franck Guiziou/

Hemis/Alamy; 285† The Courtauld Institute of Art, London; 286 © RMN/ Martine Beck-Coppola; 287 Massimo Listri/Corbis; 288 & 289 Marcelo Sayao/ EPA/Corbis; 290 Ph Mert Alas & Marcus Piggott, Styling: Katie Grand; 291 above Charles Wilp/Yves Klein; 291 below Harry Shunk–John Kender/ Yves Klein; 292 © Man Ray Trust/ADAGP, Paris & DACS, London 2009; 293 Museum Boymans van Beuningen, Rotterdam, The Netherlands/Photo © Christie's Images/The Bridgeman Art Library © Salvador Dali, Gala-Salvador Dali Foundation, DACS, London 2009; 294–295 Courtesy of the Trustees of the Edward James Foundation/V&A Images © Salvador Dali, Gala-Salvador Dali Foundation, DACS, London 2009; 296† © Salvador Dali, Gala-Salvador Dali Foundation, DACS, London 2009; 297 Audi; 298 left Fiat; 298 right & 299– 305† Courtesy of Museo Casa Mollino, Torino; 306 Ruy Teixeira; 307 Fernando Guerra; 308 left Peter Mauss/ESTO/ VIEW; 308–309 Ezra Stoller/ESTO; 310 left Ian Lambot/Arcaid; 310 right David Churchill/Arcaid; 311 Mark Bury/ Arcaid; 312–313† © Estate of Tom Wesselmann/DACS, London/VAGA, NY 2009; 314 below © Olivier Mourgue © Photo CNAC/MNAM, Dist RMN/ Jean-Claude Planchet; 314–315 Courtesy of Allen Jones; 316 Pascal Baetens; 317 Citroen; 319 Santa Maria della Vittoria, Rome, Italy/The Bridgeman Art Library; 320 Marwan Naamani/AFP/Getty Images; 321 Edison Manufacturing Co/akg-images; 322 Michael Bradley/ Getty Images; 323 left Thomas Dworzak/ Magnum Photos; 323 right Kevin Parry/Wireimage; 324 Heloise Acher/Conran Octopus; 325 © Fernand Fonssagrives. Courtesy of the Michael Hoppen Gallery; 336 Michael Potter eyephotographicworkshops.com; endpapers Wellcome Library, London.

Every effort has been made to trace the copyright holders. We apologize in advance for any unintentional omissions and would be pleased to insert the appropriate acknowledgement in any subsequent publication.

Stephen Bayley was educated at Manchester University and Liverpool University School of Architecture. He is now one of the world's best-known authorities on design and popular culture. With Terence Conran, he created the Boilerhouse Project at the Victoria & Albert Museum and London's unique Design Museum. Both the Boilerhouse and the Design Museum helped make design the popular subject it is today. Besides a curator, he has been an academic and a consultant, but is best known as an outspoken commentator on all aspects of art in everyday life. He is architecture and design correspondent of *The Observer* and contributes regularly to a huge range of national and international newspapers and magazines including *GQ*, *Car* and *The Los Angeles Times*. His many books include *Design: Intelligence Made Visible* (with Terence Conran) and *Cars*, both published by Conran Octopus, as well as *Taste*, *Harley Earl and the Dream Machine*, *The Albert Memorial* and *Life's a Pitch...* he has lectured at universities and museums throughout the world and is a familiar commentator on radio and television. In 1989 he was made a Chevalier de l'Ordre des Arts et des Lettres by the French Government and is also a Hon. FRIBA, a Fellow of the University of Wales Institute Cardiff and a Fellow of Liverpool Institute of Performing Arts. Stephen Bayley lives in central London with his wife and two children.